ETHICAL DILEMMAS IN SOCIAL SERVICE

ETHICAL DILEMMAS IN SOCIAL SERVICE

Frederic G. Reamer

Second Edition

COLUMBIA UNIVERSITY PRESS NEW YORK

Columbia University Press
New York Oxford

Library of Congress Cataloging-in-Publication Data

Reamer, Frederic G.
Ethical dilemmas in social service / Frederic G. Reamer. —2d ed.
p. cm.
Includes bibliographical references.
ISBN 0-231-06968-5
1. Social service—Moral and ethical aspects. 2. Social workers—Professional ethics. 3. Social service—United States. I. Title.
HV10.5.R42 1989
174'.9362—dc19 89-22124

Casebound editions of Columbia University Press books are Smyth-sewn and printed on permanent and durable acid-free paper

Printed in the United States of America
c 10 9 8 7 6 5 4 3 2 1

Book design by Ken Venezio

174.9362
R288
2ed

For Deborah and Emma

12-18-89 Publisher $21.55

134,818

Contents

Preface to the Second Edition ix

Preface to the First Edition xiii

1 The Nature of Ethics 1

Ethical and Nonethical Aspects of Social Work 3
The Traditional Approach to Social Work Ethics 7
The Justification of Values 13
A Closer Look at Utilitarianism 16
Toward an Ethics of Social Work 20
Central Issues in Moral Philosophy 22

2 Fundamental Ethical Issues in Social Work 35

The Duty to Aid 36
Positive and Negative Obligations 38
The Role of the State 40
The Distribution of Services and Resources 48
Justifying the Values of the Profession 55
A Guide to Ethical Decisions 60

3 Ethical Dilemmas in Service to Individuals and Families 66

Truth-Telling and Competing Interests 67
Paternalism and the Limits of Intervention 76
Divided Professional Loyalties 84
Conflicts Among Laws, Policies, and Treatment Goals 94
The Right to Confidentiality 100
The Process of Informed Consent 111

4 Ethical Dilemmas in Social Planning and Policy 123

Public Support for Social Service 124
Distribution of Limited Resources 134
The Right to Welfare 140
Government Obligation and Private Interests 149
Care for Extreme Needs 158
Ethical Aspects of Program Design 167

5 Ethical Dilemmas in Relationships Among Practitioners 178

Questioning Professional Competence 179
Complying with Agency Policy 188
Privileged Communication 197
The Use of Deception 207
Whistle-Blowing 216

6 Enduring Issues 224

The Goals of Ethical Analysis 226
The Use of Ethics Committees 229
Professional Priorities 236
The Limits of Obligation 239
Ethics and Answers 241
Of Clouds and Clocks 243

Notes 247

Index 263

Preface to the Second Edition

Since the original publication of *Ethical Dilemmas in Social Service,* the subject of professional ethics has come of age. Literature and research on professional ethics have expanded considerably in recent years, and many professional training programs now routinely address ethical issues. The growth of interest in ethical issues is evident throughout social work and other professions.

I have been heartened by the dramatic growth of interest in professional ethics, particularly social work ethics. It reflects increased awareness of the ethical dimension of practice and greater understanding of the ethical context in which professionals' judgments often are made. In short, the growth of interest in ethics reflects, to a great extent, the maturation of the professions.

All of the news, however, is not so cheery. Another reason for the recent increase of interest in ethics is the disturbing rise of ethics grievances and indiscretions in the professions. Increases in the number of formal complaints filed against practitioners for unethical conduct and violations of codes of ethics—for matters ranging from breaching confidentiality to sexual involvement with a client—have led to intense interest in professional ethics. Although it is difficult to know whether increases in ethical complaints reflect increased incidence or mere reporting, the rising numbers have moved all professions to take a hard look at the ways in which professional ethics and values are inculcated, reinforced, and enforced.

Thus, for a variety of reasons the professions are paying close attention to ethics, and this is good. I know from my extensive contact with social workers around the country that practitioners are thinking more and differently about professional ethics. They are much less likely to reduce professional ethics to some vague familiarity with a code of ethics. Instead, there is a much more thoughtful, mature grasp of ethical concepts and principles and of their relationship to hard decisions.

Readers of *Ethical Dilemmas in Social Service* have reported that they have found helpful my framework for assessing ethical issues, along with discussions of such topics as confidentiality and privileged communication, self-determination, truth-telling, the allocation of limited resources, ethical aspects of supervision and program design, the use of deception, and whistle-blowing. The majority of topics addressed in the first edition of *Ethical Dilemmas in Social Service* have stood the test of time, and, therefore, have been retained in this edition. This edition includes updated information on a number of these topics. It also contains substantially new information on topics that have recently attracted considerable attention in social work and other human service professions, such as informed consent, the phenomenon of paternalism, and the use of agency-based ethics committees.

Over the years I have become convinced that reading, thinking, and talking about ethics can make a difference. Although good practice by itself ordinarily translates into good ethics, there are times when practice principles do not illuminate or resolve troublesome ethical dilemmas, and in these cases we must draw on sound, conceptually based ethical reasoning.

I also am as convinced as ever that while serious thinking about ethics can accomplish a great deal, it cannot perform professional miracles. Practitioners who are not already well disposed toward ethical conduct may not be shaped much by even the most skillful discourse about ethics. But, despite these limitations, ethics can make a difference in the professions.

This point was brought home to me vividly shortly after I completed the first edition of *Ethical Dilemmas in Social Service*. I had been working part time as a social worker in a maximum security penitentiary. One of my responsibilities was to conduct a weekly discussion group for approximately ten inmates who were serving sentences for serious crimes, such as murder, rape, and aggravated sexual assault. At the conclusion of one of our meetings, I announced that I would need to miss the next meeting because I was scheduled to conduct a workshop on professional ethics at an out-of-state college. One member of the group asked me what "professional ethics" means, and I briefly described the kinds of ethical issues that arise in fields such as medicine, nursing, social work, journalism, business, engineering, and law enforcement. My description could not have lasted more than three minutes and elicited little reaction from the group.

During the next week I was walking through the penitentiary on my way to the group's meeting room for our first get-together following my trip. I passed through several sets of gates on my way out to the prison's yard and to the building in which we met. As I entered the yard, Bobby, one of the group's members, walked up to me waving pages torn from a magazine. This twenty-year-old, who was serving a thirty-year sentence for second-degree murder, told me excitedly that the day after my "talk" about professional ethics he had come across this magazine article on the subject. He had been working in the prison dining hall and found a copy of *Food Management,* a trade magazine for institutional food managers, on his supervisor's desk. Thumbing through the magazine, Bobby had come across an article about professional ethics in food management, addressing issues such as conflicts of interest between suppliers and buyers, bribes and kickbacks, and whistle-blowing.

I was struck—and impressed—by the fact that a magazine such as *Food Management* would publish a sophisticated article on professional ethics. I was struck even more, however, by Bobby's own reaction to the article. "This article really made me think," he said. "The authors really zeroed in on some important issues—like lying and cheating. I had never really thought about these things like that. Really makes you think."

This, I thought to myself, is what being a social worker is all about. Here's a high school dropout serving time for second-degree murder who has managed to draw connections between an article in *Food Management* on professional ethics and his own behavior. Bobby had even taken the trouble to underline short passages in the article that were particularly meaningful to him:

> We see we do things for many different reasons, many of which are contradictory, many of which change with circumstance. If we go still further we find that the degree to which we find answers to these questions depends in great

> part upon how far we've gone in looking at our ethics, morality and behavior. . . . It's not a question of to "do" or not to "do" anything. It's whether you admit what you are doing and accept responsibility for it in the broadest sense. . . . But sometimes the strings on a gift are almost invisible; they just don't become visible until some dealing many months in the future. Sometimes a gift is not what it seems.

I was moved by Bobby's insights concerning the relevance of these rather mundane ethical issues involving food vendors and managers to his own past. Bobby spent a few minutes explaining to me how he had begun thinking about his own unethical conduct.

Toward the end of our brief conversation I asked Bobby if he would lend me the article so that I could read it carefully. He promptly handed it to me and with the obvious pleasure of a gift-giver told me that I could keep the article since he had stolen it from his supervisor.

As the philosopher James Rachels has written, "The fact that rationality has limits does not subvert the objectivity of ethics, but it does suggest a certain modesty in what can be claimed for it."

Preface to the First Edition

We live in the midst of a curious era. History has known no time which has been more advanced technologically. We have invented a staggering number of tools and toys for pursuing the good life. We have greater control over our surroundings than ever before. The curiosity is that we still yearn to erase, or at least ameliorate, what throughout recorded history have been life's most stubborn and persistent problems—poverty, mental illness, crime, debilitating disease, emotional misery, physical handicaps, and various forms of injustice.

We know by now that many of our inventions have been delivered with two edges. They have brought us longer life, more convenience, and greater pleasure than many of us ever imagined possible. But there have been strings attached. Along with high-speed travel have come greater mobility and a decline in family stability. Along with the growth of industry and higher standards of living have come deteriorating cities and crime. Along with advances in high-energy physics have come dangers of nuclear holocaust.

These problems have not, of course, gone unnoticed. Along the way we have invented professions for responding to the stresses and strains of contemporary life almost as rapidly as we have invented the problems themselves. It is now possible to be trained in social work, urban planning, human services, public policy, counseling psychology, gerontology, psychiatric nursing, vocational guidance, pastoral counseling, and in many other professions which have emerged within the last hundred years. Organized efforts to help people in need are themselves not new. They have existed for centuries. But the emergence of formal professions which train and accredit practitioners is a modern phenomenon.

The so-called helping professions have spent considerable effort in recent years attempting to develop sound and effective techniques for assisting people with problems. We now have a slew of "theories" of counseling, psychotherapy, community development and organization, organizational change, social policy, and so forth. We have devised elaborate methods for testing and measuring the effectiveness of our theories, hypotheses, and hunches. We are beginning to realize, however, that embedded in our determined pursuit of effective ways of helping are dilemmas which theories and research are not able to resolve—dilemmas which have at their core important questions of right and wrong and of duty and obligation. When we struggle to decide whether we are obligated to reveal confidential information against a client's wishes, to obey an agency policy which seems unjust, to inform a supervisor about a colleague's illegal activities, to require welfare recipients to work in exchange for benefits, or to terminate services being provided to an uncooperative client, we are not faced with questions which theory and research can answer by themselves. Moreover, questions about the extent of our obligation as professionals to assist people in need, the role of government in welfare matters, and ways of distributing limited social service resources are not of the sort that theories and empirical evidence can adequately address on their own. These issues and questions are primarily ethical in nature.

The variety of ethical issues and dilemmas which face practitioners is impressive. What I have attempted here is a systematic review of the range of ethical problems which social service workers tend to encounter. In chapter 1, I acquaint readers with the nature of ethical issues generally and, in particular, with the nature of ethical issues in social service. In chapter 2, I focus more directly and in greater detail on the ethical issues I believe are the most compelling in the social service professions. The next three chapters are devoted to discussion of a series of ethical issues which arise repeatedly in the delivery of services directly to individuals and families (chapter 3), in the design and implementation of social welfare policies and programs (chapter 4), and in relationships among practitioners (chapter 5). In these chapters I have organized the discussion around actual cases which contained ethical dilemmas. My hope is that these cases will add life to what might otherwise be rather abstruse discussion of principles of ethics. I also hope that the cases will provide a useful way for practitioners, instructors, and students to begin their own discussions about ethical dilemmas in social service. The book concludes with a discussion of enduring issues related to ethics and social work, including the goals and limitations of ethical analysis, the use of ethics committees in social service agencies, and ethical priorities in the profession of social work (chapter 6).

The cases I have included are based upon actual situations which colleagues of mine and I have encountered in practice. (In each case I have altered details and changed names in order to ensure anonymity, unless the information I have drawn upon is a matter of public record.) I have not been able to provide an exhaustive selection of the wide range of ethical dilemmas which social service professionals encounter in their work; the amount of space available here simply does not permit such breadth. I have, however, attempted to include ethical dilemmas which raise what, in my experience, have been among the most persistent and troubling questions. Some of the cases show in sharp relief the ethical dilemmas which practitioners encountered. In others, the ethical dilemmas are somewhat camouflaged and more subtle. Some of the cases raise questions primarily about decisions which individual practitioners would need to make; others focus on broader questions of ethics which extend beyond the decisions an individual practitioner would need to make—for example, questions regarding the role of government in welfare matters or ways of distributing scarce or limited social service resources. Still others include discussion of ethical dilemmas which relate to both the decisions of individual practitioners *and* broader questions of social policy. My hope is that the discussion organized around the cases will help you understand that a single ethical dilemma can raise a wide variety of ethical questions and can involve a large number of people; I also hope that the case discussions will help you to develop skills for both recognizing and analyzing ethical dilemmas in practice.

You will find that in my discussion of some of the cases I venture opinions about what is right and wrong. It is important for you to keep in mind that these are only my opinions, based on conclusions I reached after thinking carefully about each case. Though my statements occasionally sound prescriptive and definitive, they represent the product of *my* attempt to apply principles of ethics to dilemmas in practice. I do not expect everyone to be convinced by my arguments or to agree with my conclusions, though I certainly do my best to be persuasive. The field of ethics is such that none of us can claim omniscience. In fact, we should be wary of claims that difficult ethical dilemmas can be resolved with tidy and simple analyses. As H. L. Mencken once observed, "For every problem there is a solution that is neat, simple, and wrong."

It is also important to keep in mind that the cases I present necessarily contain only a limited number of details. It is quite possible that the addition or subtraction of certain details would lead me to change my own opinion about the ethical aspects of these cases. I am well aware that details about the personalities of individuals, interpersonal relations, politics, economics, and our opinions about the effectiveness of social service interventions and methods of helping—details which cannot be entirely accounted for here—frequently can (and should) influence our views about how ethical dilemmas ought to be approached and resolved. What I have attempted to provide is a series of illustrations of the ways in which social service professionals can raise questions about and critically discuss and assess ethical dilemmas which arise in their work, details of which can be provided only in relatively broad outline. An important part of the challenge is to speculate about what conclusions we would reach if the details reported in these cases were altered.

I have believed for a long time that it is important for social service practitioners who encounter ethical dilemmas to have some familiarity with the ideas and methods of moral philosophy. Philosophers have thought for centuries about the justification, derivation, and application of principles of ethics. They have worked out many arguments for and against different schools of thought regarding what is right and wrong. Our approach to ethical dilemmas in social service should be as disciplined as possible. I have therefore included, whenever appropriate, material drawn from the discipline of moral philosophy. In doing so, I have tried to walk that fine line between abstract philosophy and relatively mundane case material. I want us to have an appreciation for both the forest and the trees. I also believe that it is important for us to approach the analysis of ethical dilemmas with as much reason—coupled with compassion—as possible and for us to try out our arguments on one another. There is much to be gained from such dialogue. Though we may ultimately disagree about what is right and wrong, it is important for us to anchor our opinions and judgments in reasons which we have taken the time to formulate and defend. The consequences of our opinions for the quality of individuals' lives are too important to have it any other way.

This book is intended for anyone working in the various helping professions. I rely most heavily, however, on ideas, experiences, and literature from my own profession of social work; I hope that members of other professions will not feel slighted as a result. I believe strongly, however, that social work, with its many facets, entails the range of activities which helping professionals engage in, from individual counseling and casework to community organizing and the development of social welfare policies. It has a rich tradition of social service which I believe deserves to be both highlighted and critiqued.

Many people have influenced the content of this book. I would like to thank in particular several colleagues who, over the years, have encouraged me and helped to nurture the development of my own professional ideals and convictions: Ned Gaylin, Kenneth Kahn, Peter Maida, Don Pappenfort, and Charles Shireman. I would like to thank Frank Breul for the time he took to review and comment on an earlier draft of this work. I would also like to thank John Moore of Columbia University Press for encouragement and editorial suggestions, and Gwen Graham and Crystal Williams for the clerical skill and patient assistance which they contributed to the preparation of this book. Finally, my most heartfelt thanks are due my wife, Deborah, who knows what she has meant and whose influence is scattered indelibly throughout these pages.

Good reasons must, of force, give place to better.

—WILLIAM SHAKESPEARE

ETHICAL DILEMMAS IN SOCIAL SERVICE

1

The Nature of Ethics

A number of years ago a colleague of mine, a hospital social worker, was consulted by the family of a man who lay in the hospital dying of cancer. The family spoke with my colleague on the eve of surgery, which, they hoped, would arrest or substantially retard the growth of the cancer. As one would expect, the family members were quite distraught. The surgeon had told them that there was a good chance that the surgery would not be successful and that in addition it was likely that the man would not survive the operation. Understandably, the family was grieving about the possible loss of their father and husband.

But it was not for consolation that they spoke to my colleague. Rather, it was for an opinion. The mother of the family and one of her two sons firmly believed that the man should be told, prior to his surgery, that he might not survive the operation. They believed that he had the right to know that he might soon die and that he had a right to say good-bye to his family. The mother and son felt very uneasy about telling the man about the severity of his illness—details of which had been kept from him—but felt strongly that they had an obligation to tell him the naked truth.

The second son, however, vehemently opposed the idea of informing his father in detail about his illness and the possibility of imminent death. He argued that in such an instance compassion was more important than honesty. He claimed that it would be cruel to burden his father, especially just prior to the surgery. This son insisted that the humane and decent thing to do would be to leave his father with a sense of optimism and hope.

The family was clearly divided. What was my colleague's responsibility as a social worker in this case? It was clearly her responsibility to help the family clarify the issues it faced, keep the family focused on its dilemma, and help mediate its disputes. For many social workers professional responsibility would not extend beyond helping the family reach a decision that its members could feel comfortable with. However, embedded in this case was a series of other questions that had to be addressed. Did the patient have a right to be told the truth? Did the family have a corresponding duty to be truthful with him? Should the duty to tell the truth take precedence over concern about the patient's reaction to information about his condition? Was the social worker obligated to support whatever decision the family reached? Would she have been obligated to put aside her own firmly held convictions if they had conflicted with the family's final decision? Was the worker's primary obligation to the patient or to the other family members?

These are difficult questions to answer. They broach important issues about the fundamental obligations of social workers, about the nature of our profession, and about the duties practitioners have to their clients. In short, these questions raise issues about right and wrong, duty and obligation—questions of ethics.

It is becoming increasingly apparent to social workers that their decisions as professionals frequently entail difficult questions of ethics. Is it ever permissible to break a promise of confidentiality which has been made to a client? If so, under what circumstances? Is it justifiable for a social worker to violate a law or agency regulation which she believes to be unjust? Do mentally retarded individuals have a right to community-based care which overrides the right of neighborhood residents to oppose the opening of a group home? Is it more important to spend limited public funds in an effort to revive a deteriorating community or on the construction of a new hospital, if a choice must be made?

ETHICAL AND NONETHICAL ASPECTS OF SOCIAL WORK

It is important to distinguish between the ethical and nonethical aspects of social work. The ethical aspects of the profession include questions about the obligations and duties of practitioners and about what is ethically right and wrong conduct. The nonethical aspects of the profession include questions about, for example, the effectiveness of particular intervention techniques, the proper way to prepare process notes, methods for assessing the nature of a client's problems, and ways of carrying out a cost-benefit analysis. In and of themselves these tasks require the development of technique, not the ability to judge between what is ethically right and wrong.

At times, of course, it is difficult to separate the moral and nonmoral aspects of social work. For example, our judgments about the most effective way to administer a group home for the retarded may depend in part on conclusions we reach about the kind of care we believe retarded individuals have a right to. Our conclusion about the most efficient way to administer a public aid program will ultimately rest on ethical judgments about the extent of the community's obligation to assist individuals in need.

Many decisions social workers make in their day-to-day practice include important and difficult ethical questions. Consider, for example, the following case.

> Ben Kahn was employed as a social worker at a youth service bureau, Youth-in-Need. The agency had a contract with the state Department of Social Services to provide crisis intervention to youths who had been arrested by the police for running away from home or for being ungovernable. Ben received a call at his home one evening and was summoned to the local police station to assist a sixteen-year-old girl, Bonnie, who had run away from home and who had refused to return home with her parents. The police were preparing to file a petition in juvenile court naming Bonnie as a status offender, a youth who has committed an offense that would not be considered a crime if committed by an adult.
>
> Ben arrived at the police station and met with Bonnie, her parents, and the arresting juvenile officer. The juvenile officer and Bonnie's parents described Bonnie as an irresponsible young girl who fre-

quently ran away from home and was beyond the control of her parents.

Ben met alone with Bonnie and her parents for about an hour and a half. Midway through their conversation about the family's problems Bonnie's father, Mr. Allen, briefly mentioned an incestuous relationship he had had with Bonnie during the two-year period between Bonnie's twelfth and fourteenth birthdays. Mr. Allen also mentioned that the family was meeting periodically with a therapist at a local family service agency to discuss its problems. During the conversation it appeared to Ben that everyone in the family agreed that the problems Bonnie had been having with her parents were largely due to the sexual abuse she had suffered and to the hostility Bonnie felt toward her father as a result.

Ben was also informed that Bonnie had been living with a girl friend during the past month. He arranged for Bonnie to temporarily return to her friend's home, for at least several days. In the meantime the petition charging Bonnie with a status offense was referred to juvenile court.

With the Allens' consent Ben then contacted the therapist, Marjorie Banks, who had been working with the Allens. They spoke at length about the difficulties Bonnie had been having with her parents. Ms. Banks told Ben that she had been trying unsuccessfully for months to have the Allens acknowledge that the history of incest between Bonnie and her father needed to be discussed openly if they hoped to live together and function as a family. Ms. Banks said that she had gotten "sick and tired" of the family's resistance. In fact, Ms. Banks had reluctantly concluded that Bonnie should be placed in a foster home since the family was not willing to confront its serious problems. She had advised the Allens to contact the police and report Bonnie as a runaway; she told them that a petition charging Bonnie as a status offender, or minor in need of supervision, was the most efficient way to arrange for such a placement.

After speaking with Ms. Banks, Ben concluded that placing Bonnie in a foster home would considerably diminish the chances the family had of resolving its problems. Ben felt certain that the family should be helped to understand the importance of discussing the past incest and attempting to identify and appreciate the family dynamics and circumstances which may have led to it. In short, Ben thought placing

Bonnie in a foster home was wrong and that Ms. Banks had given up on the family too quickly.

Ben faced a dilemma. He was fairly certain, based on his experience with the local juvenile court, that if Bonnie were processed as a status offender, she would be placed immediately in a foster home. And, Ben speculated, if Bonnie were placed in a foster home, there would be no incentive for the family to work on its problems. Ben also knew from his experience that if the petition were changed to one citing neglect, the Allens would be referred immediately to a family therapist used by the court, one who, in Ben's judgment, was particularly skilled at working with families where a parent has abused a child. After considerable thought Ben concluded that it would not be fair to Bonnie to have the court process her as a status offender. He felt strongly that Bonnie's running away was only a symptom of the serious problems the Allens had been experiencing as a family and that treating Bonnie as a minor in need of supervision was wrong.

Ben phoned a caseworker from the state Department of Social Services who had responsibility for screening abuse cases. He was told that since there was no evidence of current sexual abuse, a petition citing parental neglect could be filed only if Mr. and Mrs. Allen agreed to do so voluntarily. Ben met with the family and told them that he did not think it was right for Bonnie to be treated as a status offender; discussion with the family and conversations with their therapist, Ms. Banks, indicated to him that the Allens needed help as a family and needed to recognize that all of the family members should be involved.

Mr. and Mrs. Allen told Ben that they would like Bonnie to return home so that "things could be worked out." Ben reminded them that if Bonnie were processed by the juvenile court as a status offender, there was a good likelihood that she would be placed in a foster home and that as a result the family's problems would probably not be addressed. He told the Allens that it would be in their best interest to change the petition to one citing neglect, acknowledge the past abuse, and begin working in earnest on their deep-seated problems.

Several days later the Allens appeared in juvenile court for an initial screening hearing. Mr. Allen reported to the court screener that Bonnie was an incorrigible runaway. He did not mention the family's history of difficulties, nor did he mention the past abuse.

Based on Mr. Allen's testimony and the juvenile officer's report, the court screener filed a petition naming Bonnie as a status offender and scheduled an adjudication hearing. The screener then telephoned Ben and informed him that Bonnie was being petitioned as a status offender; she ordered Ben, whose agency was under contract to provide services in status offense cases, to attempt to arrange temporary foster care for Bonnie. Ben tried to persuade the court screener that Bonnie was not, in fact, a status offender and that Mr. Allen had not provided an accurate account of the family's problems. The screener insisted that Bonnie was indeed a status offender, regardless of past abuse, and reiterated her order that Ben arrange temporary foster care.

Ben thought carefully about the dilemma he faced and concluded that he could not in good conscience cooperate with a plan that treated Bonnie as a culpable status offender. He told the court screener that he would have to refuse her order and asked her to contact another agency to arrange for the foster care. Ben then contacted the Allens and shared his decision with them.

This case raises a number of important questions. How ethical was Ben's decision to disobey the order of the court screener? Was it wrong for Ms. Banks to abandon the goal of helping the Allens change their pattern of behavior and to advise Mr. and Mrs. Allen to report Bonnie to the police? Was the court screener wrong to insist that Bonnie be treated as a status offender? And, of course, there are other questions. Let us focus for now, however, on the ethical questions that might be asked about Ben's decision to discontinue service:

1. Ben was ordered by an officer of the court to assist a family that was in need of assistance. As a social worker, was Ben obligated to obey the court order and continue working with the family, despite the fact that Bonnie might be placed in a foster home and processed through the juvenile court inappropriately as a status offender?
2. Was it wrong for Ben to encourage the Allens to introduce information about the incest in court when Mr. Allen and the family might suffer serious consequences as a result (such as imprisonment or shame and embarrassment)? Or was Ben obligated to encourage the family to report the incest because it was relevant to its deep-seated problems and might have an important bearing on the outcome of the case and Bonnie's welfare?

3. To what extent should Ben have acted in accord with what he thought was the right thing to do for Bonnie's benefit, as opposed to what Mr. and Mrs. Allen preferred? To what extent was he obligated to accede to his clients' wishes?
4. Ben knew from experience that if Bonnie were processed by the juvenile court as a status offender, she would probably be placed in foster care. He knew that it would be important for Bonnie to have an advocate, such as himself, during this period to help her cope with the placement and to serve as a liaison between Bonnie and the court. Ben suspected that if he withdrew from the case, Bonnie might be without an advocate who had a good understanding of the family's problems. Should he have continued working with the family for Bonnie's sake, despite his strong feelings about the family's decision not to change the court petition?
5. Ben had some concern about the effect his decision might have on his reputation and that of his agency, Youth-in-Need. Would his decision jeopardize the agency's future relationship with the juvenile court? What effect would his decision have on his own career? To what extent should these considerations have influenced Ben's decision to discontinue service?

These questions are certainly not easy to answer. Yet the conclusions we reach when we consider ethical dilemmas such as these can have far-reaching, profound effects on the welfare of our clients, professional colleagues, ourselves, and the community at large. While it may be tempting to conclude that practitioners will never reach a consensus about the correct answers to such questions, it is important to consider what guidelines are available to social workers who face difficult ethical decisions about professional values.

THE TRADITIONAL APPROACH TO SOCIAL WORK ETHICS

It may appear at first that the boundaries between the ethical factors in the case involving Ben Kahn and those relating to social work methods and intervention techniques are blurred, that the ethical dilemmas and the dilemmas concerning technique slide into one another. This is indeed the case in some instances. Yet in most cases this blur is more illusory than real. The dilemma Ben faces contains many important questions of technique concerning therapeutic strategies for intervening with troubled families—questions related to, for example, unhealthy alliances, shifting attention away from a scapegoat or "identified patient," and so on. Conclusions Ben might reach about the use of certain treatment approaches may have important consequences for Bonnie and her family. It is hard to deny, however, that the goals Ben sets for himself and the techniques he decides to employ in his work with the Allens depend ultimately on conclusions he reaches about the nature of his obligation to Bonnie, her parents, the court, and to himself. This case contains critical questions concerning clients' rights and practitioners' obligations, and these are fundamentally ethical issues. As we will see below, the decisions Ben finally reaches about intervention techniques must be preceded by judgments he makes, implicitly or explicitly, about the ethical nature of his duties and obligations and about professional values.

Ethics in the Early Years of the Profession

Discussions of values and ethics have had an important place in social work education and practice since the beginning of the profession. Throughout the history of social work practitioners have been concerned about moral or ethical aspects of their relationships with clients. The nature of this concern has changed, however, in response both to stages in the maturation of the profession and to broader historical and political developments. It has been more intense during certain periods of the profession's history than others. In addition, the meaning of the term *moral* has changed considerably over time; for example, its meaning during the early nineteenth century was very different from its meaning today. Concern with ethical issues in social work has shifted from an emphasis upon the morality of the client to moral aspects of the practitioner's behavior and of the profession.

The English Poor Law Reform Bill of 1834 represents what is perhaps the best example of the importance of morality to those who were interested in poor relief in the nineteenth century. The Royal Poor Law Commission for Inquiring into the Administration and Practical Operation of the Poor Laws was dominated by a laissez-faire philosophy that—in the spirit of Adam Smith and David Ricardo—was critical of the Elizabethan Poor Law of 1601. The so-called classical economists believed that poverty was "the natural state of the wage-earning classes"; the poor law was seen as an artificial creation of the state which taxed the middle and upper classes in order to provide care for the wayward needy.[1]

One result of the commission's report was an end to public assistance for able-bodied persons, except in public institutions. Moreover, poverty was described in the report as a condition which resulted from the moral inferiority of individuals. As a consequence, poor relief was designed to increase "fear of insecurity, rather than to check its causes or even to alleviate its problems. At best, it would prevent starvation or death from exposure, but it would do so as economically and unpleasantly as possible."[2]

A similar attitude prevailed in the United States during this period. Though there were nominal distinctions between the "worthy" and "unworthy" poor, even those who were considered worthy were frequently condemned as moral failures; the Protestant ethic encouraged the belief that the poor suffered only from a failure to muster their own resources. This climate of opinion had particularly severe effects on Irish and German immigrants who came to the United States during the first half of the nineteenth century; the Protestant majority found it difficult to forgive and unconditionally aid these "ragged, uncouth, 'different' [un-Christian], and seemingly immoral newcomers."[3] The mission of "paternal guardians" and other representatives of private benevolent societies became the edification of the poor and the provision of careful instruction in the moral virtues of thrift, religious observance, hard work, and temperance.

The settlement house movement, beginning in the United States with the opening of Neighborhood Guild in 1886, marked a significant shift away from attributions of moral inferiority. While the members of the organized charities believed that poverty could be eliminated by moral upgrading and virtuous activity, proponents of the settlement house movement believed that the end of poverty could be realized only as a result of basic social change—by providing more jobs and better working conditions, health care, education, and housing. Poverty resulted not from moral inferiority but from inadequate social conditions, or what became known as a "poverty of opportunity."[4] Reform became more important than individual morality.

There were relatively few writings on morality and social work between the 1920s, following World War I, and the early 1950s. Once again, however, there was a significant shift in the meaning of morality in social work when the term appeared in the literature following World War II.

Whereas discussions of morality preceding this period were concerned primarily with the inchoate virtues of paupers or clients, discussions following the war and to the present have focused on moral or ethical aspects of the profession and of practitioners' professional behavior. These discussions have been of two kinds. First, they have been organized around values considered central to the profession—for instance, individual worth and dignity, self-determination, adequate living conditions, and acceptance by and respect of others. Second, they have included discussions of principles intended to serve as specific guides to social workers' relationships with their clients, colleagues, and employers—for example, with regard to protecting a client's right to confidentiality, the worker's responsibility to oppose discrimination, and the worker's obligation to avoid conflicts of interest.

Contemporary Social Work Ethics

An important example of principles intended to serve as a guide to social workers' actions is the Code of Ethics drafted by the National Association of Social Workers.[5] The current Code of Ethics includes a series of principles that cover a wide range of prescribed and proscribed behaviors for practitioners; they represent the ideas and convictions of social work practitioners and scholars about the obligations of the contemporary social worker. The Code of Ethics includes principles that relate to the social worker's (a) conduct and comportment, (b) ethical responsibility to clients, (c) ethical responsibility to colleagues, (d) ethical responsibility to employers and employing organizations, (e) ethical responsibility to the social work profession, and (f) ethical responsibility to society.

The preamble to the Code states that it is "intended to serve as a guide to the everyday conduct of members of the social work profession. . . . The social worker is expected to take into consideration all the principles in this code that have a bearing upon any situation in which ethical judgment is to be exercised and professional intervention or conduct is planned." How, for instance, might we apply the Code of Ethics to the decision Ben Kahn faced in Bonnie's case? Which principles in the Code are relevant and what do they suggest about the rightness or wrongness of Ben's decision?

Several principles included in the Code are particularly relevant to Bonnie's case and Ben's decision:

1. *The social worker should terminate service to clients, and professional relationships with them, when such service and relationships are no longer required or no longer serve the clients' needs or interests.*

From Ben's point of view this principle may support his decision to discontinue his relationship with Bonnie and her parents. Ben might argue that his assistance would not have served the family's needs; what the family needed, in Ben's judgment, was to acknowledge the sexual abuse of Bonnie by her father and the problems that may have led to and resulted from it. This could not occur if the family insisted on treating Bonnie as a status offender in court rather than as an abused child. Continuing to work with the family under these circumstances would, for Ben, have contradicted this principle. On the other hand, however, one might conclude that the court screener would not have agreed with Ben's assessment that such services would not serve the clients' needs and interests. Thus, whether this principle supports or opposes Ben's decision is not clear.

2. *The social worker should withdraw services precipitously only under unusual circumstances, giving careful consideration to all factors in the situation and taking care to minimize possible adverse effects.*

It is also difficult to know whether this principle supports or opposes Ben's decision. One might argue that Ben indeed faced unusual circumstances and that these circumstances justified the precipitous withdrawal of service. The phrase "unusual circumstances" can be defined, however, in many different ways by social workers and it is not clear whether the circumstances Ben faced were unusual in a way that justifies his actions.

In addition, the principle requires one to give "careful consideration to all factors in the situation" and to take "care to minimize possible adverse effects." We do not know, given the limited information available about Ben's decision, whether he gave careful consideration to all of the important aspects of this case; there is evidence, however, that Ben did attempt to consider possible adverse effects of his decision. He recognized that there might be adverse effects if he withdrew service as well as if he arranged for foster care for Bonnie. Ben decided to act in a manner that seemed to him to minimize the possible adverse effects. Whether he in fact did minimize these effects is difficult to know.

3. The social worker who anticipates the termination or interruption of service to clients should notify clients promptly and provide for transfer, referral, or continuation of service in relation to the clients' needs and preferences.

This principle is closely related to the preceding one. Ben apparently complied with the first part of this principle in that he promptly notified his clients and the court screener of his decision to terminate service. It is possible, however, that his actions may not have been entirely consistent with the second part of the principle that requires a social worker to make arrangements for the continuation of service.

4. The social worker should make every effort to foster maximum self-determination on the part of clients.

This principle is particularly difficult to apply to Ben's decision. Whether one concludes that this principle supports or opposes Ben's decision depends on one's definition of the term *self-determination*. The prevailing conception of self-determination in social work is of a "practical recognition of the right and need of clients to freedom in making their own choices and decisions in the casework process."[6] In Florence Hollis' words:

> Why do we put all this stress on self-direction? Because we believe it is one of the greatest dynamics of the whole casework approach. Because we believe that the soundest growth comes from within. Because we want to release the individual's own life energy to take hold of his situation. . . . But for this growth from within to occur there must be freedom—freedom to think, freedom to choose, freedom from condemnation, freedom from coercion, freedom to make mistakes as well as to act wisely.[7]

Given this definition of the concept, did Ben's decision serve to promote or discourage the self-determination of Bonnie and her parents? In fact, there appear to be compelling arguments that his decision may have both promoted and discouraged self-determination. One can argue that because Ben was not willing to act in accord with his clients' wishes to withhold from court information about the abuse Bonnie had suffered, he was violating the clients' rights to voluntarily choose a course of action and, perhaps, to make mistakes. At the same time, however, Ben might argue that he was attempting to foster the family's self-determination by refusing to cooperate with its decision to regard Bonnie as a status offender rather than as an abused child. In Ben's judgment treating Bonnie as a status offender and failing to acknowledge in court the extent of the family's past difficulties diminished the ability of the family members to effectively make decisions and manage their own lives; that is, the long-range consequences of failing to confront and resolve the family's deep-seated problems may have seriously limited the Allens' ability to act freely and thus may have contradicted the principle that requires a social worker to make every effort to foster maximum self-determination on the part of clients.

As we review these principles and apply them to Ben's decision to withdraw service from Bonnie's family, it is clear that it is at least difficult to use the Code of Ethics to help us to draw an unambiguous conclusion about the rightness or wrongness of Ben's actions. The principles in the Code do not always provide clear guidelines for acting in individual cases or, in particular, for evaluating Ben's decision; moreover, the conclusions suggested by the principles sometimes contradict one another.

What, then, is the value of these principles or, more generally, of the NASW Code of Ethics for social work practitioners? Our brief review of the Code and of a number of its principles suggests several important questions about its relevance to the resolution of ethical dilemmas in individual cases:

1. On what basis and with what justification were the principles included in the Code of Ethics selected?
2. Do the principles included in the Code of Ethics provide adequate criteria for social workers to resolve the ethical dilemmas they encounter in practice?
3. Ideally, how should social workers attempt to resolve ethical dilemmas?

THE JUSTIFICATION OF VALUES

The NASW Code of Ethics includes principles that were carefully and thoughtfully drafted by members of the NASW Task Force on Ethics. The content of the specific principles was influenced by a review of codes of ethics developed by other professional organizations and by the contributions of task force members, study groups organized to consider ethical issues in social work, and social work practitioners and scholars in general. The principles included in the Code appear to represent current professional opinion about social work values as they relate to the behavior of practitioners.

For centuries, moral philosophers have speculated about how ethical principles and values ought to be justified. Questions concerning the justification of ethical principles and values are concerned not with resolving ethical dilemmas in individual cases but, rather, with the methods used to justify the principles and values in the first place—questions of *metaethics*. Metaethical theories have traditionally been divided by moral philosophers into those that assume that absolute moral principles which guide right and wrong action can be formulated and those that assume that moral principles only represent our opinions and feelings about what is right and wrong and are thus relative. The former are referred to as *cognitivist* and the latter as *noncognitivist* theories.[8] Cognitivists believe that it is possible to derive, by using deductive or inductive logic, science, or some other formal means, ethical principles which can be used to reach conclusions about right and wrong action and that ethical principles are in fact either true or false. However, noncognitivists believe that it is not possible for one to derive, by using logic, science, or any other methods, absolute moral principles which are known to be true. One can only have an *opinion* about the suitability of a particular moral principle or have a *preference* for it. Thus, according to noncognitivists, ethical principles merely reflect our personal biases, as opposed to what can be shown to be absolutely right or wrong.

Those who believe that absolute moral principles can be derived are divided further into those who argue that empirical, scientific methods can be used to formulate such principles and those who argue that they can be known only by intuition. The former, like John Dewey, view science as a tool to be used to derive ethical principles; the latter do not accept the idea that ethical principles can be determined by using scientific methods.

Many discussions of social work ethics present ethical values and principles as having a prima facie validity that, while consistent with much popular opinion among social workers and with many contemporary practice techniques, has been based primarily on intuition or "practice wisdom," rather than on careful philosophical analysis.[9] While few members of the profession would question their merits, practitioners are often introduced to these ethical values and principles as if their validity were self-evident. As Joseph Vigilante has stated:

> Social workers have religiously clung to values over the seventy years of the development of the profession and have not done these values justice. We

seem to cling to them intuitively, out of faith, as a symbol of our humanitarianism. We have not treated them with the seriousness befitting their role as the fulcrum of practice.[10]

Contemporary philosophers have attempted to justify ethical decisions in a variety of ways. Their theories represent two major schools of thought. First, there are those who claim that certain kinds of actions are inherently right or good, or right or good as a matter of principle. Advocates of this school of thought are generally referred to as *deontologists.*[11] For instance, a deontologist might argue that it was inherently wrong for Ben Kahn to violate a contractual agreement and withdraw service, thus abandoning a family in need. Second, there are those who argue that certain actions are to be performed not because they are intrinsically good, but because they are good by virtue of their consequences. They are generally referred to as *teleologists.*[12] For instance, a teleologist might argue that Ben should have continued to work with the family, not because it was inherently right to do so, but because Bonnie and her family would in the long run be better off if they had received some help from Ben and if he had not insisted that information about Bonnie's sexual abuse be introduced in court.

Utilitarian theories, which hold that an action is right if it promotes the maximum good for everyone, have historically been the most popular teleological theories and have served as justification for many decisions made by social workers. Utilitarian theories have traditionally been of two kinds. First, there are those that justify actions that tend to promote the greatest good in situations where one of several possible actions must be performed (this is referred to as *good-aggregative utilitarianism).* Second, there are theories, such as those proposed by Jeremy Bentham and John Stuart Mill, that justify actions that tend to promote the greatest good *for the greatest number,* considering not only the quantity of goods produced but also the number of people to whom the goods are distributed *(locus-aggregative utilitarianism).*[13] The distinction between these two forms of utilitarianism is important when one considers, for example, whether to distribute a fixed amount of public assistance in a way that tends to produce the greatest satisfaction (which might entail dispensing large sums of money to relatively few people) or produces the greatest satisfaction for the greatest number (which might entail dispensing smaller sums to a larger number of people). Similar dilemmas arise whenever decisions must be made concerning the distribution of limited resources, such as medical care, nursing home beds, or a social worker's time.

A CLOSER LOOK AT UTILITARIANISM

The choice between defining an action as inherently right or good (a deontological approach) and as right because of the goodness of its consequences (a utilitarian approach) is an important one for social workers to consider because decisions and policies implemented on these bases will often have substantially different effects. For instance, while a deontologist might argue that it is inherently right to maintain an elderly person in the community as long as possible, a utilitarian might justify placing the person in an institution on the grounds that in the long run this will result in less of a burden for the person's family (a desirable consequence). Or, while a deontologist might argue that it is inherently wrong to breach the confidentiality previously afforded information shared by a client, a utilitarian might justify reporting the information to others if doing so will protect the client or someone else from serious injury.

Deontological principles can sometimes be used to justify competing points of view. For example, a deontologist who believes in the inherent value of contracts would criticize Ben Kahn for refusing to comply with the court official's mandate. However, a deontologist who believes in the inherent value of "justice" might argue that Ben was obligated to withdraw from the case because of his belief that otherwise he would be party to an unjust act.

Utilitarian principles also can be used to justify competing points of view. There appear, for instance, to be compelling utilitarian arguments both for and against Ben's decision to withdraw service from Bonnie's family.

Let us begin by examining a number of utilitarian arguments that seem to support Ben's decision to discontinue service:

1. The consequences for Bonnie and her family in the long run may be undesirable if Ben agrees to help place Bonnie in foster care where she will be treated as a status offender rather than as an abused or neglected child. The family will not be forced to confront the deep-seated problems which apparently led to and followed the abuse.
2. If Ben cooperates with a plan that treats Bonnie as a status offender, he would violate his personal commitment to treat juveniles fairly. His own

conscience and his confidence in his ability to act justly may suffer as a consequence.

3. There may be undesirable consequences for Bonnie's self-esteem, for her parents, and for the community if Ben participates in processing Bonnie as a status offender. Labeling theory suggests that youths who are inappropriately processed as offenders may come to think of themselves as offenders and, as a result, behave like offenders.[14] Labeling Bonnie's father as an abusive parent may also have adverse effects.

At the same time, however, there are a number of teleological (utilitarian) arguments that seem to oppose Ben's decision:

1. Bonnie's family is in need of service. There is a history of abuse and Bonnie has had considerable difficulty getting along with her parents. If Ben agrees to continue to work with the family there is a chance that he will be able to help them resolve some of their problems. An additional consequence to consider is that the family may receive at least some crisis intervention which may help Bonnie and her parents weather the trauma of her running away and arrest. Thus, in the long run the family members may be better off if Ben continues to work with them.
2. The family was not willing to change Bonnie's petition from a status offense petition to one citing abuse or neglect. Ben's only chance to work with the family and to develop a long-range plan for the Allens requires that he accompany them to court and participate in the processing of Bonnie as a status offender. The greatest good for the larger community may result if Ben agrees to work with the family: Bonnie's father would most likely not be imprisoned and would consequently be able to support his family. Public assistance funds would not be required to support the family, and, in addition, this family that in the past has required substantial social service, provided at public expense, might begin to work on its problems with professional assistance. The greatest good for the greatest number may result if Ben continues to work with the family.
3. If the family agrees to inform the court about the abuse of Bonnie by her father, Mr. Allen may be separated from his family. In addition to the income Mrs. Allen and Bonnie might lose as a result, they may also be deprived of whatever affection and companionship Mr. Allen provides as as a father and husband. In addition, Mr. Allen may suffer pain and

anguish. These consequences could severely diminish the family's chances of being able to resolve its difficulties in the future.

4. Several days following Ben's decision to withdraw service, the juvenile officer responsible for Bonnie's case filed a formal complaint against Ben with the state Department of Social Services and with Ben's agency, Youth-in-Need. The complaint alleged that Ben acted irresponsibly when he discontinued service. If Ben had continued to work with the family or if he had agreed to arrange for temporary foster care, he probably would have been able to avoid having a complaint filed against him, an undesirable consequence that may affect his career and the reputation of his agency.

Teleological principles, or, more specifically, utilitarian principles have traditionally been the most popular guides to ethical decisions made by social workers. One reason utilitarianism has been so popular in the profession of social work is that it appears to foster generalized benevolence; a principle that requires one to perform acts that result in the greatest good for the greatest number is, on the face of it, appealing to professionals whose primary mission is to provide aid to those in need. Utilitarianism also captures our intuition about what constitutes morally right action, and, in its classic form it appears to provide specific guidelines for resolving ethical conflicts. Bentham's original presentation of utilitarianism in *An Introduction to the Principles of Morals and Legislation* (1789) suggests that by examining the "intensity, duration, certainty, propinquity, fecundity, and purity" of the consequences of various actions, one could determine which acts ought to be engaged in: "actions are right in proportion as they tend to promote happiness; wrong as they tend to produce the reverse of happiness." If Ben had been a strict utilitarian, he would have examined all of the possible consequences of the options available to him and decided which action was most likely to result in the greatest good for the greatest number.

Despite its initial appeal, however, utilitarianism has been criticized extensively ever since it was formally introduced by Bentham in the eighteenth century.[15] One can imagine, for instance, how difficult it would have been for Ben to actually calculate the total happiness or general good that might result from continuing to work with Bonnie's family, as opposed to disobeying the court screener and terminating service. How could Ben have assigned quantitative values to Bonnie's happiness, to Mr. Allen's anguish if he had been removed from the home, or to the community's burden if the family required public assistance? Thus, one serious problem with utilitarianism is the difficulty of assigning quantitative values to consequences of actions that are frequently qualitative in nature. In addition, it is difficult to make comparisons between individuals. For example, how can we know whether the trauma Bonnie might suffer if she is processed as a status offender is worse than the trauma her parents might suffer if she is processed as an abused child? Are the consequences of Ben's decision to withdraw service as they relate to his career more or less important than the consequences of his decision for Bonnie's mental health? These are certainly difficult questions, and utilitarians have not yet provided satisfactory answers to this critical problem of interpersonal comparisons.

A related problem concerns the kinds of consequences that should be considered when one is attempting to determine the rightness of particular acts. Utilitarians have not been consistent in their definitions of *good,* and it is not clear in many instances exactly what goods are to be valued and pursued and for what reasons. Bentham, for example, is known as a *hedonistic utilitarian* because of the value he placed on pleasure as opposed to pain. John Stuart Mill, however, argued that mere pleasure is not to be the sole criterion for evaluating consequences, as indicated by his well-known statement, it is "better to be Socrates dissatisfied than a fool satisfied." The state of mind of Socrates might be less pleasurable than that of a fool, but, according to Mill, Socrates would be more content than a fool. For Mill there are "higher" and "lower" pleasures, though he is not too clear about the characteristics of these various pleasures. G. E. Moore, on the other hand, believed that some states of mind, such as those of acquiring knowledge, had intrinsic value apart from the pleasure they produced. Philosophers who take this point of view are known as *ideal utilitarians.*[16]

Utilitarians have also not been clear about whether consequences that are expected to obtain in the future should be considered in addition to consequences that are expected to be immediate. Should consequences for residents in Bonnie's neighborhood be considered, or must one also consider possible consequences for the entire city or county? The extent and scope of the consequences to be considered under utilitarianism are not clear.

Perhaps the most serious problem with utilitarianism, however, is that technically it may permit subordination of the rights of a few individuals if a greater aggregation of good results. Thus, the right Bonnie may have to be treated by the juvenile court as an abused child could be ignored under utilitarianism if processing her as a status offender would result in a greater aggregation of good (for instance, because of benefits that might accrue to Bonnie's parents or to the larger community). In its most extreme applications utilitarianism technically permits the punishment of an innocent person if doing so would have generally desirable consequences. A compelling example appears in Dostoevsky's classic, *Crime and Punishment*:

> Look here; on one side we have a stupid, senseless, worthless, spiteful, ailing, horrid old woman, not simply useless, but doing actual mischief, who has not an idea what she is living for herself, and who will die in a day or two in any case. . . . On the other side, fresh young lives thrown away for want of help, and by thousands, on every side. A hundred thousand good deeds could be done and helped, on that old woman's money which will be buried in a monastery! Hundreds, thousands perhaps, might be set on the right path; dozens of families saved from destitution, from ruin, from vice, from the lock hospitals—and all with her money. Kill her, take her money and with the help of it devote oneself to the service of humanity and the good of all. What do you think, would not one tiny crime be wiped out by thousands of good deeds? For one life thousands would be saved from corruption and decay. One death, and a hundred lives in exchange—it's simple arithmetic![17]

TOWARD AN ETHICS OF SOCIAL WORK

My brief review of ethical theories as they relate to social work appears, at first, not to have advanced our ability to resolve the difficult ethical dilemmas that confront practitioners. While deontological and teleological points of view have an initial appeal, it is clear that both approaches to making ethical decisions suffer from serious weaknesses. The deontological approach, which claims that certain acts are inherently right and thus ought to be engaged in, fails to provide guidelines for resolving conflicts of opinion among practitioners. The teleological (utilitarian) approach, on the other hand, which claims that the rightness of an act is determined by the goodness of its consequences, seems unwieldy and impractical; utilitarians have not determined how consequences that are qualitative in nature can be quantified. Nor have they solved the problem of interpersonal comparisons or the problem that the rights of a few can be subordinated for a presumably greater good.

Do these serious difficulties with traditional ethical theories compel us to conclude that any attempt to derive guidelines for resolving ethical dilemmas in social work practice is necessarily ill fated and destined to fail?

Do these difficulties require us to resort to an extreme form of subjectivism or relativistic ethics where one opinion or conclusion is as acceptable as another? No, they do not.

Thus far we have attempted to answer the question that has challenged moral philosophers for centuries: What normative theory of ethics should be used to resolve ethical dilemmas in individual cases? The evidence available to date suggests that this question in this form cannot, in fact, be answered satisfactorily. A supreme ethical theory which has been able to stand up to sustained and careful scrutiny has not yet been formulated. Theories that require one to consider the goodness of consequences are as susceptible to criticism as theories that depend on assumptions about the inherent goodness of individual actions. Yet, our inability to provide unambiguous guidelines for determining right and wrong action cannot lead us to abandon the search. The ethical dilemmas will not disappear if we abandon our pursuit of principles to guide us in resolving them.

The fact that philosophers and social workers interested in ethical issues have not been able to reach determinate conclusions about right and wrong action may merely indicate that we have not been asking the appropriate questions. A more realistic and appropriate goal, though one that is certainly no less compelling, is to provide social workers with guidelines for the analysis of ethical dilemmas in the profession, guidelines which consider how ethical principles should be justified in the first place and how social workers can systematically approach the resolution of ethical dilemmas. While social workers may continue to disagree about the ultimate rightness or wrongness of certain acts and while a supreme ethical principle may never be derived, being able to identify the ethical aspects of a given case and to understand the strengths and limitations of particular ethical arguments can advance the morality of social workers considerably. As Dorothy Emmet has stated:

> In these days when few of us think that we can look up the answers to moral problems at the back of the book, we may get further if we are prepared to take the risk of developing our powers of making moral judgments, rather than sit back and let these powers atrophy because of our uncertainties. . . . It would do no harm for social workers themselves to do more of it during their own training. Even if the result is to drive us back on to some moral principles or values for which we can give no further reasons, there will be a difference between holding them in this way *after* a process of critical heart-searching and just asserting them dogmatically. At any rate we can learn . . . to see moral questions as problematic and open ended, which means that

they can be thought about and discussed and also see there are reasonable ways of going about this.[18]

Our task, then, is to begin an outline of the fundamental ethical issues in social work and to consider ways in which social workers can systematically approach ethical dilemmas in practice. Our goal is not to generate a series of rigid ethical principles to be applied in practice; the efforts of philosophers throughout the ages suggest that this approach will be filled with considerable difficulties. Rather, our goal shall be to develop guidelines for what we will refer to as *ethical analysis,* guidelines that will assist social workers in their efforts to identify and reason about ethical dilemmas encountered in practice.

If we are to concern ourselves with the ways in which social workers can approach the resolution of ethical dilemmas in practice, we must first identify the range of ethical issues with which social workers ought to be concerned. What are the ethical issues that social workers encounter in their day-to-day practice? Are some more compelling than others? Are there ethical issues that are currently not receiving attention from practitioners that deserve attention?

If we are to develop an adequate understanding of ethical issues in social work, it will be important for us to be guided by an understanding of ethical issues generally and to appreciate the content and traditions of the broad field of ethics and moral philosophy. The ethical issues that we encounter as social workers are a subset of ethical issues in general and should be treated as extensions of them. Thus, a brief review of the central issues in ethics that have occupied the attention of moral philosophers throughout the ages will provide an important guide to our examination of ethical issues in social work.

CENTRAL ISSUES IN MORAL PHILOSOPHY

Moral philosophers have traditionally identified three central questions within which most, if not all, ethical issues can be subsumed.[19] First, why should one be concerned with morality and ethics, in the sense of considering one's obligations to other individuals, especially when these obligations conflict with one's own interests? Second, whose interests, in addition to our own, should we be concerned with, and in what manner should goods and resources be distributed among individuals? And third, what actions and resources are to be considered worthwhile, good, and desirable on their own account, and for what reasons? These three questions have been referred to as, respectively, the *authoritative, distributive,* and *substantive* questions of ethics.

The Authoritative Question

Our decisions to intervene in clients' lives in certain ways tend to be influenced by several factors. We sometimes consider available evidence from research regarding the effectiveness of a particular treatment technique. Or, we may be influenced by a particular theory of human behavior, though there may be no empirical evidence to establish its validity. We may also be influenced by the apparent success of our experiences working with clients who have particular problems and by the experiences of our colleagues and supervisors. And, finally, we may be influenced by our values, our beliefs about what is right and wrong, or good and bad, in a particular situation.

The factors that tend to influence social workers' decisions about how to intervene in clients' lives can be generally classified as *technical, empirical,* and *ethical.* Technical factors relate to beliefs that certain methods of social work practice are appropriate for use with clients who present certain traits and problems. These beliefs are based on theories of social casework and policy and on experiences social workers have had throughout the years using a variety of social work approaches in a variety of settings and with a variety of clients. They are based on what many social workers refer to as "practice wisdom." Very often these beliefs are shaped by the training one has received and by the method or methods of social work that are used by one's professional colleagues.

Empirical factors relate to science and to what is known from research about the effectiveness or likely consequences of specific social work approaches. For example, a practitioner's decision to use task-centered casework with a twelve-year-old child who is having difficulty completing school assignments may be based on a systematic review of the empirical evidence concerning the effectiveness of this method with children experiencing school problems. Or, a decision to reduce the caseloads of public aid workers may be influenced by research evidence that there is an inverse relationship between caseload size and client satisfaction with service.

Ethical factors relate to conclusions that are based on an analysis of what is right and wrong, or good and bad, in a moral sense. For example, while empirical evidence may suggest that runaways who are briefly incarcerated tend to run away less than comparable runaways who are returned home, the argument that it would be fundamentally wrong, in a moral or ethical sense, to incarcerate a youth who is considered by law not to be responsible for his acts may be viewed by some as the critical reason for avoiding incarceration. That is, the ethical grounds may supersede the empirical factors.

The degree to which technical, empirical, and ethical factors should guide social workers' decisions about how to intervene in clients' lives has been the subject of extended debate.[20] It is argued by some that empirical evidence of the effectiveness of specific social work approaches cannot replace the intangible evidence one accumulates after years of practical experience working with clients. Others argue that guidelines based on a careful analysis of results of research should influence decisions in practice. And still others argue that to be guided ultimately by factors other than those based on beliefs about what is morally right or wrong, or about duty and obligation, is unacceptable.

It is certainly important to consider technical, empirical, and ethical factors when one is faced with a decision about how to intervene. Certainly our own professional experiences, the experiences of our colleagues, and theories of social work provide valuable information about the possible consequences of various social work strategies. Research that has been carefully designed and conducted can provide valuable tests of various social work techniques. And, of course, it is important to raise questions about the ethical aspects of various approaches. Ideally, the conclusions we reach based on research, professional experience, theories of social work, and ethical guidelines would be consistent with one another. We know from experience, however, that such consistency is frequently not achieved. Research findings may contradict what a previously untested theory of treatment has asserted. Ethical guidelines may conflict with traditional agency practices. And these, of course, are the difficult cases.

Technical, empirical, and ethical factors all have a place in our decisions as social workers. However, ethical beliefs about what is right or wrong must serve *in the final analysis* as the primary justification of a particular social work intervention. This is so for several reasons. First, decisions about what intervention would be the most desirable in a given case necessarily reduce to questions about how to define the term *desirable*. Insofar as these questions entail questions about the preferences of individual practitioners, they concern values. And insofar as questions of values ask what is right or wrong, or good and bad to value, they are ethical. For example, one social worker may argue that, based on her experience and review of relevant theories, the most desirable intervention for juvenile delinquents is the one that reduces recidivism rates to the greatest extent. Another worker may argue that the most desirable intervention is the one that results in the greatest degree of compensation for victims. Or, while one worker may argue that, based on her experience, it is important to inform dying patients of their impending deaths as soon as possible, another may argue that her experience suggests withholding such information until the patient specifically asks for it. Decisions about which worker's view has the greatest merit necessarily rests on questions of values and, hence, on questions of ethics.

Empirical evidence can at times help us make such decisions. Research on the effectiveness of specific social work techniques can help resolve disagreements about the likely outcomes of certain interventions. However, empirical evidence by itself cannot be translated directly into decisions about the most appropriate treatment strategy. One major difficulty with basing decisions about intervention strategy on the results of empirical evidence is that a single set of empirical results can be interpreted differently by different people. An example of this can be found in a study of the effects of secure detention and community-based services on the recidivism rates of juveniles arrested for status offenses, such as running away from home, ungovernability, and truancy.[21] Results gathered from eight states consistently indicate an absence of significant differences between the effects of these two interventions. These results cannot, however, be translated directly into policy concerning the detention of status offenders. For example, these results suggest to some that community-based services are no more effective than traditional detention and, thus, provide evidence that this approach is not effective and should not be continued. These juvenile offenders should be locked up for a short period of time if for no other reason than to satisfy our natural desire for retribution. To others these results suggest that detention of juveniles does not have a deterrent or rehabilitative effect any greater than that of community-based services. Therefore, these results suggest that the rather severe intervention of secure detention does not result in greater protection to the community than do community-based services and is therefore not warranted. The difficulty with these interpretations is that the empirical evidence does not lead to a clear, unambiguous conclusion about the desirability of alternatives to detention. Decisions about the use of secure detention must ultimately rest on beliefs we have about the sanctity of values such as freedom, justice, and desert.

Thus, while research can provide valuable information about the effects of specific social work strategies, normative conclusions cannot be deduced directly and immediately from the empirical evidence itself. There is no logical connection between empirical, descriptive statements of fact and ethical judgments. This difficulty is referred to by moral philosophers as the *is-ought* problem:

> It is often said that one cannot derive an "ought" from an "is." This thesis, which comes from a famous passage in Hume's *Treatise,* while not as clear as it might be, is at least clear in broad outline: there is a class of statements of fact which is logically distinct from a class of statements of value. No set of statements of fact by themselves entails any statement of value. Put in more contemporary terminology, no set of *descriptive* statements can entail an *evaluative* statement without the addition of at least one evaluative premise. To believe otherwise is to commit what has been called the naturalistic fallacy.[22]

A related problem with the use of empirical evidence as the primary basis for making practical decisions relates to fundamental questions about the validity and reliability of data gathered in research. These questions, frequently debated by philosophers of science, concern such issues as the ability of researchers to construct accurate operational measures of the concepts studied, limits on the ability of researchers to make inferences about causal relations between variables, and the effects of research procedures themselves, which may bias empirical results.[23] It is well known, for instance, that social work researchers have considerable difficulty operationalizing variables that are of primary concern to practitioners, variables such as mental health, self-awareness, ego strength, autonomy, and competence.[24] It is difficult to obtain agreement among social workers about the most accurate indicators of these concepts; this is a problem of content validity. As a result, it is frequently difficult to know whether research findings indicating that, for instance, casework is not effective are a consequence of the inability of researchers to accurately measure outcome or are solid evidence of the ineffectiveness of our efforts.[25]

A serious limitation in social work research also results from researchers frequently being unable to control for extraneous variables when testing the effects of specific interventions. Random assignment of subjects to experimental and control groups is often not possible, and, thus, factors such as historical events, contemporaneous events, and the effects of testing and maturation are frequently not controlled for. As a result, social work researchers must frequently rely simply on correlations between specific interventions and measures of outcome. Our ability to make inferences about the causal relationship between social work efforts and outcome is thus quite limited.

It is clear, then, that technical factors, based on professional experience and theories of social work, and empirical factors, based on research, cannot by themselves justify practice decisions in social work. The very nature of our decisions requires us to address questions of values and ethics. This is not to say that nonethical considerations such as economic constraints, empirical evidence, practice techniques, or political compromises should not enter into professional judgments. Of course they should and frequently must. The inescapable conclusion, however, is that our professional decisions must be justified ultimately by statements (implicit or explicit) that a particular decision is *right* or *wrong* for specific reasons and has consequences that are considered *good* or *bad*. The very use of terms such as *right* or *wrong* and *good* and *bad* to represent professional preferences and values leads us in the end to ethical concepts and ethical issues.

The Distributive Question

The distributive question asks, whose interests, in addition to our own, should we be concerned with and in what manner should goods and resources be distributed among individuals? As one might expect, philosophers have answered the first part of this question in a variety of ways. Their arguments have ranged from those asserting extreme forms of altruism, where an individual is concerned with everyone's interests other than his or her own, and those asserting extreme forms of egoism, where an individual is concerned with only his or her own interests. Between these extremes are arguments to the effect that individuals ought to be concerned with the interests of others, though not the interests of everyone. These arguments sometimes state that one should be concerned only or primarily with the interests of persons who lack certain skills or resources (for example, vocational skills or adequate housing) or who belong to a certain community, religion, race, economic or social class, or to some other restricted group.

The debate regarding whose interests individuals ought to be concerned with is an important one for social workers to consider. The traditional mission of the profession has depended on assumptions about obligations individuals have to care for and give to one another. In the early years of the profession these assumptions were frequently based on religious beliefs about obligations to assist the wayward needy to learn Christian virtues. More recently these assumptions about caring and giving have been based on beliefs that members of a democratic society incur fundamental obligations to aid those who have suffered the undesirable consequences of a way of life organized around a system of free enterprise. It is these beliefs that have served as the foundation for many contemporary social welfare programs, including public assistance programs for the poor, elderly, and disabled, food stamps, medical aid for the needy, disaster relief, federal subsidies and loan guarantees for failing corporations, services for the chronically ill, public housing, mental health services, and many other publicly and privately financed programs.

It is important to consider, however, the extent to which there is in fact an ethical obligation to aid those in need and the extent to which such efforts, while perhaps desirable and commendable, are not required in a moral sense. The positions we take in this debate can, in fact, have extremely important consequences. If we assert that citizens of a democratic society have an obligation to aid those in need (which would, of course, first require a detailed definition of what constitutes need), we would then organize ways to provide such aid. Decisions would be made about the extent to which government agencies should assume responsibility for providing aid, and these decisions would depend upon assumptions about the place of the state in the lives of its citizens. However, if we deny that citizens of a democratic society have an obligation to aid those in need, social services and financial assistance would depend on the voluntary efforts and generosity of private citizens and services that can be purchased from private vendors under market conditions fostered by free enterprise.

The second part of the distributive question—which concerns the manner in which goods and resources should be distributed—has also been the subject of considerable debate among philosophers. It has been argued by some (Karl Marx, for example) that goods and resources should be distributed based on need. Others, such as David Hume, Jeremy Bentham, and other utilitarians, have argued that the greatest happiness will result the more nearly equal is the distribution of goods and resources. And still others have argued that a just distribution is based on dealing with people according to their merits. According to Aristotle, for instance, the criterion of merit is virtue, and justice is achieved by distributing goods in accordance with the extent of one's virtue or goodness of character. Other criteria of merit cited by philosophers have included ability, social status, contribution, intelligence, and wealth.

As we shall see below, guidelines for distributing goods and resources are critical in a field such as social work. Practitioners must frequently make decisions about the distribution of services, financial aid to individuals, agencies, and communities, facilities, time, and other resources, and these decisions have important effects upon individuals. The reasons we provide to justify the distribution of resources in particular cases must be given careful consideration.

The Substantive Question

The third central question of moral philosophy asks what actions and resources are to be considered worthwhile, good, and desirable on their own account, and for what reasons. An important distinction is made here between actions and resources. When we raise ethical questions about actions—such as whether to breach client confidentiality or to withhold public assistance payments from individuals who have reported false information—we ordinarily ask whether the actions are right, wrong, or obligatory. We ask whether they ought or ought not to be done. When we raise ethical questions about resources—such as the value of social services, public assistance programs, a social worker's motives or intentions, or mental health facilities—we ask whether they are morally good or bad. Thus, when we make judgments about the morality of actions, we make judgments of moral obligation, or what philosophers refer to as *deontic* judgments. When we make ethical judgments about resources, we make judgments of moral value, or what philosophers refer to as *aretaic* judgments.

Earlier I briefly reviewed the criteria philosophers have used in their judgments of moral obligation. These included deontological criteria, where certain actions are considered to be inherently right or wrong, or right or wrong as a matter of principle, and teleological criteria, where the rightness of actions is determined by the goodness of their consequences. Judgments of moral value have also been approached by philosophers in a variety of ways. The questions philosophers have asked concerning judgments of moral value have been of two principal types: What things or resources should be considered good? and Of those things or resources that are considered good, which are to be valued most?

What Is Good? Philosophers have been preoccupied with this question for centuries. A number of candidates has been suggested as things that are good for their own sakes, including life, truth, beauty, self-esteem, trust, happiness, knowledge, benevolence, freedom, peace, friendship, and so on. The conclusions social workers reach about what things are good certainly have important consequences. If we value trust, can we ever justify revealing information shared by a client in confidence? If we value knowledge, can we justify spending tax revenue on parades and carnivals rather than on educational programs for the handicapped? If we value freedom and self-determination, can we justify interfering with a client who has decided, after considerable deliberation, to commit suicide?

Philosophers have frequently argued that judgments about what one ought to do (judgments of moral obligation) in particular cases are to be determined by judgments of value or judgments about the meaning or definition of *good.* Thus, if we accept that freedom is good, then we ought to act in ways that promote and enhance freedom—for example, by encouraging clients to select and purchase social services rather than assigning services to them. Or, if we accept that truth is good, then we ought to act in ways that are consistent with this belief—for example, by providing candid assessments to clients who request reports about their progress. However, a traditional difficulty encountered is that actions suggested by these beliefs frequently seem to conflict. For example, if we simultaneously value self-esteem and truth, it may be that reporting the truth to a client about his or her progress will result in diminished self-esteem. If we value equality and economic security, it may be that an equal distribution of community development funds among communities with different degrees of need will result in a lower degree of economic security than would result from an unequal distribution. Or, if we value the right to self-determination and the right to life itself, we encounter a very difficult conflict of duty when a troubled client expresses his or her intention to commit suicide. In fact, it frequently occurs that ethical decisions in practice do not involve choices between values which seem good and bad, but choices between values which, when considered independent of one another, seem good. These cases represent the greatest challenges for social workers who concern themselves with ethical dilemmas.

Conflicts of Duty. One of the classic discussions of conflicts of duty is found in the opening passage of Plato's dialogue concerning civil disobedience, the *Crito.* In short, Socrates was condemned to death by the state for corrupting the youth of Athens with his teachings. He was accused, tried, and convicted in a manner considered by many to have been quite unjust. Friends offered to arrange a plan that would allow Socrates to escape from prison, a plan which Socrates ultimately rejected. The story contains, however, a compelling description of Socrates' conflict of duty. Socrates provided arguments to show that he ought not to break state laws by escaping. First, he argued that we ought never to harm anyone and that escaping would harm the state since the state's laws would be violated. Second, if one remains living in a state when one could leave it, one tacitly agrees to respect its laws. But in Plato's *Apology* Socrates is presented as saying that if the state spares his life on the condition that he cease teaching Athens' youth, he will not obey, because the god Apollo has assigned him to teach, and his teaching is necessary for the good of Athens. Thus, Socrates had to decide between his duty to obey the state, which would require him to cease teaching, and his duty to obey the god Apollo, which would require him to teach for the good of the state. His decision involved not only an appeal to values but a further decision about which values take precedence. The dilemma faced by Socrates was not unlike those faced by modern-day social workers, like Ben Kahn in the Allen case, about conflicting values and the precedence they should have over one another.

The Oxford philosopher W. D. Ross has provided a useful distinction between what he refers to as *prima facie* duty and *actual* duty in his famous discussion of conflicts of value and duty in his work, *The Right and the Good.*[26] A prima facie duty is an action we ought to perform, *other things being equal,* or independent of other ethical considerations. For example, according to the NASW Code of Ethics, Ben Kahn had a prima facie duty to "make every effort to foster maximum self-determination on the part of clients." The difficulty for Ben, however, was that this prima facie duty, whereby, according to one interpretation, he should have respected the

Allens' wishes to process Bonnie as a status offender. conflicted with another prima facie duty to "terminate service to clients, and professional relationships with them, when such service and relationships . . . no longer serve the clients' needs or interests." In Ben's judgment his prima facie duty to act in accord with Bonnie's needs and interests—which would entail having Bonnie treated by the court as an abused child—should take precedence over his prima facie duty to foster his clients' self-determination. Thus, Ben concluded that his *actual* duty required him to refuse to cooperate in a plan which would process Bonnie as a status offender. An actual duty follows, then, an attempt to reconcile two or more conflicting prima facie duties.

Conflicts among prima facie duties frequently occur in social work and decisions about one's actual duty in instances when they conflict represent what are perhaps the most compelling ethical challenges for practitioners. These are, in a phrase, the hard cases. These are the cases that require one to make difficult, frequently painful choices among options, none of which, oftentimes, seems entirely satisfying in the end. These are the cases in which one must decide, for instance, whether information shared by a dangerous client in confidence should be shared with others, whether community residents should be displaced in order to rehabilitate a deteriorating neighborhood, or the extent to which one should interfere with a client who has carefully and thoughtfully decided to harm him- or herself. As Alan Donagan has said in his *The Theory of Morality:* "it is possible, by breaking one moral prohibition, to entangle yourself in a situation in which, whatever you do, you must break another: that is, in which you are perplexed *secundum quid.* Can common morality provide consistent contrary-to-duty prescriptions for such cases?"[27]

There have been, as one might expect, many opinions ventured about the ways in which individuals should reconcile conflicts among prima facie duties to determine one's actual duty. W. D. Ross, for instance, claims that prima facie duties, such as justice, fidelity, reparation, and gratitude, are self-evident to all "thoughtful and well-educated people" who "have reached sufficient mental maturity and have given sufficient attention" to these duties. Concerning propositions reflecting prima facie duties, such as that people ought to promote the good of others, keep promises, or tell the truth, Ross states: "The moral order expressed in these propositions is just as much part of the fundamental nature of the universe (and, we may add, of any possible universe in which there were moral agents at all) as is the spatial or numerical structure expressed in the axioms of geometry or arithmetic."[28] In the end, however, Ross acknowledges that he does not provide a principle that resolves in an unambiguous manner conflicts among prima facie duties. Problems resolving differences of opinion remain.

A second point of view concerning guidelines for resolving conflicts among prima facie duties and determining actual duties is based on a variant of the principle of utilitarianism. It holds that an actual duty in a case where prima facie duties conflict is that which results in the least harm. As Donagan says:

> What [common morality] provides depends on the fact that, although wrongness, or moral impermissibility, does not have degrees, impermissible wrongs are more or less grave. The explanation of this is simple. Any violation of the respect owed to human beings as rational is flatly and unconditionally forbidden; but the respect owed to human beings may be violated either more or less gravely. It is absolutely impermissible either to murder or to steal; but although murder is no more a wrong than stealing, it is a graver wrong. There is a parallel in criminal law, in which murder and stealing are equally felonies, but murder is a graver felony than stealing. In general, every wrong action impairs some human good, and the gravity of wrong actions varies with the human goods they impair. Although there is room for dispute in some cases as to whether or not this action is a graver wrong than that (for example, whether theft of one's reputation is worse than theft of one's purse), when they find themselves trapped . . . in a choice between wrongs, not only do most moral agents have opinions about whether those wrongs are equally grave, and if they are not, about which is the graver; but also, if they adhere to the same moral tradition, their opinions on these questions largely agree. And, given that wrongs can differ in gravity, it quite obviously follows from the fundamental principle of morality that, when through some misdeed a man is confronted with a choice between wrongs, if one of them is less grave than the others, he is to choose it. This precept is a special application of a more general principle which I shall refer to as the principle of the least evil, and which was already proverbial in Cicero's time: namely, *minima de malis eligenda*—when you must choose between evils, choose the least.[29]

Attempting to determine actual duties in cases where prima facie duties conflict represents, as we shall see, what is consistently the most critical ethical dilemma facing social workers. Much of our attention in the remaining chapters will be devoted to a consideration of this task.

The central questions of moral philosophy thus encompass a wide range of ethical issues and problems. They include such basic questions as why one should be concerned with morality and ethics—a question of metaethics—as well as questions of normative ethics, such as in what manner should goods and resources be distributed among individuals? The central ethical questions for the profession of social work encompass an equally wide range of issues and problems. As I observed earlier, the fundamental ethical issues in social work must be considered a subset of fundamental ethical issues in general and should be derived from them. Thus, consideration of the central issues in moral philosophy—including the authoritative, distributive, and substantive questions—has now brought us to the important task of identifying the central ethical issues in social work.

2

Fundamental Ethical Issues in Social Work

Earlier I distinguished between questions of metaethics and questions of normative ethics. You will recall that questions of metaethics involve an analysis of the meaning and definitions of ethical terms such as *good* and *bad, right* and *wrong;* normative ethics, on the other hand, involves the application of ethical standards and values in order to judge whether specific actions, institutions, and ways of life are right or wrong, or good or bad. Thus, the question What is the meaning of the term good? is one of metaethics, while the question Should services and resources be distributed among individuals on the basis of need? is one of normative ethics.

Just as the central questions in ethics and moral philosophy concern issues of metaethics and normative ethics, in general so do the fundamental ethical questions in social work; as I observed earlier, they derive from the central questions in ethics and moral philosophy. The fundamental ethical questions in social work also concern such basic issues as the meaning of ethical terms, the justification of values, the nature of ethical obligation, and the distribution of goods and resources.

The particular ethical questions which concern social work reflect the special status of the profession as one whose practitioners are vested with various degrees of authority to intervene in the lives of individuals. The critical concept here is *authority*. Social workers routinely occupy positions of authority whose status enables them to act in ways that directly or indirectly affect the lives of individuals. Because social workers occupy positions of authority, where authority is defined as the ability to influence the activities, events, and welfare of others, it is vitally important to consider guidelines for their professional decisions and actions. Charles Frankel has referred to this central feature of the profession of social work as the "problem of authority":

> In simple terms, . . . attempts to solve the "problem of authority" represent a search for a framework of principles to guide individuals in determining the course of social action which they should follow; or, in more general social terms, it is an attempt to find principles which will establish the relative priority that should be given to the various systems of authority functioning in a society. In struggling with the problem of authority, in other words, philosophers have been seeking to work out a comprehensive framework of fundamental beliefs and values which will generate and control the formulation of a coherent set of proposals for social policy.[1]

Several important questions derive from the problem of authority. Under what circumstances are social workers obligated to intervene in the lives of others? What limits should we place on our interventions? In what manner should the services and resources over which social workers have control (for example, social service funds, mental health services, staff time) be distributed among individuals? As we shall see below, the most important ethical dilemmas encountered by social workers can be considered within the context of these questions. Let us turn to an examination of these fundamental ethical issues in social work.

THE DUTY TO AID

The profession of social work has traditionally urged concern for children, the poor, the disabled, the invalid, and the mentally ill. The mission of the profession has been based on the enduring assumption that members of society assume an obligation to assist those in need, especially those who seem unable to help themselves. Moreover, social workers have traditionally argued that care of those in need cannot be left entirely to the voluntary efforts of private citizens and organizations; the state, in the form of federal, state, and local government, must assume significant responsibility for its organization and distribution.

The proposition that society incurs an obligation to provide aid to those in need and that the state has an obligation to assume portions of this responsibility has not, however, been uniformly endorsed. Indeed, there have been arguments to the effect that members of society do not in fact have an obligation to aid those in need and, while charity and other voluntary efforts of assistance may be commendable and encouraged, there is no reason to believe that the state has a special responsibility to provide such aid. A more extreme position maintains that it is in fact wrong in an ethical sense for the state to assume such responsibility. According to Robert Nozick, for example:

> Our main conclusions about the state are that a minimal state, limited to the narrow functions of protection against force, theft, fraud, enforcement of contracts, and so on, is justified; that any more extensive state will violate persons' rights not to be forced to do certain things, and is unjustified; and that the minimal state is inspiring as well as right. Two noteworthy implications are that the state may not use its coercive apparatus for the purpose of getting some citizens to aid others, or in order to prohibit activities to people for their *own* good or protection.[2]

The arguments for and against these various positions demand attention, especially in an era in which increases in need seem to coincide with diminished public and private funds available for aid. Government agencies and private citizens and organizations must routinely make hard choices among competing claims of those in need. The positions we take on issues concerning the duty to aid and the role of the state thus have direct and significant consequences for human welfare.

An important aspect of the general issue regarding the duty to aid concerns the choice social workers must frequently make between intervening in individuals' lives in order to provide assistance and alleviate suffering and avoiding intervention so as to respect individuals' apparent right to freedom from interference. These choices often involve very difficult conflicts of duty, that is, choices between the prima facie duty (to use Ross' term) to aid those in need and the prima facie duty not to interfere with the freedom of individuals to manage their own lives as they wish. These decisions represent choices between what I will refer to as, respectively, *positive obligations* and *negative obligations*.

POSITIVE AND NEGATIVE OBLIGATIONS

At times it seems very difficult to know where to draw the line between withholding interventions into individuals' lives in order to avoid interfering in their affairs and intervening to help correct intolerable living conditions, self-destructive or threatening behavior, and emotional misery. These are the cases that test the strength of our convictions about individuals' rights to self-determination, freedom, and well-being. On the one hand, we are tempted to avoid paternalistic acts and to respect the preferences individuals have for certain foods, clothing, and music. On the other hand, as social workers we often find ourselves drawn by a commitment to help those whose preferences do not seem benign, either because they threaten the welfare of others or because they are self-destructive. The push and pull between these two ideals is frequently laden with profound ambivalence and angst. This is the tension that represents perhaps better than any other the Scylla and Charybdis of social work.

Imagine, for example, the following circumstances encountered by a young social worker employed by a major hospital in St. Louis.

> Gloria Wade is a seventeen-year-old mother who has been living with her husband and two-month-old daughter in St. Louis for almost eight months. Gloria was raised in a rural community in eastern Kentucky; it was here that she met her husband, Lester, nearly a year ago. Soon after they were married, Gloria and Lester moved to St. Louis. Lester was having difficulty finding work in their Kentucky community and speculated that work might be easier to find in St. Louis, a city he once visited briefly as a child.
>
> Gloria had taken her daughter, Louise, to the emergency room of the local hospital at least once a week ever since Louise was born. In each instance Gloria reported that Louise was suffering from either a head cold or diarrhea. Following Gloria's seventh visit, the pediatrician on duty in the emergency room forwarded a memo to the hospital's social work department suggesting that Gloria might be neglecting her daughter; Louise's hospital record indicated gradual weight loss, chronic head colds, and diarrhea during the six-week period. In addition, the record noted that when Gloria brought Louise to the hospital, the baby was frequently left in a chair unattended.

Marcia Simmons, the hospital social worker who investigated referrals from the emergency room, arranged to visit with the Wades in their home. Marcia located the Wades' apartment in the basement of a building in a deteriorated section of St. Louis. The windowless apartment included two small rooms, a bathroom, and a large closet which contained a small refrigerator, sink, and stove. In her statement summarizing her visit Marcia described the apartment as "hot, cramped, and dirty." Marcia also reported that the Wades did not have a crib for Louise; the baby slept on a sofa where it appeared likely that she could fall off. Marcia concluded that, in her judgment, Gloria was neither well informed about nor prepared for child care. She mentioned to Gloria that the hospital would like to arrange for a series of visits from a visiting nurse who would help Gloria and Lester learn more about child care.

Marcia reported to her supervisor that Gloria "became very defensive" when the idea of the visiting nurse was suggested. Gloria claimed that she knew how to care for her child and that Louise was not suffering any unusual illness. Gloria refused, in fact, to allow the hospital to send a visiting nurse to her home. She adamantly denied that any serious problem existed.

The dilemma Marcia Simmons and her supervisor faced involved a choice between respecting Gloria's preference to raise her child as she wished and requesting a court order which would require the Wades to accept a visiting nurse or face having Louise placed temporarily in foster care. In more formal terms, Marcia and her supervisor faced a choice between a *negative obligation* to avoid interfering with Gloria's freedom to choose how to care for her child and the *positive obligation* to intervene in the Wades' lives, contrary to Gloria's wishes, in order to protect Louise's welfare. At what point, they speculated, is it justifiable to ignore clients' preferences in pursuit of some "greater" good? If Louise had been battered, there would be little question about the right of the social workers to intervene. But is Louise's condition as described in the emergency room records and in Marcia Simmons' report such that intervention opposed by Gloria Wade is justifiable? Is Louise's right to well-being more important than Gloria's right to raise her child as she wishes? If so, for what reasons?

The distinction between positive and negative obligations is based in part on a distinction made by the philosopher Sir Isaiah Berlin in his classic discussion of positive and negative liberty.[3] *Positive liberty* concerns the freedom to act as one wishes and the abilities and resources necessary for one to fulfill one's purposes; negative liberty concerns freedom from coercion and interference. *Negative liberty* is perhaps best exemplified in John Stuart Mill's essay *On Liberty,* where he presents arguments against interference by the state in the lives of its citizens.

Over the years philosophers have debated about the proper balance between interference in the lives of individuals in order to provide services and alleviate suffering (in accord with positive liberty) and freedom from interference and coercion (in accord with negative liberty). As Berlin states:

> The freedom which consists in being one's own master, and the freedom which consists in not being prevented from choosing as I do by other men, may, on the face of it, seem concepts at no great logical distance from each other—no more than negative and positive ways of saying much the same thing. Yet the "positive" and "negative" notions of freedom historically developed in divergent directions not always by logically reputable steps, until, in the end, they came into direct conflict with each other.[4]

The choice between intervening to assist those in need and avoiding intervention in order to respect an individual's right to freedom is frequently based on assumptions that certain values—for example, the right to life, health, food, and shelter—take precedence over other values, such as an individual's right to freedom. Such assumptions are themselves based on assumptions about the proper relationship between social welfare institutions and individuals—in particular, the nature of the state's responsibility to provide aid to those in need at the expense, perhaps, of some degree of freedom of other citizens.

THE ROLE OF THE STATE

Debate concerning the obligations of the state, or government institutions, to promote and maintain welfare has an ancient history. The balance between private and public responsibility for welfare has shifted over time and across nations, reflecting widely varying views concerning the proper role of the state. History has taught us that the consequences of shifts in this delicate balance can range from profound neglect to gratuitous interference in the lives of individuals.

The involvement of federal, state, and local government in the provision of welfare in modern times takes many forms. Its activities include large-scale income maintenance programs, social security, unemployment compensation, medical assistance, aid to the disabled, and vocational training and employment. It is important to note, however, that the involvement of the state in welfare matters is a relatively recent phenomenon.

The Growth of the Welfare State

The growth of government responsibility for problems of social welfare began largely out of concern for the poor. At the end of the Middle Ages, the developing nation-states of western Europe had to contend with the problem of poverty. As economies and governments developed on a national scale, poverty became a national problem. National laws and ordinances concerning the treatment of the poor, vagrancy, and begging were enacted and ordinarily administered by local authorities.[5] They frequently cited the individual's duty to work, the community's duty to provide work for the able-bodied and relief for the disabled, and forms of punishment to be inflicted on those who failed to comply.

Substantial changes in the treatment of the poor came about during the second half of the eighteenth century as a result of the Industrial Revolution and the American and French Revolutions. National governments had to become increasingly concerned about problems resulting from large concentrations of poor people. As a result, national strategies were developed throughout western Europe and the United States in an effort to respond to the needs of the poor. The welfare programs and poor laws which resulted were regarded for the most part as concessions that eighteenth- and nineteenth-century life required. Though certain individuals supported national welfare strategies for altruistic reasons, widespread support depended upon arguments that aid to the poor was necessary in order to preserve the social order.

It is in these early attempts to devise national welfare programs that contemporary programs have their roots. For example, what is frequently referred to as the *welfare state*—where a national government accepts responsibility for some basic level of economic security and health of its citizens—has its origins in eighteenth-century Prussia and the *Landrecht,* or civil code, of 1794. This document, which is at least somewhat reminiscent of modern welfare legislation, stipulated that: "(1) it is the duty of the State to provide for the sustenance and support of those of its citizens who cannot . . . procure subsistence themselves; (2) work adapted to their strength and capacities shall be supplied to those who lack means and opportunity of earning a livelihood for themselves and those dependent upon them; (3) those who, for laziness, love of idleness, or other irregular proclivities, do not choose to employ the means offered them by earning a livelihood, shall be kept to useful work by compulsion and punishment under proper control; (6) the State is entitled and bound to take such measures as will prevent the destitution of its citizens and check excessive extravagance; and (15) the police authority of every place must provide for all poor and destitute persons, whose subsistence cannot be ensured in any other way."[6]

Since the earliest attempts at national policies the growth of governmental involvement in public welfare has been accompanied consistently by considerable debate concerning the proper limits of intervention by the state. This was especially apparent, for instance, during the period in which social insurance was formally introduced in Imperial Germany by Bismarck in the late nineteenth century, following, as it did, the laissez-faire policies of the eighteenth century discouraging the provision of aid to the poor.

The Limits of the Welfare State

The debate concerning the limits of state intervention has historically centered on the compromises that necessarily inhere in systems of government which simultaneously value individual freedom and social security. History has demonstrated that attempts by any nation to design programs to care for its poor and disabled have required some sacrifice of individual freedom, either as a result of regulations which prohibit certain activities—such as subjecting people to harsh labor or unsafe living conditions—or those which require certain activities—such as paying taxes to support welfare programs or sending one's children to school.

Thoughtful arguments have been offered over the years both in favor of and opposed to extensive governmental involvement in welfare matters. Supporters of governmental sponsorship of welfare programs have argued that an economic system based entirely on principles of free enterprise does not provide adequate protection to individuals who suffer the sometimes tragic effects of unemployment, physical and mental disability, and old age. Proponents of government sponsorship of welfare programs frequently point to the turbulent and unsettling Depression years following 1929 as evidence of the misery that can result from an unpredictable system of free enterprise unsupported by national welfare policies. They point out that when western societies moved from agrarian to industrial economies, individuals lost control over much of their economic well-being. Workers became subject to factors such as unemployment, market fluctuation, and harsh labor practices and working conditions. Opponents of government involvement in welfare programs argue that government interference in the private market inevitably results in a series of unwanted consequences which, in the long run, jeopardize welfare rather than safeguard it. In particular, such critics frequently claim that attempts by government to guarantee employment, impose price controls, subsidize housing, and provide generous public assistance benefits substantially increase the likelihood that incentives for investment will be destroyed, taxes will increase, and incentives for individuals to train and seek advancement will diminish. In addition, government-sponsored programs will result in constraints on individual freedom. Opponents of extensive government involvement in welfare programs generally claim that both freedom and well-being are best protected and promoted under conditions of a competitive market which is not subjected to regulations imposed by national welfare policies.[7]

The enduring debate concerning the role of the state in welfare policy represents one of the most pressing conflicts of values with which social workers must be concerned. The fundamental conflict is between the value of freedom (from government interference) and the security or welfare which results from government-sponsored programs. Practitioners who are in positions to design or endorse welfare policy frequently encounter situations which require difficult choices between these values.

In 1979, for example, the Chrysler Corporation, the third largest automobile manufacturer in the United States, declared that its financial difficulties were so severe that loan guarantees by the federal government would be necessary to avert sudden bankruptcy. In short, Chrysler was experiencing a serious cash flow problem and did not have enough money to pay its regular bills: the corporation's obligations had been accumulating at the rate of nearly $100 million per month while revenues had been steadily declining. Critics accused Chrysler of general mismanagement, in particular of spending erratically on maintenance and repairs, neglecting domestic operations while expanding abroad, and failing to respond to the demand for smaller automobiles.

Before requesting assistance from the federal government, Chrysler attempted to acquire further credit from its bankers. The banks refused, and the corporation thus turned to the federal government for loan guarantees totaling $1.5 billion.

Considerable debate ensued concerning the merits of federal assistance to the financially troubled corporation. There were claims that federal loan guarantees to Chrysler would sound the death bell for free enterprise in the United States. A federal bail-out of a beleaguered corporation would set a dangerous precedent, resulting in more harm than good for the nation's welfare. As a result of state intervention in the free enterprise system, major industries would lose their incentive for maintaining productive and efficient operations; this would hasten the arrival of a stagnant economy, high unemployment, and large welfare rolls. Said one banker who urged the Senate Banking Committee to reject the request for aid: "There isn't any avoiding the fact that [this] is an attempt by the government to move economic resources to places where they wouldn't otherwise go. Such distortions inevitably lead to less productivity, and therefore fewer jobs."[8]

At the same time, however, there were many vocal supporters of federal aid to Chrysler. Their arguments generally rested on claims that the federal government had an obligation to protect the welfare of thousands of individuals who would be adversely affected if Chrysler were forced to declare bankruptcy. These proponents of federal assistance argued that the welfare of the individuals and communities which depended on the corporation should take priority over an abstract concern about safeguarding principles of free enterprise. As the chairman of Chrysler stated: "the central and critical issue at stake in Chrysler's survival is people and jobs. If government wants to do something about unemployment, if it wants to prevent increased welfare dependency and government spending, if it wants to offset an $8 billion imbalance of automotive trade with Japan, let it approve Chrysler's legitimate and amply precedented request for temporary assistance."[9]

The volatile debate concerning Chrysler is a good example of the controversy which periodically erupts concerning the role of the state in matters which ultimately affect the welfare of individual citizens. Was there in fact an obligation on the part of the federal government to guarantee loans to Chrysler in order to protect the jobs of thousands of workers? What obligation did the federal government have to millions of taxpayers who might eventually need to support unemployed workers who would qualify for various welfare benefits? Conversely, what obligation did the federal government have to refuse loan guarantees to Chrysler in order to avoid threatening the foundation of a free enterprise system whose efficiency and productivity in principle depend upon the absence of government intervention? Would the long-term effect of loan guarantees be a decline in the net welfare of the nation, which would be more substantial and damaging than the suffering which would be brought about if the loans were not made?

The Clash of Laissez-Faire and Mercantilism

The philosophical debate concerning the role of the state in welfare matters has endured for centuries, stemming at least since the time of Plato and from the time of the decline of the kinship system in ancient Athens under the statesman Cleisthenes. The most significant chapter in the debate for social welfare was in the early nineteenth century, when mercantilist and laissez-faire doctrines clashed. Mercantilism was then the dominant economic principle in Britain and other major European nations. A central assumption under mercantilism was that the primary sources of a nation's power were a large population and precious metals. As a result, activities of the economic market were highly regulated, emigration was prohibited, and protective tariffs were imposed. It was assumed that "*Under prevailing conditions,* increases in heads would increase real income per head" and that, in order to discourage idleness, repressive poor laws needed to be imposed.[10]

In contrast to mercantilism, the doctrine of laissez-faire was based on an assumption that human welfare could be promoted and sustained if labor were allowed to find its own price in the market, if the creation of money were subject to a gold standard, and if goods and services were allowed to be freely exchanged between nations.[11] Adam Smith trusted, for example, that some of the increases in wealth which resulted from a free market economy and laissez-faire would eventually find their way to the poor.

A number of major mercantilist policies designed to protect and encourage prosperity in Britain, including the Corn Laws, the Navigation Acts, and the Settlement Acts, spurred the great debate between free trade and protection.[12] Critics of Adam Smith and laissez-faire argued that social welfare and national security brought about by government intervention were more important than the pursuit of profit under conditions of a free market:

> The prosperity of a nation depends on the achievement of a balance between the several productive processes of that nation, and only extensive governmental intervention can assure the achievement of such an equilibrium between the interests of agriculture, commerce and manufacturing. The free market could not be relied upon to bring about a natural reconciliation of individual and national interests. Only governmental regulation could ensure that the long-term needs of the nation were not jeopardized by the short-term interests of individuals and sectional groups.[13]

One of the critical differences between mercantilism and laissez-faire—both of which were hospitable to capitalism—was that national welfare policies which entailed government intervention were consistent in principle with the tenets of mercantilism but not of laissez-faire. In fact, the growth of the state's role in welfare can be attributed in large part to a declining confidence, following the Great Depression of the 1870s, in the ability of a free market to promote and sustain individual welfare.[14] It is interesting to note that the Passenger Acts passed between 1842 and 1855, which were designed in part to discourage the mistreatment of paupers shipped to the United States by private firms, represent a significant move toward the development of government regulation.[15] The European nations which began to industrialize in the later years of the nineteenth century—most notably France, Prussia, Italy, and Russia—did so with extensive involvement of government in the formulation of economic and welfare policy. Government intervention was much more moderate in Britain, which was still attached to a laissez-faire and free trade doctrine. Germany, on the other hand, which had a history of government involvement in economic policy, became under Bismarck the first so-called welfare state in Europe.

The development of contemporary national welfare programs has been influenced greatly by the early twentieth-century economic theories of John Maynard Keynes. Keynes drew on his understanding of mercantilist principles and applied them to problems of economic and social welfare in Britain. Keynes suggested that employment and investment could be stimulated by creating a system of "flexible exchanges and international cooperation."[16] He argued that the "outstanding faults of the economic society in which we live are its failure to provide for full employment and its arbitrary and inequitable distribution of wealth and incomes."[17] In response, Keynes claimed, government must become actively involved in economic and welfare policy: "The State will have to exercise a guiding influence on the propensity to consume, partly through its scheme of taxation, partly by fixing the rate of interest, and partly, perhaps, in other ways."[18] As Robert Pinker has pointed out, these "other ways" included extensive social services, public investment programs, and, in general, a close association between the state and private enterprise (such as cooperative enterprise sponsored jointly by public and private organizations).[19]

The spirit of some of Keynes' proposals was later carried forth by Sir William Beveridge, who, in his 1942 study of British social security, foreshadowed and influenced the development of social welfare policy in every major nation of the world. The Beveridge Report outlined a comprehensive plan of social programs as "an attack upon want."[20] The central concept of the report was the principle of a national minimum income needed for subsistence and was based on an assumption that individuals have a right to freedom from want to which the state must respond. His plan was somewhat different from the one that existed in most other nations in that the level of benefit was to be determined by need rather than by past contributions or past earnings.[21] Beveridge was at the same time, however, concerned about harmful effects of governmental involvement in welfare: "the State in organizing security should not stifle incentive, opportunity, responsibility; in establishing a national minimum, it should leave room and encouragement for voluntary action by each individual to provide more than that minimum for himself and his family."[22]

The extent to which national governments now intervene in welfare matters has grown considerably since the innovations of the nineteenth and early twentieth centuries; yet substantial variation still exists among nations in the degree to which governments involve themselves in welfare matters. In the United States, for example, it is clear that there is still considerable opposition to many government-sponsored programs, despite the burgeoning of welfare programs since the Depression of 1929. The vociferous debate surrounding the proposed loan guarantees to the Chrysler Corporation reflects the fundamental ambivalence of Americans toward state intervention. In both Britain and Sweden, on the other hand, there is a greater acceptance of government involvement in welfare policy. The history of the relationships the governments of these countries have had with private industry suggests, for example, that public support of financial assistance for a major failing corporation that is considered central to the economic welfare of many people would be much more widespread than the support Americans showed for federal aid to the Chrysler Corporation.

Decisions concerning the role of the state in particular welfare matters, of course, cannot be made simply by considering the traditions of relationships between government and private citizens in various nations. Because they necessarily include judgments about rights, duties, and obligations as they relate to human welfare, these decisions are, in the end, ethical ones. Political ideology and debate about economic doctrine certainly tend to determine the final content of many of these decisions; but the decisions are in principle and by necessity ethical.

The decisions social workers face which require judgments about the role of the state take many forms. They must be made by practitioners who work directly with individuals, families, and groups (for example, decisions concerning whether the state should remove a possibly neglected child such as Louise Wade from her parents) as well as by social workers in policy and planning positions.

One of the most persistent dilemmas social workers face concerning the role of the state is related to the distribution of limited services and resources. Decisions must frequently be made about the manner in which, for example, social services, public assistance funds, housing, and food stamps should be distributed and by whom these resources should be distributed (whether the state or private agencies). The scarcity of social workers' resources is a perennial problem. Debate concerning the criteria for distribution represents one of the most pressing ethical issues in social work.

THE DISTRIBUTION OF SERVICES AND RESOURCES

In a small community which recently built a twenty-five-bed facility for elderly people, decisions must be made about which of thirty-three elderly who have submitted applications will be admitted. Should the applicants be ranked according to the severity of their medical problems? Should those who are able to pay for their maintenance in the facility be accepted before those whose care must be paid for by public assistance funds? Should an individual who has contributed much to the community, such as a former mayor, be admitted before someone who has been considered less valuable to the community—for example, a former resident of skid row or a chronic offender? Should twenty-five names be selected at random from this group of thirty-three? Certainly the answers we provide to these questions and the criteria we establish for distributing limited services and resources have important consequences for human welfare. The ability of individuals to feed, clothe, shelter, and educate themselves is often directly affected by the manner in which social workers apportion various resources.

The resources may include, for example, money, time, counseling services, nursing home beds, jobs, or staff. Recipients may include individuals, social services agencies, families, or cities. In each case, however, the dilemma is the same: According to what criteria should limited resources be distributed? This is a central question which must be addressed in any discussion of distributive justice.

The distribution of scarce or limited resources in social service has generally been guided by four criteria. At times these criteria have been considered independent of one another, at times in combination. They are: *the principle of equality; the principle of need; the principle of compensation;* and *the principle of contribution.*

The Principle of Equality

The principle of equality represents one of the most valued concepts in the field of social service. The proposition that individuals should have equal access to services and resources has an intuitive appeal which has made this principle among the most enduring in social work.

The idea of equality appears, at first glance, uncomplicated. Individuals with similar problems should have equal claim to services and resources such as counseling, nursing home beds, and financial assistance. The apparent simplicity of the principle of equality is, however, deceiving. Attempts to apply this principle to the actual distribution of services and resources have, in fact, been filled with difficulties.

Equality means different things to different people. To some it suggests that those who qualify to receive certain services or resources ought to receive them in equal shares. This interpretation of the idea of equality emphasizes the *outcome,* or the product, of a particular distribution; equal shares should be distributed to eligible recipients.

This interpretation differs considerably from one which emphasizes specific *procedures* for distributing services and resources or, in particular, equality of opportunity.[23] What is important here is not that services and resources be distributed equally, but that individuals (and communities, organizations, and so on) have equal opportunities to compete for them. The emphasis is on process rather than outcome.

Another interpretation of the principle of equality is particularly relevant to cases in which services and resources are limited and cannot possibly be distributed equally among eligible individuals. If thirty-three elderly people apply for admission into a new facility which has only twenty-five beds, it is not possible to distribute the beds equally among them. One possible application of the principle of equality under such circumstances is to select twenty-five of the thirty-three individuals randomly and to provide beds for them. Under this arrangement each of the thirty-three individuals would have an equal chance of being admitted to the facility.

There is thus an important distinction between arrangements where individuals have an equal opportunity to compete for services and resources and those which provide an equal chance under lottery conditions to receive services and resources. Equality of opportunity allows individuals to pursue services and resources at their own pace; those who are first in line or who are most persistent are often rewarded for their efforts. The results of a random selection of individuals for services and resources are not, however, affected by individual determination.

The consequences of distinctions among equality of opportunity, equality under lottery conditions, and actual equality can be critical for people in need of aid. It is commonly believed that certain services and resources must be distributed as nearly equally as possible among individuals. This is ordinarily the case with municipal services such as police and fire protection. Other services and resources are traditionally made available on a first-come, first-served basis, or according to the principle of equality of opportunity. Examples include living units in public housing complexes and nursing home beds. Some services and resources, such as renal dialysis machines and membership in treatment groups, have at times been distributed according to a lottery.

Frequently, however, those responsible for distributing limited services and resources rank individuals according to their degree of need and apportion accordingly. Under this arrangement the twenty-five elderly individuals with the greatest need for institutional care, based perhaps on measures of physical disability and ability to care for one's self at home, would be provided beds. The outcome of this arrangement could of course be substantially different from the outcome of a lottery or a race to be first in line.

The Principle of Need

What constitutes need is itself a complicated issue. Difficult decisions must be made concerning the relative importance of various needs and the relative intensity of individuals' suffering. Is Mrs. Golumb's need for a nursing home bed, considering her recent stroke and broken hip, greater than Mr. Shoreman's need, considering his terminal cancer of the stomach? What indicators should be used to determine whether one city has a greater need for community development funds than other cities which have applied for aid? Is the local crime rate a less important indicator of need than the number of individuals on welfare? To what extent should the likelihood that the recipient of aid will benefit from assistance (a form of social, as opposed to medical, triage) be considered?

Perhaps the most popular contemporary statement concerning the obligation to aid those in need is found in John Rawls' work, *A Theory of Justice*.[24] Rawls' theory assumes that individuals who are formulating a moral principle by which to be governed are in an "original position" of equality and that each individual is unaware of his or her own attributes and status that might represent relative advantage or disadvantage. Under this "veil of ignorance" it is assumed that individuals will derive a moral principle which protects the least advantaged. Rawls' "difference principle," which states that goods must be distributed in a manner designed to benefit the least advantaged, includes a requirement to aid those in need and provides an important safeguard against applications of classic utilitarianism which might sacrifice the needs of the disadvantaged for a greater aggregation of good.

According to Alan Donagan, however, there are limits on the obligation one has to provide aid to those in need.[25] Donagan argues that there is a duty to promote the well-being of others and that this duty derives from their character as "rational creatures, not from their desert."[26] This duty primarily includes contributing to the upbringing and education of children, especially of orphans; helping those who have duties which, as a result of bereavement, injury, illness, or desertion, they can perform only with help; restoring to a condition of independence those who have been incapacitated by illness, accident, or injury; and caring for those who are crippled, deaf, or blind, or are chronically ill or senile. However, Donagan attaches two important qualifications to his discussion of the duty to aid. First, no one is morally obliged to promote the well-being of others at disproportionate inconvenience to oneself: "One does not fail to respect another as a rational creature by declining to procure a good for him, if that good can be procured only by relinquishing an equal or greater good for oneself."[27] Second, one has the right to expect those in need to assume some responsibility for their welfare: "Genuine benevolence, or willing the well-being of others, is willing that they live a decent human life, and so being prepared to help them in their efforts to do so; it is not an interminable bondage to alleviating the woes brought upon themselves by those who make little or no effort to live well."[28]

The Principle of Compensation

An additional problem we encounter in our attempts to define need concerns the distinction between past need and present need. Ordinarily we think about providing aid to individuals whose present needs seem to warrant assistance. But frequently social welfare policies take into consideration the needs of specific groups of individuals in past generations and their effect on present generations. This is particularly the case when past generations are considered to have been deprived of needed services and resources because of discrimination. As a result, many contemporary social welfare policies are earmarked for members of specific ethnic or racial groups (for example, Native Americans and blacks) whose ancestors were denied services and resources which were made available to other citizens. Contemporary policies which include quotas for admitting minimum numbers of individuals of certain ethnic and racial groups to educational institutions, vocational training programs, and jobs are examples of attempts to distribute services and resources based not only on the needs of the current generation but on the needs and deprivations suffered by past generations as well.

There is considerable controversy about the extent of the obligation we have to provide special or preferential treatment to individuals who descend from groups which have suffered discrimination in the past. The argument on one side is that while the consequences of past discrimination are unfortunate, the contemporary generation should not be held accountable for the injustices of its forebears. Providing preferential treatment to descendants of groups which were treated unfairly in the past at the expense of members of the contemporary generation results, it is argued, in forms of "reverse discrimination" which are equally unjust. The argument on the other side is that the current generation has an obligation to right the wrongs of past generations and that preferential treatment is necessary in order to restore some semblance of equality and equal opportunity among various ethnic and racial groups, both in the present and in the future. The extent to which we believe in a principle of redress where members of the current generation have a duty to compensate for injustices of past generations thus represents a vital question of ethics.

The Principle of Contribution

The final principle which guides the distribution of services and resources is that of contribution. This principle too has been applied in many different ways and with many different intentions. A simple interpretation of this principle is that services and resources should be distributed to individuals in proportion to the contribution they have made toward their production or support. But this is a vague interpretation. In practice the principle of contribution has guided the distribution of services and resources in various ways.

Perhaps the simplest example of distribution based on contribution is when clients exchange payment for specific services and resources, such as counseling, dental care, and child care. Individuals who contribute toward the support of these services receive them; individuals who choose not to pay for these services do not receive them, unless they are provided free of cost (in which case they are distributed according to some other principle, such as need). This principle thus involves a relatively simple exchange of fee for a service which is provided almost immediately and depends on the ability of clients to pay.

Another version of this arrangement involves the exchange of fees for a service or resource which is to be provided in the future and which is prorated based on the amount of an individual's contribution prior to its delivery. Examples of welfare resources which are distributed in this manner are private pensions and insurance. Participants in these plans ordinarily contribute a fixed amount of money on a regular basis (for example, monthly or annually) to a fund which is invested and in turn used to support individuals who contributed in prior years. In principle a participant, or his or her beneficiaries, receives income years after the payments began and in proportion to the total amount contributed. Once again, resources from such funds are distributed only to those who have contributed to their support and growth.

The principle of contribution has also been applied in yet a third way. This application differs significantly from those which are based on fees for service or benefits provided immediately or in the future. It is instead based on the nonmonetary contribution of individuals in exchange for services and resources. Recall, for example, the case where thirty-three individuals have applied for twenty-five beds available in a recently constructed home for the elderly. Assuming that their physical disabilities, medical needs, and demands on family members are similar, should a bed be given to a former mayor of the city before it is given to a former resident of skid row? In the instance where three renal dialysis machines must be distributed among five patients, should the prominent benefactor of the hospital be cared for before a severely retarded woman? Can we say that the contributions of these individuals to the well-being of the community should enter into our decisions? Should past contributions be considered as important as present contributions or the prospects of future contributions? Are these criteria to be preferred to a simple lottery?

These, of course, are difficult questions to answer. But, as with most ethical questions, we cannot afford to abandon them because of their difficulty. They will not disappear; that we know. Decisions concerning the distribution of social services and resources must be made.

The extent to which we decide to rely on the principles of equality, need, compensation, and contribution certainly requires thoughtful justification. Are there in fact good reasons for distributing certain counseling services and social security benefits according to the principle of contribution while we distribute police protection based on the principle of equality and welfare payments on the principle of need? Are there good reasons for considering need a more important value than equality, or equality a more important value than contribution? Again we are faced with the task of resolving conflicts among basic values which in the end directly guide welfare policy and social workers' decisions.

The decisions social workers make concerning their duty to aid those in need, the role of the state, and the distribution of limited services and resources ultimately depend, then, upon assumptions about the rights individuals have to certain services and resources and the obligations social workers have to assist people in need. These assumptions, in turn, depend upon the values social workers subscribe to and the values practitioners consider to be central to the profession.

JUSTIFYING THE VALUES OF THE PROFESSION

Concern with the justification of values and ethical principles in general has occupied the attention of philosophers consistently from the time of the ancient Greeks to the present. Perhaps the preeminent debate among philosophers who have been concerned with the justification of values and ethical principles has centered on whether values and principles that serve as absolute, impartial, and objective ethical guides can in fact be derived.[29] On the one hand, there are those who argue that there is a true and valid ethical code that can be applied impartially in order to judge the morality of specific actions, decisions, and intentions. On the other hand, there are those who deny that there is a true and valid ethical code which is equally applicable to all individuals at all times. Proponents of the first position are referred to as *absolutists;* proponents of the second are known as *relativists.*

Absolutists and Relativists in Social Work

The debate between absolutists and relativists has important bearing on our examination of ethical issues in social work. If one believes that conclusions concerning ethical values and guidelines reflect only *opinions* about the rightness and wrongness of specific actions and that objective standards do not exist, there is no reason to even attempt to determine whether certain actions are *in fact* right or wrong. One opinion would be considered as acceptable as another. However, if one holds that absolute ethical standards do or can in principle exist, it is sensible to attempt to identify the content of these standards and to subsequently judge the rightness and wrongness of particular actions according to them.

The popularity of relativism and absolutism has waxed and waned throughout the ages. Belief in absolutism has generally coincided with belief in the dogmas of orthodox religion, in particular, Christian monotheism; it has tended to fade, with accompanying increases in the popularity of relativism, during times of widespread religious skepticism. In recent years, however, there has been a declining tolerance of relativism and a yearning for ethical standards that would serve as moral lodestars for individuals who find the perplexity and instability of contemporary life disconcerting.

The quest to provide a rational justification of principles that would enable us to separate right and wrong has been, without question, the most important and challenging problem of moral philosophy. Philosophers such as Plato, Aristotle, Kant, and Mill have considered such a pursuit worthwhile. Others, such as Hume, Marx, and Nietzsche, have not. Events of our modern era have, however, inspired many contemporary philosophers to pursue in earnest the justification and derivation of ethical standards:

> In a century when the evils that man can do to man have reached unparalleled extremes of barbarism and tragedy, the philosophic concern with rational justification in ethics is more than a quest for certainty. It is also an attempt to make coherent sense of persons' deepest convictions about the principles that should govern the ways they treat one another. For not only do the divergences among philosophers reflect different views about the logical difficulties of justification in ethics; the conflicting principles they uphold, whether presented as rationally grounded or not, have drastically different implications about the right modes of individual conduct and social institutions.[30]

Concern about the needs for ethical standards in social work practice has also swelled in recent years, though academic concern about the value base of the profession has been prominent primarily since the 1950s. Many practitioners during the early years of the profession maintained and were guided by strong beliefs in Christian values. One might even argue that in later years the widespread belief in Christian values was replaced by widespread belief in secular values, in particular, those associated with the period commonly known as the "psychiatric deluge."[31] Beginning in the 1960s, however, relativism experienced a surge of popularity in the profession. Influenced by the unsettling effects of the civil disturbances of that decade and by the rise of skepticism about conventional social institutions and standards, significant numbers of social workers began to question the validity of professional codes of ethics which suggested specific standards for judging right and wrong. The result was a tendency on the part of many practitioners to resist espousing specific ethical standards and values and especially the temptation to impose any particular value or values upon clients, whether they be individuals, families, or communities.[32] What had been described in earlier years as "deviance," such as single-parent families, the use of drugs, and certain sexual mores, began to be more respected or at least tolerated by many practitioners as reflections of life-styles and preferences of certain age and ethnic groups that were merely "different" from those of conventional society. Social workers experienced a dramatic shift in their threshold of tolerance for unfamiliar ways of life.

It was during the 1960s that social work, along with many other professions, found itself in the midst of its closest brush with relativism. Since this era, however, there has been a gradual resurgence of interest in the development of ethical standards. The interest in values and standards has not concerned the morality of the preferences and life-styles of clients, as it did in earlier chapters of the profession's history. Rather, the concern has been focused on the ethics of practitioners—on the justifications provided for intervening or failing to intervene in clients' lives, the acceptability of specific forms and methods of intervention, and the criteria used for distributing services and resources. The willingness of practitioners to tolerate relativism and the absence of standards as they relate to their own actions and decisions has diminished significantly. While social workers tend to acknowledge that absolute, objective ethical standards which would serve as unambiguous guides to specific actions and decisions can perhaps not be derived, there is widespread belief that the actions they perform and the decisions they make frequently have ethical content that warrants thoughtful attention. The belief that relativism or intuitionism provides an acceptable strategy for making difficult ethical decisions has grown somewhat anachronistic. As Dorothy Emmet has stated: "Part of our trouble is the prevalence of the idea that moral standards are personal, subjective and emotional, and so are not matters into which intelligence enters, and for which reasons, maybe good reasons, can be given and communicated to other people."[33]

If we accept the propositions that good reasons may be given for concluding that certain actions and decisions of social workers are ethically right and ethically wrong and that certain values should take precedence over others in cases of conflict, it is important to consider as a next step the standards according to which such judgments should be made. How can we justify certain fundamental values for the profession which would serve as the foundation for the formulation of ethical guidelines for social workers? Is it possible to derive ethical guidelines for the profession in a manner which is more compelling than a simple appeal to intuition?

The Problem of Justification

Philosophers who have maintained that ethical principles can in fact be justified have proposed over the years a variety of arguments about the proper way to achieve such justification. As I noted in chapter 1, these arguments have ranged from claims that the rightness of a moral judgment can be known only by intuition to claims that it can be known by appealing to religious doctrine or by relying on empirical measurements of the amount of, for instance, happiness that results. The attempt to identify the determinants of the rightness of a moral judgment has been referred to by Alan Gewirth as the "problem of the independent variable," which concerns "whether there are any objective independent variables that serve to determine the correctness or rightness of moral judgments."[34]

Most of the arguments philosophers have presented concerning the justification of moral judgments and principles have had difficulty standing up under sustained scrutiny. Earlier I noted the problems involved in arguments that empirical observations of individuals' attitudes, behavior, or attributes can lead to normative conclusions or principles; there is no logical connection between empirical or descriptive statements of fact and evaluative conclusions. This is the heart of the is-ought problem, or what G. E. Moore referred to as the "naturalistic fallacy,"[35] where factual judgments are mistaken for evaluative ones. We know what it means to say that the statement "Carl Smith is being removed from the home of his biological parents and placed in foster care" is true; it is difficult to know, however, how we would determine whether the statement "Carl Smith ought to be removed from the home of his biological parents and placed in foster care" is true.

I have also noted the difficulties with the arguments of intuitionists who claim that the rightness of a moral judgment can be determined by immediate intellectual inspection and without proof or consideration of the judgment's consequences. People inevitably disagree about what intuition suggests is right and wrong and there are no standards offered by intuitionists to settle such differences of opinion. The argument that in such cases certain individuals are simply "morally blind" does not assist us in our efforts to know whose judgments are to be respected.

Perhaps the most popular version of intuitionism has been that commonly known as the "moral point of view."[36] The origin of the moral point of view can be traced to Adam Smith's argument that individuals are likely to reach agreement in their moral judgments only by assuming the position of an impartial spectator or of an "ideal observer."[37] An ideal observer is one who has such characteristics as being informed, impartial, fair, dispassionate, calm, willing to universalize, considering the good of everyone, and so on. Thus, a social worker who is in a position to decide the morality of, for instance, breaching confidentiality, withdrawing service, or recommending that a certain community receive public funds would obtain as much information as possible about the nature and circumstances of the phenomenon of concern, take into account the various interests of all who may be affected by his or her decision, and, from an impartial position, weigh the various considerations against one another in order to determine what course of action would result in the greatest balance of favorable consequences over unfavorable ones.

Arguments in favor of the theory of the moral point of view have suffered from two apparently fatal difficulties. First, the characteristics that are to be held by ideal observers are such that no individual can be shown ever to possess them. Consequently, it cannot be known that a moral conclusion is one that has been or would have been reached by an ideal observer. Second, the characteristics of ideal observers are themselves not morally neutral; the assumption that individuals who make moral judgments *should* be informed, impartial, fair, objective, dispassionate, and so forth, is itself a normative or moral judgment.[38]

Is it the case, then, that any attempt to justify an ethical principle or judgment is bound to encounter insurmountable difficulties? Is such thinking about ethics destined, as Wittgenstein said, "to run against the boundaries of language?"[39]

In *Reason and Morality* the philosopher Alan Gewirth has provided what is perhaps the most compelling contemporary discussion of these questions.[40] Following a series of complex—and controversial—philosophical arguments and derivations, Gewirth ultimately claims that human beings have a fundamental right to *freedom* and *well-being* and that there are three core "goods" that human beings must value: *basic goods*—those aspects of well-being which are necessary for anyone to engage in purposeful action (for example, life, health, food, shelter, mental equilibrium); *nonsubtractive goods*—goods the loss of which would diminish a person's ability to pursue his or her goals (for example, as a result of being subjected to inferior living conditions, or harsh labor, or as a result of being stolen from, cheated, or lied to); and *additive goods*—goods which enhance a person's ability to pursue his or her goals (for example, knowledge, self-esteem, material wealth, education) beyond those included under basic goods.

Although questions can be raised about the technical merits of some of Gewirth's philosophical assumptions and derivations, his arguments about the nature of basic human duties and rights—and the resolution of conflicts among them—have particular relevance to social work practice. Gewirth's claims provide a useful framework for examining central values and value conflicts in the social work profession.

A GUIDE TO ETHICAL DECISIONS

Applications of Gewirth's claims about basic human duties and rights are of two kinds and both have implications for social work. *Direct applications* of Gewirth's framework concern relationships among individual people. Under the direct applications actions are morally right if they permit others to pursue their goals with freedom and well-being. These applications include duties and obligations regarding freedom (the duty not to interfere with others by the use of violence, coercion, or deception); basic goods (the negative duty not to interfere with the basic preconditions of human action —life, health, food, shelter, mental equilibrium—and the positive duty to assist others in acquiring the basic preconditions of human action when such assistance can be provided without comparable cost to oneself); nonsubtractive goods (the duty not to break promises, cheat, steal, live, or subject others to inferior living or working conditions); and additive goods (the duty to foster the development and distribution of goods which enhance individuals' ability to pursue their goals, such as income, material possessions, self-esteem, education, and to compensate for individuals' disabilities and for past interferences that diminished the ability of groups of individuals to fulfill their purposes).

Under the indirect applications, Gewirth's framework suggests various social rules that have a bearing on the social work profession. First is the justification of social rules concerning the voluntary nature of associations (in keeping with individuals' right to freedom). If there are to exist specific associations and rules, then all the association's members must voluntarily consent to membership and rules, as, for example, in tenants' rights organizations, self-help groups such as Alcoholics Anonymous, and trade unions. However, since voluntary agreements will not necessarily protect each person's right to freedom and well-being, there is justification for a second category of rules resembling the criminal law whereby provisions are made to permit interference with the freedom of those who represent a threat to others. A third category of rules concerns the "method of consent," whereby individuals can freely discuss and criticize a government and vote for and against its policies and representatives. This indirect application is primarily concerned with institutional arrangements which promote and protect individuals' rights to these civil liberties rather than with acts of individuals. Finally, there is the justification of social rules concerning the provision of basic goods, nonsubtractive goods, and additive goods; this justification concerns the idea of the supportive state and the promotion of welfare.

Gewirth recognizes that the various duties and rights people have sometimes conflict and that choices sometimes need to be made among them. In *Reason and Morality* he argues that in cases of conflict there must be a hierarchy among values, and he offers a series of guidelines to help make these difficult choices (or, to use Ross' terminology, to identify one's actual duty among conflicting prima facie duties):[41] 1)If one person or group violates or is about to violate the rights of another to freedom and well-being (including basic, nonsubtractive, and additive goods), action to prevent or remove the violation may be justified. Whether the action to prevent or remove the violation is justified depends on the extent to which the violation jeopardizes an individual's ability to act in the future. 2) Since every individual has the duty to respect others' right to the goods that are the necessary preconditions of action (freedom and well-being), one duty takes precedence over another if the good that is the object of the former duty is more necessary for the possibility of action and if the right to that good cannot be protected without violating the latter duty. 3) Rules governing interactions among individuals can, in particular cases, override the duty not to coerce others. Such rules must, however, meet several conditions: any coercion permitted by the rules must be necessary to prevent undeserved coercion and serious harm; such coercion must not go beyond what is necessary for such protection; the rules which permit occasional coercion must be imposed by the procedures of the method of consent.

These criteria for revolving conflicts of value and duty can be applied to the resolution of conflicts encountered by social workers. In particular, these criteria suggest the following guidelines in instances when values and duties conflict:

1. *Rules against basic harms to the necessary preconditions of action (such as life, health, food, shelter, mental equilibrium) take precedence over rules against harms such as lying or revealing confidential information or threats to additive goods such as recreation, education, and wealth.*

This guideline would justify a decision by Marcia Simmons, for example, to report to an officer of the court information shared with her in confidence by Gloria Wade if it could be established that breaching the promise of confidentiality was necessary in order to protect Louise's basic well-being. That is, Louise's right to basic well-being (a necessary precondition of action) would supersede Marcia's obligation to keep her promise regarding confidentiality. This guideline would also justify admitting a very disabled, destitute individual who cannot arrange care for him- or herself to a home for the elderly before admitting a prominent citizen who is less disabled and whose family can arrange for in-home care until a bed is available. The threat to the well-being of the destitute individual and to his or her ability to act in the future is more important than the enhanced reputation which the home for the elderly might enjoy (an additive good) as a result of caring for a prominent citizen.

2. *An individual's right to basic well-being (the necessary preconditions of action) takes precedence over another individual's right to freedom.*

In general, this guidelines suggests that individuals have a right to freedom and to act as they wish unless their actions threaten the welfare of others. Thus, an intervention required to protect Louise Wade's right to basic well-being that is introduced contrary to Gloria's wishes—such as a court order requiring Gloria to accept the services and advice of a visiting nurse—would supersede Gloria's right not to have her freedom interfered with. Louise's basic well-being is more necessary for the possibility of future action than is Gloria's freedom to act as she wishes. This guideline also suggests that admitting a very disabled, destitute individual to a home for the elderly should have priority over the freedom of the home's staff to admit a less disabled prominent citizen who has resources to arrange in-home care until a bed is available.

In addition, this guideline has important implications regarding diminished freedom for social workers that may result from the obligation to provide aid to those who lack or stand to lose basic goods—for example, when a social worker is required against his or her wishes to work overtime (which results in diminished freedom) in order to care for an elderly client whose health is failing rapidly.

3. *An individual's right to freedom takes precedence over his or her own right to basic well-being.*

In general, this guideline suggests that someone who chooses to engage in self-destructive behavior should be allowed to do so if it can be established that the individual is making an informed, voluntary decision with knowledge of relevant circumstances and that the consequences of the decision will not threaten the well-being of others. Temporary interference with an individual who threatens to engage or actually engages in behavior which results in basic harm to him- or herself is justifiable in order to determine whether the conditions of voluntariness and informed choice have been met. The guideline requires, however, that if these conditions have been met, further interference must be discontinued. Thus, if it were clear that Gloria Wade had made an informed, voluntary decision to live by herself in a "windowless, deteriorated, cramped, and dirty" apartment, she should be permitted to do so, providing that the welfare of others is not threatened as a result. However, if the welfare of a dependent is threatened by Gloria's choice of living conditions, it would be justifiable to interfere with her freedom.

In instances, for example, when a client chooses to engage in apparently self-destructive behavior, such as remaining in a troubled marriage or abusing alcohol or drugs, the guideline justifies temporary interference with the acts in order to determine whether the individual is in fact acting voluntarily and with knowledge of the consequences of the behavior. However, if it can be established that the basic welfare of others is not threatened by his or her action, that he or she has no dependents whose basic welfare would be threatened, and if others would not be required to provide support if he or she is incapacitated, interference with the client must cease. While these conditions may be difficult to satisfy in many cases, they can frequently be satisfied.

4. *The obligation to obey laws, rules, and regulations to which one has voluntarily and freely consented ordinarily overrides one's right to engage*

voluntarily and freely in a manner which conflicts with these laws, rules, and regulations.

For example, the rules which govern participation in a professional organization, such as the National Association of Social Workers, to which members voluntarily consent, generally override the freedom of individual members to act in a manner inconsistent with the organization's rules. It is this guideline which permits NASW to discipline or censure members who violate its standards of professional conduct, despite the fact that in doing so the freedom of individual members may be interfered with. This guideline also suggests that social workers are ordinarily obligated to abide by the rules and regulations of their employers and to obey the law.

5. *Individuals' rights to well-being may override laws, rules, regulations, and arrangements of voluntary associations in cases of conflict.*

Thus, the obligation to obey laws, rules, and regulations is not absolute. Situations can arise where, because of a threat to an individual's basic well-being, a law, rule, or regulation can justifiably be violated. At what point violation is justifiable is highly debatable and requires considerably more discussion. For now, however, let us simply acknowledge that, in principle, such violation may, on occasion, be defensible. Further, the rules of professional associations which have been entered into voluntarily should not be complied with if they threaten the well-being of individuals. For example, the rules governing an organization of clinical social workers will ordinarily not conflict with any individual's right to basic well-being. However, a voluntary association of practitioners who incorporate and conspire to submit fraudulent vouchers to a local unit of government for services not rendered is not justifiable because of the injury caused to the well-being of taxpayers. The same reasoning would apply to a consortium of private agencies which conspires to create a monopoly on services provided to a particular group of clients, thus prohibiting competition from other agencies and, perhaps, inflating the cost of service. This guideline also suggests, for instance, that it would be wrong for a voluntary association made up of staff of a county department of planning to deny needed financial assistance to residents of a city because the current mayor defeated the individual endorsed by the county commissioner in a recent election.

This reasoning suggests further that it would be wrong for the voluntary association made up of the members of the Wade family to agree not to provide adequate care and basic goods for Louise; Louise's well-being takes precedence over the freedom of the family—a special case of a voluntary association—to deprive her of basic care.

6. *The obligation to prevent basic harms such as starvation and to promote public goods such as housing, education, and public assistance overrides the right to retain one's property.*

This guideline applies specifically to the justification of taxation required to provide aid to those in need and to prevent basic harms. It justifies the assessment of taxes and the use of revenue to assure that children such as Louise Wade are provided with adequate care, either in their own homes or in foster homes or other residential settings. Tax revenues might be used to support the work of public social service agencies or to purchase service from private agencies and individuals.

These six guidelines can be usefully applied in instances when social workers encounter conflicts of values and duties. As we shall see in our discussion of cases in the remaining chapters, these guidelines provide useful criteria for organizing our examination of ethical dilemmas in social work practice. It is important to keep in mind, however, that a series of guidelines, no matter how specific, cannot provide solutions to which everyone will always agree. Our review of various schools of thought in moral philosophy has taught us to beware of claims that particular theories of ethics can provide unambiguous, undebatable solutions to moral dilemmas. The very nature of guidelines is such that applications of them to individual cases inevitably require considerable interpretation, speculation, and inference, all of which invite and ordinarily result in some measure of disagreement and debate. Such disagreement and debate may concern the validity of the guidelines themselves as well as their particular application in specific cases. This is to be expected and encouraged. The value of ethical guidelines is in their ability to help one organize one's thinking and to provide a systematic guide for practitioners who encounter difficult ethical decisions. Let us move now to a detailed examination of ethical dilemmas in social service.

3

Ethical Dilemmas in Service to Individuals and Families

The professional activities of social workers can be described in various ways. In general, social workers provide services to assist people in their efforts to achieve their goals and cope with life's difficult problems. They are concerned with problems such as poverty, learning and behavioral disorders, family crises, crime and delinquency, disability, and mental illness. Practitioners work with communities and organizations, with the young and old, and with individuals whose problems are acute and chronic. Social workers also use a variety of interventions in their work, including traditional casework, behavioral techniques, family counseling, and group therapy.

Though the activities of social workers vary considerably, what is common to all of them is a concern with human welfare. As we have seen, however, the path toward promoting and maintaining welfare is not always a clear one. Social workers frequently face dilemmas concerning the merits of various courses of action: Should the worker intervene? If so, how should the worker intervene and with what constraints? Whose interests should be considered primary? Must the worker always tell the truth? Is it ever appropriate to reveal information shared in confidence by a client? As we observed earlier, the answers to these questions often depend not only (or primarily) on our judgments about the effectiveness and efficiency of particular social work interventions but on the consideration of what is right and wrong from an ethical point of view as well.

Social workers encounter a wide variety of ethical dilemmas in their work with individuals and families. In general, these dilemmas involve decisions concerning intervening in clients' lives in the first place, the nature of social workers' and clients' relationships during the time services are provided, the role of government in clients' lives, and the distribution of limited resources. I will focus on a number of specific ethical issues which frequently emerge in social work. These dilemmas include difficult questions concerning truth-telling in relationships with clients, providing services against a client's wishes and the issue of paternalism, conflicts between social workers' obligations to their employers and to their clients, conflicts between the law and treatment goals, the right to confidentiality, and the process of informed consent.

TRUTH-TELLING AND COMPETING INTERESTS

CASE 3.1 Anne Rawlings was a fifteen-year-old girl who had an I.Q. of 52 and was considered mildly retarded. She functioned at the intellectual level of an eleven-year-old. Anne suffered brain damage as a result of complications during her birth. She spent the early years of her life with her parents, two brothers, and three sisters. When she was seven years old, Anne was admitted to the first grade of the local public elementary school. The school did not have a special program for retarded children; Anne made little progress in school, and after two years in the first grade the principal asked the Rawlings to try to locate a private school for their daughter.

Shortly after Anne's tenth birthday her parents separated and, several months later, divorced. Anne and the other children were placed in their mother's custody. Three months following the divorce, Mrs. Rawlings decided that she could no longer care for Anne and filed an application to have her placed in a state school and hospital for the mentally retarded. She claimed that raising Anne was extremely frustrating for her; she tried to be patient with Anne and to understand her limitations, but Mrs. Rawlings was becoming more and more short-tempered as time passed.

Anne's aunt and uncle, Mr. and Mrs. Sanford, were distressed about the possibility that their niece might be placed in an institution. They loved Anne deeply and enjoyed her company. Mr. and Mrs. Sanford agreed to raise Anne themselves. Anne moved to the Sanford's home and seemed to adjust well. She was not able to read or write and spent much of her time watching television and strolling around the rural neighborhood and nearby park. Her mother visited occasionally for several months though her visits became less and less frequent over time.

At age fourteen Anne required much the same care she had needed as a young child. She was able to clothe and bathe herself most of the time, though she frequently needed detailed instructions and help from her aunt and uncle. Anne sometimes helped clean house. She was not allowed to cook, however, because she had severely burned herself with boiling water on two occasions.

One evening Mrs. Sanford was helping Anne get ready for her bath and noticed a swelling in her niece's abdomen. She took Anne to a local doctor who discovered, much to the Sanfords' surprise, that Anne was five months pregnant. Mr. and Mrs. Sanford were shocked and saddened. They found it difficult to believe that someone had taken advantage of their retarded niece. Anne apparently was not aware that she was pregnant; she occasionally complained of mild stomach pains, but did not ask questions about her bulging stomach. The Sanfords wondered whether Anne could understand what pregnancy was all about.

Dr. Blefary, the family's physician, suggested that the Sanfords contact the local office of the Children's Social Service Bureau to arrange to have Anne's baby adopted; he also suggested that Anne should not be told about her pregnancy or about plans to have the baby adopted. Dr. Blefary was concerned about confusing and distressing Anne and felt that it was in her best interests not to be informed about the baby.

The Sanfords had a difficult decision to make. Should they tell Anne about the baby? Should the baby be placed in adoption? They contacted a social worker at the Children's Social Service Bureau to discuss the dilemma. The social worker, Martha Bowens, agreed with

Dr. Blefary; Anne should not be told about the baby. The Sanfords reluctantly and with great misgivings accepted the advice of Dr. Blefary and Ms. Bowens and explained to Anne that the doctors thought that the swelling in her stomach was due to an infection; Anne was told that she would go to the hospital to have the problem corrected. Anne then asked many questions about the swelling, though the Sanfords were not certain that Anne fully understood and accepted their explanation.

The Sanfords also agreed that the baby should be adopted. Mrs. Sanford was developing cataracts and Mr. Sanford was himself recovering from a mild stroke. It simply was not realistic for them to care for Anne's baby. About one month prior to the birth of the baby, Ms. Bowens told the Sanfords that it was time to begin locating a family that would be willing to accept Anne's child. She referred the Sanfords to Maria Adair, the social worker in charge of the adoption division within the Children's Social Service Bureau. After reviewing the case, Ms. Adair told the Sanfords that she believed Anne should be informed about the baby; she felt strongly that Anne had as much right to the truth as any other client.

The Sanfords were very upset at this sudden turn of events. They could not bear the thought of telling Anne about the baby; Anne loved children, and the Sanfords could not imagine asking their retarded niece to approve adoption. Ms. Adair sympathized with the Sanfords, but explained to them that she felt compelled to tell Anne the truth about the baby and its prospective adoption.

This case raises a number of important ethical questions about the general subject of truth-telling in social work. To what extent does a social worker have an obligation to be truthful in his or her work with clients and colleagues? To what extent do clients and others have a right to be told the truth? Should Anne be told about the baby and involved in the decision concerning adoption? Whose interests should be considered primary? Anne's? The baby's? Mr. and Mrs. Sanford's? The social workers'?

The Right to Know

The question concerning Anne's right to know about the baby is a fundamental one for several reasons. First, it requires us to consider, in particular, the rights of the retarded. Is it wrong to withhold information from a retarded individual when, as is often the case, we assume that he or she is not capable of making informed, competent decisions? If there are instances when it is permissible to withhold information from retarded individuals, what is the nature of these instances? When is it not acceptable to withhold information? These questions regarding the particular rights of retarded individuals also suggest broader questions about the rights of clients generally to be informed about decisions by practitioners which directly affect them. When is it acceptable to withhold information from a client on the grounds that it is in his or her "best interests"?

In 1975 the President's Committee on Mental Retardation enumerated a series of rights of retarded individuals.[1] Among them are the right to manage one's own affairs and the right to reasonable protection from harm. The claim that retarded individuals have the right to manage their own affairs suggests that Anne Rawlings may have a right to be informed about the baby and to participate in any decision concerning the baby's future. At the same time, however, the claim that retarded individuals have a right to reasonable protection from harm suggests that it may be permissible to withhold information about the baby from Anne on the grounds that as a result she would be protected from the emotional trauma which might follow from knowing about a baby which would eventually be taken from her and placed in adoption.

This case thus represents a compelling example of an instance where two prima facie rights seem to conflict. The conflict in this case is primarily between the right to be told the truth and to manage one's own affairs (the right to freedom) and the right to protection from harm (the right to well-being). Are the rights of the individuals involved in this case best protected if Anne is or is not told the truth about her baby?

Philosophers have had different opinions about the need to always tell the truth. Deontologists, those who claim that certain moral principles are inherently right or wrong, frequently claim that it is never permissible to intentionally lie or withhold information. Perhaps the best known statement in this spirit is that of the eighteenth-century German philosopher Immanuel Kant.

> The duty of being truthful . . . is unconditional. . . . Although in telling a certain lie I do not actually do anyone a wrong. I formally but not materially violate the principle of right. . . . To be truthful (honest) in all declarations,

therefore, is a sacred and absolutely commanding decree of reason, limited by no expediency.

Thus, the definition of a lie as merely an intentional untruthful declaration to another person does not require the additional condition that it must harm another. . . . For a lie always harms another; if not some other particular man, still it harms mankind generally, for it vitiates the source of law itself.[2]

An opposing point of view claims, however, that it is not only permissible but necessary to lie or withhold information in certain instances in order to avoid harmful consequences. Proponents of this teleological line of reasoning argue that it is foolish and shortsighted to always tell the truth when there are clearly cases when the truth results in greater harm than would follow a lie. For example, Mrs. Smith tells Mrs. Jones' estranged husband, who has threatened to kill Mrs. Jones, that Mrs. Jones is not in Mrs. Smith's home, when in fact she is. According to the teleological point of view, such a lie is permissible and justifiable because of the harm it prevents. To tell the truth in such an instance in order to abide by the principle that one should never lie would be to commit a senseless act of what J. J. C. Smart refers to as "rule-worship":

Suppose that there is a rule R and that in 99 percent of cases the best possible results are obtained by acting in accordance with R. Then clearly R is a useful rule of thumb; if we have not time or are not impartial enough to assess the consequences of an action it is an extremely good bet that the thing to do is to act in accordance with R. But is it not monstrous to suppose that if we *have* worked out the consequences and if we have perfect faith in the impartiality of our calculations, and if we *know* that in this instance to break R will have better results than to keep it, we should nevertheless obey the rule? Is it not to erect R into a sort of idol if we keep it when breaking it will prevent, say, some avoidable misery? Is this not a form of superstitious rule-worship (easily explicable psychologically) and not the rational thought of a philosopher?[3]

There appear to be instances when, regrettably, it is better to lie or withhold information than to tell the truth. In general these are instances when a lie must be told or information must be withheld in order to avoid a more serious threat to an individual's basic well-being, such as the loss of life or serious emotional trauma. We need not accept this conclusion casually and without misgivings. Indeed, we reach this conclusion not because we choose to willingly and with ease but because we must. It is justified as an extension of the conclusion we reached above that one duty (for example, protecting basic well-being) must sometimes take precedence over another (the duty not to lie or withhold information that may help individuals pursue their purposes) if the good that is the object of the former duty is more necessary for the possibility of action and if the right to that good cannot be protected without violating the latter duty (guideline 1).

If we accept that there are occasional instances when it is permissible to lie or withhold information, we must specify the circumstances under which such actions are justifiable. Are such actions justifiable only in extreme cases when they are necessary in order to save a life? Is deception, in the form of a lie or withheld information, also justifiable in order to avoid profound emotional misery, such as when a fragile client or dying patient has asked for the truth about his or her condition? In particular, does the case of Anne Rawlings qualify as an instance where the threat of a client's well-being is severe enough to permit the deliberate withholding of information about the impending birth of her child? These, of course, are the difficult questions.

There are arguments both in favor of and opposed to a decision to tell Anne about her baby. The Sanfords, Dr. Blefary, and Martha Bowens seem primarily concerned about the anguish they expect Anne to suffer if she is made aware of her baby; they especially fear her reaction upon learning in addition that the baby would be taken from her and placed in adoption. To the Sanfords the choice is clear: Anne must be protected at all costs from being told about the baby. Her ability to comprehend details concerning pregnancy and childbirth is limited, they assume, and she must be protected from such disturbing and confusing information. They cannot bear to imagine the trauma she might experience if she were to learn of the baby and its fate. The Sanfords also cannot bear, perhaps, to imagine the difficulty they may have caring for Anne if she learns about the baby.

What are the arguments in favor of informing Anne about the baby? First, it can be argued that Anne has the right to information which may help her understand the drastic physiological changes she is and will be experiencing. It might be argued that if the Sanfords are concerned about Anne's emotional welfare, they should do everything possible to help her cope with the confusion surrounding the changing shape and sensations of her body. In addition, it might be argued that Anne will likely experience some degree of emotional trauma whether or not she is told about the baby and that the likelihood of minimizing her anguish is greater if she is given the opportunity to understand the truth about her condition as opposed to being left to speculate about the mysterious swelling in her stomach. In the end, Anne's ability to fulfill her purposes with some degree of freedom and well-being may be enhanced if she is helped to understand the sequence of events which will conclude with a very sudden disappearance of the swelling.

Each of these various arguments for and against informing Anne about the baby appears at least somewhat compelling. Each appears to have Anne's interests at heart. Recognizing that the Sanfords and the social workers from the Children's Social Service Bureau must make a decision, which arguments are the most persuasive? The weight of the arguments appears to be on the side of informing Anne about the baby and its prospective adoption. Though Anne's intellectual capacity is limited, she is able to engage in purposeful behavior and has rights to well-being and limited freedom. Her right to well-being is comparable to that of any individual, mentally competent or incompetent. Her right to freedom is limited only to the extent that her behavior represents a threat to the freedom and well-being of others (as would be the right to freedom for any individual, such as a criminal offender, whose behavior represents a threat to others) or to herself.

Anne's right to well-being requires that everything possible should be done to enable her to fulfill her purposes in the future. In general it can be argued that being told the truth and having available information relevant to one's welfare is important if one is to be able to carry out one's life plans, no matter how modest they may be. Being lied to and having relevant information deliberately withheld will, in the long run, tend to frustrate one's plans. It might be argued that Anne is not capable of fully understanding and appreciating the truth about her condition; however, evidence does not exist which suggests that a mildly retarded individual is unable to comprehend at least the rudimentary aspects of pregnancy and childbirth.[4] It is indeed likely that Anne will be upset and confused upon learning the truth; her well-being may suffer as a result, and this is to be regretted. But the threat to her long-term well-being may be greater if she is not told the truth. If she is not told the truth about the baby, she will lack important information relevant to her own future. It is also conceivable that she would somehow learn the truth later in her life; such an experience could damage deeply her mental health and diminish somewhat her ability to establish and maintain trust in her relationships with others.

Modified Utilitarianism

An important point must be made about the justification of this conclusion to tell the truth to Anne Rawlings about her baby. This conclusion is *not* based on a straightforward utilitarian calculation designed to estimate whether the greatest good would result from informing Anne about her baby. Under a conventional utilitarian approach we would not be required to act in Anne's best interests or with her welfare as a primary consideration. In principle, her interests could be sacrificed for some greater aggregation of good which might benefit other individuals (such as Anne's aunt and uncle, her parents, or the social workers from the Children's Social Service Bureau). Instead, the conclusion to tell Anne the truth about her baby is based on our best guess about the consequences of the decision for *her* freedom and well-being. Regrettably, we cannot know whether our guess is the correct one. We only know that we make it with her interests as our primary concern and that the decision represents a sincere effort to enhance the quality of Anne's life.

This is not a trivial conclusion; the history of social service is filled with instances when the welfare of individual clients has not served as the primary reason for decisions to intervene in a certain manner. Too often the expected effects of a decision on the convenience of a caretaker or a social worker have been considered more important than anticipated consequences for the welfare of clients themselves. Practitioners may, and likely will, disagree about whether telling Anne the truth is or is not in her best interests. This is to be expected. The important point is that the debate among workers must be about the consequences of the decision primarily for Anne's welfare and only secondarily for the welfare of others. It is her welfare that is most threatened.

Should we take this conclusion to mean that the worker's responsibility is to always act in order to protect the freedom and well-being of his or her client, regardless of the consequences for other individuals? Is there an inviolable obligation to consider the welfare of one's client more important than the welfare of others who may have competing interests? Apparently not, and the reasons will become clear as we consider further the ethical dilemmas presented in the case of Anne Rawlings.

Whose Interests Are Primary?

Up to this point our reasoning has been guided by a primary concern for the freedom and well-being of Anne. We have been concerned about the effects of a decision to tell her about the baby for her welfare. Now we must consider an additional question: If Anne is made aware of her pregnancy and the impending birth, should she be denied the opportunity to care for the baby once it is born? On the one hand, a strict interpretation of Anne's right to freedom suggests that she ought to be allowed to care for the baby if she so wishes. The problem, of course, is that Anne's prima facie right to freedom seems to conflict with the baby's (future) prima facie right to well-being, assuming that Anne's ability to care for and raise a child is severely limited. We thus have a classic conflict of rights. How can such a conflict be settled? To what extent should a concern about the welfare of Anne's baby be balanced with a concern for Anne's freedom to choose and for her own well-being?

In my discussion of conflicts of rights and duties in the previous chapter, I concluded that an individual's right to basic well-being (the necessary preconditions of action such as life, health, and mental equilibrium) takes precedence over another individual's right to freedom (guideline 2). In this case, then, the baby's right to basic well-being takes precedence over Anne's right to choose to raise it herself if it can be established that Anne is unlikely to be able to competently care for the baby. This conclusion is based on the central assumption stated earlier that one duty takes precedence over another if the object of the former duty (the baby's well-being) is more necessary for the possibility of action and if the right to that good cannot be protected without violating the latter duty (to protect Anne's right to freedom).

This resolution suggests, then, that it would be wrong to be primarily concerned with Anne's welfare when considering the possibility of placing the baby in foster care. In this instance the baby's interests must be considered primary; the threat to its well-being is greater than the threat to Anne's freedom, which would follow from being denied the opportunity to care for the child. The consequences for Anne may be tragic, and this is sad and unfortunate. The consequences for the baby are more compelling, however, and should be considered primary.

It appears, therefore, that the individual whose interests should be considered primary in any given case depends on the relative threat to the well-being of those likely to be affected by a worker's decision. When we considered whether or not Anne should be told the truth about the baby, we concluded that her interests must be considered before those of her aunt and uncle, her doctor, and the social workers from the Children's Social Service Bureau. However, when we consider whether or not Anne ought to be permitted to care for the baby if she desires to do so, we must conclude that the interests of the baby take precedence over Anne's.

These conclusions suggest, then, that a social worker is not obligated to always place the interests of his or her clients above the interests of other individuals. In general it is sound practice to act in a manner which enhances and protects the freedom and well-being of one's clients; there are relatively rare instances, however, when the interests of others must unfortunately take precedence over the interests of one's own clients. In these cases the justification for placing the interests of others above those of one's clients must be that the welfare of the other individuals is seriously threatened and that the welfare of the other individuals can be protected only by sacrificing to some extent the interests of one's clients.

PATERNALISM AND THE LIMITS OF INTERVENTION

CASE 3.2 The police dispatcher warned Michael Bunker to expect something unusual. Michael turned his car into the alley off of Ellicott Street and saw a woman who appeared to be about seventy years old rummaging around in the cluttered yard beside a dilapidated garage. Michael stopped for a moment to collect his thoughts, got out of his car, and cautiously approached the woman.

Michael was a social worker with the city's Department of Human Resources. His responsibilities included responding to cases encountered and referred by the police department which required some form of social service—emergency food and shelter, public aid, or health care. Earlier that morning he had received a call from the police department; an elderly woman had been lingering for days in a residential area on the city's west side. The woman appeared to be spending most of her time searching through rubbish which had accumulated in an alley and dragging discarded junk into an old garage.

The police officer who responded to the call was able to find the woman and spoke with her casually as she continued about her business of searching and collecting. She reported her name as Helen and told the officer that she had been living in the garage for three weeks; she claimed to have the owner's permission to stay there. She told the officer that she recently moved to the garage from her home in Parkville, on the other side of town, because her husband recently died and because she did not want to live with her daughter and son-in-law. Helen claimed that she was content with her new home and had no interest in being taken back to Parkville.

The police officer attempted to locate the owner of the garage in order to confirm Helen's story, but to no avail. He then requested the police dispatcher to contact the Department of Human Resources; the police officer assumed that it would be best for a social worker to try to assist Helen.

As Michael Bunker began to walk toward Helen, he took a quick look around. The thirty-foot garage had no windows, appeared to have no locks, and had a large hole in the roof. The neighbor who phoned the police had reported that Helen slept on one of two broken-down couches which she apparently dragged into the garage by herself.

Michael told Helen that he was from the city's Department of Human Resources and that he had come to see if she needed some help. Helen refused to tell Michael her last name and shouted, "I don't need no help. I have my daughter and a home in Parkville." Michael explained to Helen that he was in a position to arrange for food, health care, and a place to live. Helen simply ignored Michael and continued sorting through a pile of old newspapers. Extremely frustrated, Michael excused himself, told Helen that he might return the following day, and began searching for neighbors who might be able to provide some additional information about Helen.

According to Alma Torrez, "Helen has been out on the streets for six years. She says she's not old, just over twenty-one. That woman is afraid—she doesn't want to go to an old folks' home to die. But the little kids throw rocks at the garage and they hit her with rocks, too. And sometimes they break her door down and then run away." Alma

> Torrez and several other people from her apartment building occasionally gave Helen some food. They also allowed her to bathe and stay in the building's basement during storms. In return, Helen cleared trash from the area surrounding the building and picked up decaying apples. "She works all day fixing things and clearing out her yard." Alma told Michael. "When I first met her, it was three o'clock in the morning and she was walking around picking up all the wood in the alley. She's real clean and strong. There are broken tree branches in her yard and every day she picks some up and throws them in the garage. She says that she has to have a place by herself and doesn't want to be moved by anyone. Maybe that's why she keeps collecting rocks and boards. She told us she gathers them to someday build a home."
>
> Michael drove back to his office not knowing what to think. Here was a woman who was obviously quite resourceful and independent, though rather confused. She was managing to take care of herself without any serious burden to other people. Yet her living conditions were decrepit and dirty. She appeared to have no income and lived off the generosity and scraps of neighborhood residents. Michael was genuinely torn. Should Helen be allowed to live her life under such conditions, or was he, as an employee of the city's agency charged with providing emergency assistance to those in need, obligated to arrange for Helen to be moved and for food and medical care?

The dilemma faced by Michael Bunker is not unlike many dilemmas social workers encounter in their day-to-day practice: Under what circumstances is a social worker obligated to intervene in the life of a client who refuses or resists assistance? This case raises important questions about paternalism and the duty to aid, in particular the distinction between positive and negative liberty. Michael Bunker recognizes that Helen is a woman living in what many people would consider deplorable conditions. On the surface it appears that her living conditions limit her ability to engage in activities which many people find enhance the quality of their lives. It appears that a variety of services, including shelter, public assistance payments, and medical care, might increase Helen's opportunities for leading a more comfortable life. Aid provided in the form of such services would be in pursuit of what I earlier referred to as positive liberty, or aid designed to enhance an individual's ability to fulfill his or her goals. Michael also recognizes, however, a competing point of view: Despite the good intentions of those who seek to provide aid to those in need, individuals ordinarily have the right to chart the course of their own lives, even if the course appears to be a harmful, self-destructive one. Respecting an individual's right to manage his or her own affairs in this fashion represents what I have referred to as negative liberty.

Protection from Harm

The central question in cases where an individual who seems to be in need of aid resists assistance must concern the identification of those circumstances which warrant intervention despite the individual's protests. Are Helen's living conditions of a sort that justify coerced intervention by the city's Department of Human Resources? If so, on what grounds?

A popular response to these questions is that coerced intervention is justifiable if an individual's activities and behavior represent a serious harm to other individuals or to him- or herself. If we are to respect the rights of others to freedom and well-being, it would be justifiable to provide Helen with assistance to the extent necessary in order to protect these rights. Helen's activities do not, however, appear to represent such a threat. The owner of the garage in which she lives has agreed to allow Helen to use it as a home. Helen has not taken property from neighbors without their permission, and she has not asked them for assistance. The food and shelter with which neighbors have provided Helen have been given voluntarily. But what about the threat Helen's activities represent to her own welfare? What obligation does Michael Bunker have to protect Helen from the consequences of her own behavior?

The debate concerning the obligation to prevent individuals from harming themselves is an ancient one. On one side there are those who argue that the right to self-determination entails the right to engage in activities which may result in harm to oneself. Any interference on the part of others is viewed as unwarranted and wrong. Proponents of this point of view argue that it is permissible, for example, for a client to choose to continue living with an abusive spouse if he or she so wishes or for a troubled client to refuse counseling. Perhaps the strongest statement which has been made by adherents of this point of view is that it is even wrong to interfere with a client's choice to end his or her own life.[5]

On the other side, of course, are those who argue that members of society have an obligation to protect one another from self-destructive behavior and that it is sometimes necessary to interfere with another individual's intentions for that person's own good. According to this point of view, it would be not only permissible but necessary to insist that Helen be provided with secure shelter, food, and medical care. If she is not able to protect herself from the harmful consequences of her own decisions, it is necessary for others to do so for her.

The debate concerning the proper balance between clients' right to engage in apparently self-destructive behavior and social workers' obligation to prevent harm centers on a concept which has long endured in the mainstream of social work practice: self-determination. The tension has been between those who believe in clients' right to set their own goals and, possibly, to make mistakes, and those who claim that there are instances when clients can develop the ability and wherewithal to make informed choices only if they follow professional advice and are provided with professional assistance. It is illustrated vividly in the following passage by Felix Biestek:

> The principle of client self-determination is the practical recognition of the right and need of clients to freedom in making their own choices and decisions in the casework process. Caseworkers have a corresponding duty to respect that right, recognize that need, stimulate and help to activate that potential for self-direction by helping the client to see and use the available and appropriate resources of the community and of his own personality. The client's right to self-determination, however, is limited by the client's capacity for positive and constructive decision making, by the framework of civil and moral law, and by the function of the agency.[6]

Clearly, difficult decisions must on occasion be made by social workers either to strongly encourage or insist that clients avail themselves of specific professional services and courses of action or to respect a client's right to refuse assistance and, as David Soyer describes it, the client's "right to fail."[7]

A Closer Look at Paternalism

The concept of paternalism, though not the term itself, has been bandied about regularly since the time of Aristotle, who argued in his *Politics*—written in the fourth century B.C.—that some degree of paternalism is justifiable in a society in which certain elite individuals are clearly more informed and wiser than others. The classic commentary on paternalism, however, appeared in the nineteenth century in John Stuart Mill's essay *On Liberty*. Following the publication of this essay in 1859, Mill came to be regarded as the principal spokesman for antipaternalism, especially with respect to the excesses of government intervention. In *On Liberty* Mill presents what has become the standard citation for antipaternalists: "[The] sole end for which mankind are warranted, individually or collectively, in interfering with the liberty of action of any of their number, is self-protection. That the only purpose for which power can be rightfully exercised over any member of a civilized community, against his will, is to prevent harm to others. His own good, either physical or moral, is not a sufficient warrant. . . . Over himself, over his own body and mind, the individual is sovereign."[8]

Since the publication of *On Liberty* there has been considerable debate about the nature of paternalism and its justification. Concern with the problem of paternalism among contemporary philosophers was especially noteworthy during the 1960s, largely because of the widespread attention being paid then to issues of civil rights and liberties. Debate during those unsettling years about the rights of, for example, the mentally ill, prisoners, and children gave rise to considerable philosophical controversy concerning the limits of government intervention and the rights of citizens under the care of the state. Professional practices that had previously been unchallenged were called into question. Is it permissible to sterilize a mildly retarded female adolescent "for her own good"? Does she have the right at least to participate in the decision? Is it permissible to require a ward of the state to accept a blood transfusion despite his protests? Do individuals committed to a state department of mental health have the right to the least restrictive alternative?

It is no accident that what is widely regarded as the seminal contemporary essay in the philosophical literature on paternalism appeared in the midst of national controversy about civil liberties. In his 1968 essay, "Paternalism," Gerald Dworkin, a moral philosopher, defines *paternalism* as "interference with a person's liberty of action justified by reasons referring exclusively to the welfare, good, happiness, needs, interests, or values of the person being coerced."[9] For him, examples of paternalism include laws that justify civil commitment procedures on the basis of preventing the client from harming him- or herself, require members of certain religious sects to have compulsory blood transfusions, make suicide a criminal offense, require motorcyclists to wear safety helmets, and forbid persons from swimming at a public beach when lifeguards are not on duty.

Dworkin's definition of paternalism is thus restricted primarily to interferences with the actions of individuals that, to use Mill's term, are self-regarding. Philosophical discussions of paternalism since Dworkin's original formulation have expanded this definition to include interference with individuals' access to information, emotional condition, and so forth, in addition to actions per se. In her prominent essay on the justification of paternalism, the philosopher Rosemary Carter defines a paternalistic act more broadly as "one in which the protection or promotion of a subject's welfare is the primary reason for attempted or successful coercive interference with an action *or state* of that person."[10] In a more detailed definition, Allen Buchanan, a philosopher concerned with medical ethics, describes paternalism as "interference with a person's freedom of action or freedom of information, or the deliberate dissemination of misinformation, where the alleged justification of interference or misinforming is that it is for the good of the person who is interfered with or misinformed."[11] Though Carter's and Buchanan's definitions of paternalism are more comprehensive than Dworkin's, all contain the element of coercion or interference that is justified by references to the good of the individual who is being interfered with.

Paternalism can thus take a variety of forms in the practice of social work. In general, there are three categories into which paternalistic actions can be placed: interference with an individual's intentions or actions; deliberate withholding of information; and deliberate dissemination of misinformation. Interference with the intentions or actions of an individual can include, for instance, requiring that a client be hospitalized against his or her wishes, restraining a self-destructive client with force, or insisting that a client accept an offer of assistance or a particular service. Withholding information or providing misinformation can also occur under a variety of circumstances where it is believed that clients may harm themselves if they have access to truthful information.

Debates about the justification of paternalism ultimately reduce to debates about conflicts among various rights and duties. Paternalism essentially entails a conflict between the right of clients to well-being and their right to freedom from interference or coercion. There are also corresponding conflicts among the social worker's simultaneous duties to protect the client from injury or harm, promote maximum self-determination on the part of the client, and avoid gratuitous intervention in clients' lives.

The inclination to assist people who experience problems in living is what tends to draw us to the profession of social work. However, because of our abiding interest in helping, we must be particularly attentive to any tendency to become excessively intrusive in the lives of our clients. Paternalism in social work is not always inappropriate. At times it is even obligatory. Paternalism becomes a problem, however, when the attributes of our clients and the situations in which they find themselves do not strictly demand actions that may be in their interests but run counter to their wishes. The assertion that we know what is best for others may in some rare instances be true. Too often, however, it is presumptuous.

We must be especially careful to justify paternalistic acts because of the ease with which this concept can be misused to exercise excessive social control. The term *paternalism*—which implies that one's actions are motivated by an altruistic interest in a client's welfare—can be and has been used as camouflage for actions that in fact are inspired by individual or organizational self-interest. Unfortunately, claims that clients need to be restrained, deceived, or administered services for their own good are sometimes little more than rhetoric designed to justify actions that are ultimately designed to keep order or sustain an organization and its method of operation. Because of this problem of "pseudopaternalism," it is important to recognize that the conditions that must be met to justify paternalistic acts are stringent and that the burden rests primarily with the potential paternalist.

The Right to Choose

In the previous chapter I concluded that an individual's right to freedom takes precedence over his or her own right to basic well-being (guideline 3). This guideline suggests that an individual who chooses to engage in self-destructive behavior should be permitted to do so, provided that the individual is making an informed, voluntary decision with knowledge of relevant circumstances and possible consequences and that the consequences of the decision are not likely to threaten the well-being of others. It is necessary to consider the likely effects of the decision on others in order to be consistent with the guideline that an individual's right to basic well-being takes precedence over another individual's right to freedom (guideline 2).

It appears that in Helen's case it would be permissible for Michael Bunker to interfere temporarily in order to determine, to the best of his ability, whether Helen is indeed making a voluntary and informed decision to live under her present conditions and to make her aware of the assistance available to her. If it appears that the conditions of voluntariness and informed choice have been met, further interference would not be justifiable. Interference might be justifiable if it appeared that Helen's ability to make a voluntary and informed decision is severely limited due to, for example, severe mental illness. Interference would also be justifiable if it appeared that Helen's activities represented a serious threat to the freedom and well-being of others.

This may be considered by some a debatable conclusion. It may be argued, for instance, that anyone who chooses to live as Helen has by definition suffers from an inability to make informed, rational choices and that her decision to live under her present conditions only demonstrates the severity of her mental illness. It may in fact be that in some cases an individual's decision to engage in what appears to be self-destructive behavior is the result of serious mental illness and that in these instances interference is justifiable. But it would be difficult to establish that in all such cases an individual's decision is the product of serious mental illness. As Alan Gewirth has said: "It may be contended that the conditions of voluntary consent are never fulfilled in such cases, that only abysmal ignorance or deep emotional trauma can lead persons to extreme measures like these. While this is true in many cases, it would be difficult to prove that it is true in all."[12] The difficult task for social workers in such cases, then, is to judge whether the individual who has refused assistance is able to make a voluntary, informed choice and whether the freedom and well-being of others is threatened by the individual's decision.

DIVIDED PROFESSIONAL LOYALTIES

CASE 3.3 Jane Gimble's supervisor walked into her office and handed her a slip of paper on which was scribbled "327—get there as soon as you can." Jane, a social worker on the neurosurgery unit at County Hospital, finished her telephone conversation, walked to the nurse's station on the third floor, and pulled the chart for the patient in Room 327 of the intensive care unit. The patient, Sharlene Thomas, age seventeen, had been admitted to the hospital twelve days earlier with a gunshot wound. Sharlene underwent emergency surgery to dislodge a bullet from her head. After the surgery she contracted meningitis and pneumonia. Sharlene was unconscious; she was receiving antibiotics intravenously and nasal/gastric tube feedings. Six days following her admission to the hospital, Sharlene's condition worsened; diagnostic studies revealed that she was suffering from a cerebrospinal fluid leak. Surgery was planned for the next day to repair the leak.

According to Dr. Frey, the hospital's chief of neurosurgery, Sharlene would be permanently blind in both eyes as a result of the wound and had suffered extensive brain damage. She would not be able to live without the aid of a respirator and would never regain consciousness. Dr. Frey recommended that "all life support systems be withdrawn" and that nature be allowed to take its course.

The following day Jane Gimble attempted to contact Sharlene's mother, who was listed as her guardian, in order to discuss her daughter's case and Dr. Frey's recommendations. She was unable to find a telephone listing for the family and decided to drive to the home to see Mrs. Thomas. Jane discovered that Mrs. Thomas was herself an invalid, bound to a wheelchair because of severe arthritis. Mrs. Thomas told Jane that Sharlene was the fourth oldest of eleven children who ranged in age from two to twenty-five. Before being shot, Sharlene was living in a halfway house in a neighboring county. Mrs. Thomas explained that Sharlene had been incarcerated for ten months following a conviction for armed robbery. She also told Jane that Sharlene had "suffered from drugs for nearly four years but got clean after her arrest."

Jane Gimble learned that on the weekend of the shooting, Sharlene was on a two-day home visit from the halfway house. She had earned the visit because of her performance in a vocational training program. Sharlene had been anxious to visit her boyfriend, Leonard. When she arrived at her mother's home on the first night of her two-day leave, Sharlene found out that Leonard had hanged himself in a jail cell following an arrest for aggravated assault. According to Mrs. Thomas, "Sharlene was real sad, but not in a real bad way." Later that evening Mrs. Thomas rushed to Sharlene's bedroom after hearing a loud noise and found Sharlene slumped on the floor, bleeding, with a gun by her side. Mrs. Thomas told Jane that she was sure that the shooting was an accident; her daughter would never have committed suicide. She told her that she wanted the hospital to do everything it could to keep Sharlene alive.

Jane Gimble met with Dr. Frey the following day to discuss her meeting with Mrs. Thomas. She told Dr. Frey that Mrs. Thomas wanted the hospital staff to do everything they could to keep Sharlene alive. Dr. Frey shook his head and told Jane that he knew it was a mistake to keep Sharlene alive; he had seen many such cases and in each one the patient could be kept alive only with extraordinary measures. The coma was irreversible. At best, Sharlene would be severely damaged and would require constant care which would have to be paid for with public aid funds. He could not justify spending hundreds of thousands of dollars of taxpayers' funds on a patient who would likely remain comatose. It was much more important to use the limited money available for medical care of public aid recipients on patients who had some reasonable chance for recovery. Dr. Frey told Jane that it was her responsibility to persuade Mrs. Thomas to approve the hospital's plan to withdraw the extraordinary measures being used to sustain Sharlene. He said he would talk with Mrs. Thomas himself but that he could not afford the time to travel to her home to see her. Dr. Frey reminded Jane that whether or not she agreed with the recommendations of the medical staff, she was obligated as an employee of the hospital to represent its point of view.

She told Dr. Frey that she did not think she could try to convince Mrs. Thomas to approve a course of action that would hasten her daughter's death; she believed her responsibility as a social worker was to help Mrs. Thomas make a decision and to provide her with support. But she was troubled with second thoughts: What obligation did she have to follow the recommendations of the medical staff of the hospital for whom she worked? Did she have an obligation to follow Dr. Frey's advice so that more money would be available for other patients who have a better chance for survival and for leading relatively normal lives?

This case raises three significant and interrelated issues. First, Jane Gimble is torn between acting in accord with the recommendations of the medical staff of the hospital which employs her and advocating on behalf of Mrs. Thomas, whose wishes clash with Dr. Frey's. Does she have an obligation to protect the interests of Mrs. Thomas and Sharlene in this case, even if doing so requires her to defy Dr. Frey's recommendation? Or, is Jane obligated, as an employee of the hospital, to obey the recommendations of its medical staff? Second, who has the right to decide Sharlene Thomas' fate, Dr. Frey or Mrs. Thomas? Finally, to what extent should the cost of the care required to keep Sharlene Thomas alive affect conclusions about the extent to which extraordinary measures will be taken? How should the answers to these questions affect Jane Gimble's obligations as a social worker?

Divided Loyalties

It is not uncommon for social workers to feel torn between satisfying the interests of various parties, such as employers and clients, whose intentions conflict. Public aid workers are at times faced with choosing to abide by departmental regulations and approving assistance to needy clients who do not technically qualify for benefits. Practitioners in private agencies must occasionally choose between complying with policies regarding intake criteria and agreeing to serve individuals in need who do not meet eligibility requirements. Similarly, Jane Gimble faces a choice between supporting the point of view of her employer, as represented by Dr. Frey, and supporting the wishes of Mrs. Thomas.

A popular point of view is that social workers are obligated to abide by the policies and regulations of the agencies which employ them. As Charles Levy has said:

> The social worker owes specific ethical responsibilities to his employing agency. Foremost among these is the responsibility to act for, and represent the agency loyally and well—not without some thought to, and responsibility for inequities and injustices that the agency may inflict on others, but unequivocally nonetheless—unless or until he severs his relationship with the agency. This is not a matter of blind and rigid loyalty without regard for its consequences, but a contracted obligation in the sense that if the social worker works for an agency, he works for and not against it. Second, the social worker does what the agency employs him to do in fulfilling the agency's declared purpose and service function, not something else.[13]

In fact, the guideline presented earlier, that the obligation to obey laws, rules, and regulations to which one has voluntarily and freely consented (such as agreements to support the official points of view of the agency by which one is employed) overrides one's right to engage voluntarily and freely in a manner which conflicts with these laws, rules, and regulations (guideline 4), suggests that social workers have an obligation to abide by agency policies.

But is this a guideline by which one is obligated to abide in all cases, regardless of the consequences? It appears not, as I have suggested in the guideline which states that individuals' rights to well-being may override laws, rules, regulations, and arrangements of voluntary associations in cases of conflict (guideline 5). Thus, ordinarily social workers are obligated to adhere to agreements they enter into with employers to act in a manner which is consistent with agency policy. There are instances, however, regrettable though they may be, when the threat to someone's well-being may require one to violate agreements with his or her employers. An extreme example of such an instance is provided by the case of a social worker employed by a private family service agency who was prohibited, according to agency policy, from offering service to clients who had large, unpaid bills for services rendered. A client who had not paid her bill in over four months called the worker one afternoon in an apparently suicidal state and pleaded with the worker to see her. The worker consented to a meeting with the client, contrary to agency policy.

Few would argue that it was wrong for this worker to see the client under these emergency circumstances. This case demonstrates that there are instances when it is permissible to violate agency rules in order to protect the basic well-being of an individual, in that rules against basic harms to the necessary preconditions of action (such as life, health, food, shelter, mental equilibrium) take precedence over rules against harms such as lying or deceiving (or violating agency guidelines). The difficult challenge, of course, is deciding whether the circumstances in the case of Sharlene Thomas are such that it would be permissible for Jane Gimble to defy Dr. Frey's recommendation and to advocate instead in Mrs. Thomas' behalf.

Our attention in this case must be focused on the responsibility Jane Gimble has to her agency and the responsibility she has to Mrs. Thomas and to protect Sharlene's welfare. One way to examine this case is to compare the nature of the goods which each of these responsibilities entails. The hospital's threatened goods include the consistency with which its social work employees represent the point of view of its medical staff to patients and their families. A lack of consistency may undermine smooth working relationships between medical and social work staff. Acts of insubordination may also threaten the traditional authority of medical staff in the hospital. The goods belonging to Sharlene Thomas which are threatened include life itself. Because life is a more basic good and is more necessary for the possibility of action than is the maintenance of smooth working relationships among hospital staff and traditional lines of authority, it can be argued that Jane Gimble is not obligated to abide by Dr. Frey's recommendation *simply* because the hospital maintains a policy that social work staff should represent the opinions of medical staff to patients. If Jane Gimble agrees to endorse Dr. Frey's recommendation, she should do so on the grounds that withdrawing extraordinary measures is necessary in order to protect certain individuals' rights to basic well-being. It does not appear, however, that Sharlene Thomas' right to basic well-being would be protected by withdrawing extraordinary medical care; on the contrary, withdrawing such care appears on the surface only to further threaten her well-being. This suggests that a decision to withdraw extraordinary care must depend on evidence that the well-being of others would be threatened if Sharlene continued to receive extensive treatment.

A question which remains to be considered, then, is whether Jane Gimble's responsibility as a social worker requires her to support Mrs. Thomas' wish to have the hospital sustain Sharlene indefinitely, or whether she has the responsibility to persuade Mrs. Thomas of the futility of extraordinary lifesaving efforts in Sharlene's case, and of the hospital's need to instead divert its resources to patients who have some likelihood of recovering. Thus, the ethical dilemma Jane Gimble faces entails difficult questions concerning the distribution of limited resources in addition to questions related to conflicts of interest between a social worker's employer and client.

The Extent of Care

The question of the extent to which resources should be spent to care for a critically ill patient is a troublesome one—and one which is forever present in the medical profession. At what point should a physician cease treating the illness of a dying patient aggressively and shift his or her efforts to the less expensive task of making the patient as comfortable and free of pain as possible before his or her death? How much weight should be given to the wishes of a relative or guardian? Similar questions are frequently asked in the social welfare field. How much money should be spent caring for clients who display little change in their behavior after massive amounts of aid? Is it justifiable to spend millions of dollars of public funds to support the treatment of severely disturbed juvenile offenders, retarded or psychotic adults, or chronic alcoholics if there is relatively little evidence that professional interventions are effective?

The case of Sharlene Thomas includes an additional complication. It might be argued that if Sharlene were insured by a private company, neither Jane Gimble nor the hospital's medical staff would be in a position to deny her long-term care. However, Sharlene's care is being paid for by state and federal funds. Does this fact alter the nature of the obligation Jane and the hospital have in this case? The sad fact of the matter is that it may. If Sharlene were privately insured, she would have the right to as much care as allowed under the conditions of her policy. But because her care is supported by funds drawn from a finite pool supported by tax revenues, serious questions concerning the distribution of limited resources necessarily arise. Individuals who are in a position to affect the allocation of these funds, such as the hospital's medical and social work staff, have an obligation to try to distribute them in a manner which, to the greatest extent possible, minimizes suffering and enhances health. As a result, difficult decisions must sometimes be made to favor one patient over another.

It is clear to all of the parties involved in this case—Dr. Frey, Jane Gimble, Mrs. Thomas—that Sharlene's condition is grave. Her coma appears to be irreversible, she is blind, she has suffered extensive brain damage, and she can be sustained only with the aid of a respirator. She has no reflexes, no movement, and a flat electroencephalogram. On the average, her care is costing $1,250 per day.

A strictly utilitarian approach to this case would perhaps suggest that the greatest good for the greatest number would result if Sharlene were allowed to die and if the funds being used to provide her care were diverted to the care of other patients whose care must be supported with public funds and whose chances of survival are greater than Sharlene's. But another utilitarian might view the case differently and argue that the greatest good for the greatest number would result by allowing Sharlene to live so that she can serve as a subject for medical research.

An alternative to the utilitarian point of view is to act in accord with the

Hippocratic principle, which requires a physician to do what he or she believes will most benefit the patient. But this guideline is also subject to various interpretations. One physician might argue that it is in Sharlene's best interests for the hospital's medical staff to do all they can to keep her alive as long as possible. Another physician might take the point of view that there is an obligation for the medical staff to put an end to her suffering and to allow her to die peacefully.

A balanced view of this case suggests that it is important to consider both the obligation to protect Sharlene's right to basic well-being and the obligation to distribute limited public aid resources in a manner which provides the greatest degree of health care possible to each individual who requires medical assistance. This is not a strictly utilitarian conclusion. Our interest here is not in distributing available funds so that the greatest aggregate amount of health care is provided; rather, our interest is in providing to the greatest extent possible competent health care *for every individual,* including Sharlene Thomas. A strictly utilitarian approach would not necessarily pay close attention to Sharlene's welfare.

How can a reasonable balance be achieved between Sharlene's interests and the interests of others whose lives might be saved or enhanced with the money being spent to sustain her? While no formula exists which would permit us to determine how much money should be spent caring for Sharlene before extraordinary measures are withdrawn, an outline of possible procedures can be provided. It would seem appropriate for the hospital to assemble a team of medical staff who have considerable experience with patients who have suffered traumas and medical complications similar to Sharlene's. The members of this team would monitor Sharlene's condition regularly (perhaps daily or every other day) in order to determine the likelihood that Sharlene could ever survive without extraordinary medical care. If there were no such evidence that Sharlene could survive without such care after monitoring her condition for a specified period of time agreed upon by the medical team, extraordinary measures would be withdrawn so that nature could take its course and so that hospital and general health care resources could be diverted or conserved for patients who have a greater likelihood of recovery. It is indeed unfortunate that such life-and-death decisions must be influenced by the availability of public funds. But these conditions are givens in contemporary times; we cannot allow the remorse we feel about having to make such decisions to discourage us from thinking carefully and compassionately about them.[14]

Implications for Practice

The conclusion that Jane Gimble's primary responsibility is to act in a manner which protects individuals' rights to basic well-being and that this is more important than simply complying with hospital policy which requires social work staff to endorse the views of medical staff is not based on an assumption that a social worker must always place the interests of clients above the interests of others, though ordinarily he or she should; similarly, we cannot conclude that a social worker should always place the interests of his or her employer above the interests of others. In each case when a choice must be made among competing interests, the worker's responsibility is to assess to the best of his or her ability the extent to which the individuals involved are threatened with the loss of basic goods (freedom and basic well-being) which are necessary in order to engage in action and to act in a manner which is designed to minimize such a threat. There will be times when a social worker's decisions will be based on an assumption that the client's interests are primary, and times when the interests of others must be considered primary (for example, a spouse or children whose welfare is threatened by a client's behavior).

These conclusions have important implications for the relationships between a social worker and his or her clients, colleagues, and employers. One of the central tenets of social work practice is that a worker must spend time cultivating relationships which are based on feelings of trust and confidence. It is generally considered critical that employers, colleagues, and especially clients be able to assume that a social worker is trustworthy and dependable. However, the conclusion that there may be instances which require a worker to choose among the competing interests of these various parties suggests that a social worker may sometimes be obligated to act in a manner which runs against the wishes of his or her clients, colleagues, or employers.

This possibility need not, however, represent a serious threat to the sanctity of the relationships which effective social work is generally considered to depend upon. It is indeed important that a client, colleague, or employer have confidence that a social worker can be depended upon to represent his or her interests. Such confidence is the foundation of the helping relationship. However, it would be less than fair for a social worker to enter into any such relationship without acknowledging that in any professional relationship the possibility exists that conflicts of interest will emerge, conflicts which may require that the interests of one party be considered before those of another. Rather than view the possibility of such choices as a threat to the integrity of relationships, the *possibility* of conflicts of interest, no matter how remote, would be better viewed as an indispensable characteristic of relationships, one which should be recognized as a premise from which relationships derive rather than as an unanticipated consequence. The individuals with whom social workers enter into professional relationships have a right to be made aware of the possibility that a worker may at some point have to make a difficult choice among competing interests. It would be wrong to leave clients, colleagues, and employers with the impression that their interests will, without exception, be considered primary.

Relationships between social workers and their clients, colleagues, and employers do in fact depend on trust. However, a relationship founded on an assumption that a worker will never, under any circumstances, consider the interests of another individual more pressing is to some extent blind to the exigencies of life. A deep, solid sense of trust can be developed between a practitioner and a client, colleague, or employer who is made to understand the nature of the difficult choices social workers sometimes face. This trust, however, must be based on a clear understanding that while the worker is ordinarily concerned with the interests of his or her clients, colleagues, and employers, occasions can arise when the interests of others must be considered primary because of a serious threat to their freedom and well-being. Jane Gimble faced such a dilemma when she realized that the interests of the hospital and of other patients conflicted with the interests of Sharlene Thomas. The conclusion that she should consider the interests of Sharlene and other patients as primary is based on an assumption that the threat to their well-being is more compelling than the threat to the welfare of the hospital.

It is important to note that the outcome of the course of action which I have argued Jane Gimble should endorse may not differ from the outcome of Dr. Frey's recommendation. In each case, the final result may entail withdrawing Sharlene's extraordinary medical care. There is a meaningful difference, however, in the justifications of these courses of action. Dr. Frey insisted that Jane Gimble endorse his point of view because of a hospital policy which requires social work staff to represent the opinions of medical staff to patients. This justification is less defensible than one based on a careful analysis of the various threats to the basic well-being of

Sharlene and other patients who stand to be affected by the decision in this case.

It is unfortunate that we cannot feel happy about the conclusion this case seems to force us to accept. However, it is often the case that resolutions of ethical dilemmas do not leave one feeling joyful. Ethical dilemmas frequently demand a choice between two unpleasant options. What is important is that in these regrettable instances we have good reasons to support our belief that we are making the right choice.

The conclusion that Jane Gimble should endorse a plan which may result in withdrawing Sharlene's extraordinary care and in opposing Mrs. Thomas' wishes places her in an unenviable position. It may be difficult for her to develop an effective, supportive relationship with Mrs. Thomas when she feels compelled to agree with a decision which may result in hastening Sharlene's death. The challenge for her is a substantial one. If it appears that she cannot provide Mrs. Thomas with the kind of support and assistance she needs, Jane Gimble should do her best to refer Mrs. Thomas to someone who can.

This case is a very sad one, and it requires several hard decisions. But it is characteristic of many instances in social work when painful choices must be made among a number of unappealing options. These choices must be made, however, despite the sorrow we may feel about the possible consequences.

CONFLICTS AMONG LAWS, POLICIES, AND TREATMENT GOALS

CASE 3.4 Rachel Sahlins had been seeing Jan Stanhouse as a client for nearly two months. Rachel worked as a caseworker for the Child Care Association and had been meeting regularly with Jan to discuss problems surrounding her recent separation and divorce. Jan had a two-and-one-half-year-old daughter, Grace. Jan first came to the Child Care Association shortly after Grace's second birthday; Grace had begun crying a great deal each night, and Jan was becoming less and less patient with her. Jan came to the agency very concerned that she might "fly off the handle pretty soon" and hurt Grace. She knew Grace was upset about her parents' separation and wanted a social worker to help settle Grace down.

Jan's divorce had been a traumatic one. She had married her

husband, Chris, when she was eighteen years old and had given birth to Grace two years later. Jan's first year of marriage had been happy. She had been anxious to leave her parents' home and believed that with Chris she had a new life ahead of her. Jan had run away from home several times as a teenager, twice after resisting sexual advances by her stepfather. The state placed her in foster care for sixteen months when she was thirteen years old, after her parents were brought to court on a neglect petition.

During the second year of their marriage, Chris and Jan began to argue more and more. Very often their arguments concerned whether or not they would have a child. Chris was very anxious to have a baby; Jan, however, wanted to wait another two years or so. Jan complained that she was not ready to be tied down at home caring for an infant. Several of the arguments between Chris and Jan became very heated and ended with Chris slapping Jan. On two occasions Jan left Chris and spent several days with her sister and her family. After talking with her sister, Jan decided that having a baby might help bring her and Chris closer together.

Grace was born, and for several months Jan and Chris lived a relatively tranquil life. Before long, however, Jan and Chris again began arguing regularly. After several weeks of constant fighting, Jan took Grace and again moved in with her sister and her family.

On a recent visit to the Child Care Association, Jan told Rachel that she was afraid that Grace may have been abused by her new boyfriend, Larry. Jan had noticed a bruise on Grace's buttocks and heard Grace make several vague comments about being afraid of Larry. Jan showed Rachel Grace's bruises.

Rachel was quite confused. She had serious doubts about Jan's ability to care adequately for Grace. She suspected that Jan resented having to care for Grace by herself, especially considering that Jan was reluctant to have a baby in the first place. Rachel also wondered what effect Jan's having been abused herself might have on her ability to care for Grace. She also recalled that when Grace was three months old, Jan had brought her to a hospital emergency room for what was later determined to be a failure to thrive.

Rachel ended her session with Jan and went to talk with her supervisor, Margaret Oates, about the case. Rachel described the history of her relationship with Jan and conveyed her concern about

Jan's feelings and ability to care for Grace. She told Mrs. Oates that she feared for Grace's safety and that she believed that Jan, and not her boyfriend, may have been responsible for the bruises on Grace. Mrs. Oates advised Rachel to comply with the state law which requires social workers and other professionals to report suspected cases of abuse to the Department of Social Services.

Rachel left Mrs. Oates' office not knowing what to do. She knew that technically she was required to report Jan to the Department of Social Services. She believed that Grace was in some danger, but her evidence was rather circumstantial and not very conclusive. At the same time Rachel felt that if she reported Jan to the Department of Social Services, she would not be able to continue a therapeutic relationship with Jan and might jeopardize whatever chance she had to help Jan resolve her problems. She knew that Jan feared having Grace taken from her; Jan told Rachel on several occasions that she wanted to work out her problems on her own and that she "didn't want any of those state people messin' with me and my baby." Jan also told Rachel that if the state came around looking for her, she would take Grace and move "somewhere far from here." She was afraid Grace would be placed in foster care just as she had been as a teenager.

Rachel believed that Jan could be helped to resolve some of the problems which appeared to be affecting her relationship with and her ability to care for Grace. She also believed that Jan was finding her relationship with Rachel meaningful and helpful. But continuing to work with Jan involved some risk for Grace. Rachel did not know whether it was more important to sustain a therapeutic relationship with Jan in the hope that she could help her become a more responsible parent or to report the case to the Department of Social Services in order to comply with the state regulation and to protect Grace from the risk of further injury.

It is tempting to approach this case in a primarily teleological fashion. On the surface it seems difficult to argue with a strategy which would be designed to ensure, to the greatest extent possible, Grace's welfare. But beneath the surface lie several questions which must be addressed before such a conclusion can be reached. Is it more likely that Grace's welfare will be protected if Rachel reports the case to the Department of Social Services or if she continues to work with Jan on her own? How should Rachel reconcile what appears to be a conflict of interest between Jan and the state, as represented by the Department of Social Services? Does Rachel have an obligation to obey a state law which requires her to report the case to the Department of Social Services, even though it is at least possible that doing so would not be in Grace's best interest? To what extent is Rachel obligated to act in accord with Jan's wishes?

Relative Risk

It seems clear that Rachel's primary obligation is to ensure, to the greatest extent possible, Grace's welfare. This may require her to pursue a course of action which conflicts with Jan Stanhouse's wishes. Whether or not it does remains to be seen. But there appears to be little doubt that the individual whose freedom and well-being are most threatened in this case is Grace. Certainly Jan's welfare is also threatened; her ability to live her life and to raise her daughter as she wishes may be threatened if Rachel reports the case to the Department of Social Services. It is possible that the department would remove Grace from Jan's home and place her in foster care, and that Jan herself may suffer ill effects from an investigation into her own behavior as a parent. However, the threat to Grace's welfare must take precedence over the threat to Jan's. It can be argued that because of her age, Grace's ability to withstand the threat to her welfare is less than Jan's ability to withstand whatever threat reporting the case to the Department of Social Services represents to her. This does not require us to conclude that Rachel necessarily has an obligation to report the case to the department. That is a separate question. Rather, it suggests that in case of conflict Grace's welfare must take precedence over Jan's.

There appear to be several possible threats to Grace's welfare. If she remains with her mother, there is the possibility that she will be abused, either by Jan or her boyfriend, Larry. If the case is reported to the state Department of Social Services, there is the possibility that Grace will be removed from her home and placed in foster care. One must then consider the psychological and emotional harms which often result from placement because of inadequate efforts to reduce a child's length of stay in foster care, incompetent foster parents, the lack of adequate follow-up or after-care services, and the lack of continuity and coordination of services.[15]

It appears that Rachel must make a choice between two options, each of which entails risks and possible benefits: reporting the case to the department and continuing to work with Jan Stanhouse without reporting the case. Ethical dilemmas frequently seem to demand such hard choices. However, a closer look at the details of many ethical dilemmas will often suggest additional options which are at first not apparent. Such is the case with the dilemma which Rachel faces.

The State's Interests

Let us first examine why the state law requires social workers and other professionals to report suspected cases of abuse to the Department of Social Services. Presumably the reasons are a concern for the welfare of children whose abuse may go undetected and a concern about the harm children who remain with abusive parents or guardians may suffer. At the same time, however, it is clear that state social service agencies also recognize the risks involved in removing children from their homes and placing them in foster care. Several states, in fact, have introduced a system of incentives designed to encourage private agencies to attempt to return children to their parents.[16] In 1971, for example, New York City introduced a program where for each child returned home after being in foster care for more than one year, a private agency received $400 to be used to help prepare the family for the child's return.[17] In 1973 the California State Department of Health recommended that any savings that "accrue by diverting children from placement by maintaining them at home" should be made available by the state to the counties to be used for preventive services.[18]

It appears, then, that state governments have recognized that in some instances it is important to encourage the placement of children and that in others it is important to encourage the maintenance of children in their own homes. The guiding principle appears to be the assumption that the course of action taken should be that which is believed to afford the greatest protection to a child's welfare.

A reasonable resolution in the case of Jan and Grace Stanhouse would be to act in accord with the state's legitimate interest in monitoring and protecting Grace's welfare, without jeopardizing Rachel Sahlins' efforts to help Jan with her problems, and to enable Grace to receive competent care in her mother's home. An important characteristic of this strategy is that it would attempt to protect the freedom and well-being of Jan and Grace, while considering Grace's welfare primary. It would also take advantage of the relationship Rachel has established with Jan.

Evidence of Abuse

The evidence available to Rachel indicates that either Jan or her boyfriend, Larry, may have hit Grace. Rachel's first duty must be to assess whether Grace is being regularly or severely beaten and abused. She should explain to Jan that she is concerned about Grace's welfare and believes that it is important for her to have an opportunity to talk with Larry about his relationship with Grace. Through her conversations with Larry, Jan, and Grace herself Rachel should do her best to determine whether Grace has in fact been abused. If it appears that Grace has been hit on occasions but has not been abused, Rachel should probably attempt to work with Larry and Jan on alternative ways of disciplining Grace and on alternative ways of handling their frustrations.

If it appears that Grace has been abused and that it would be dangerous for her to be left in Jan's care, Rachel would have no choice but to report the case. Rachel would, of course, need to explain to Jan in detail the reasons for her actions. It may be that as a result Rachel would not be able to maintain a therapeutic relationship with Jan. However, Rachel's first obligation under these circumstances would be to protect Grace. Whether or not she remained in a position to help Jan would be important, but secondary.

The important point here is that *if* Rachel acquired evidence that Grace had been abused, it would not be permissible for her to disobey the state law which requires professionals to report suspected cases of abuse to the Department of Social Services (in accord with guideline 4). However, if it appeared that Grace had occasionally been hit by her mother or Larry, Rachel would not be required to report the case, since occasional physical discipline by a parent that does not result in bodily injury, however undesirable, is not ordinarily considered abuse.

Throughout, Rachel would need to do her best to make it clear to Jan that she wants to help Grace, Larry, and Jan get along well and resolve whatever problems they have. It is conceivable that at some point Jan would object to Rachel's efforts to determine whether or not Grace has been abused. Jan may feel threatened and betrayed by Rachel's inquiries. If this were to occur, Rachel should talk with Jan about her feelings and explain

Rachel's intentions. Rachel should not, however, fail to report the case to the Department of Social Services simply to keep her relationship with Jan intact, assuming that Grace has in fact been abused. It is important to reiterate that Rachel's primary obligation is to Grace. It is her welfare that is most threatened.

THE RIGHT TO CONFIDENTIALITY

CASE 3.5 The McNallys had been clients of Art Bulaich's for almost three months. Art had a private practice and specialized in marriage and family counseling. Several months ago Art received a telephone call from Bev McNally. Bev told Art that she and her husband, Hal, were having serious problems and that a former client of Art's had recommended that she contact him. Bev briefly described to Art the difficulties she and Hal had been having. Hal began drinking heavily about a year earlier, shortly after he was passed over for a promotion he had expected. According to Bev, not receiving the promotion was a serious blow to Hal's self-esteem; he became despondent and began drinking more and more heavily. He ordinarily had two drinks after work and before dinner, and two or three drinks during the remainder of the evening. As each evening wore on, Hal became more difficult to be around. Bev claimed that he was becoming increasingly cantankerous and abusive. It was getting to the point where she simply did not enjoy being with her husband.

Bev had urged Hal to see a counselor, but Hal refused. He argued that he "didn't need help from a damn shrink" and that Bev was overly concerned about his drinking problem. Hal admitted that he was drinking more than he used to, but insisted that he had his drinking under control.

Several months passed without much change in Bev and Hal's relationship. One evening Hal returned home from work and began fixing his usual drink. Bev arrived home a short time later only to be berated by Hal for not having his dinner prepared. Bev explained that she had stopped by the local office of Alcoholics Anonymous to get some information for Hal about its program. Hal slammed down his drink and began screaming at Bev to stop interfering in his life and to leave him alone. Bev began crying and told Hal that their marriage "was in serious trouble" and that she would leave him if he did not try to get some help. She then ran to their bedroom, slammed the door, and cried herself to sleep.

The following morning Bev calmly told Hal that she wanted them to see a marriage counselor and that if Hal refused, she would file for a divorce. Hal looked at Bev, his eyes filled with tears, and told her that he knew it was time for him to get some help and to stop his drinking and that he would do whatever was necessary to save their marriage. That afternoon Bev telephoned her friend, Stephanie Grich, who suggested that Bev contact Art Bulaich.

Art suggested that Bev and Hal make an appointment to see him to discuss in greater detail their respective views of their problems. During their first meeting both Bev and Hal reaffirmed their commitment to the marriage and agreed that the most pressing problem was Hal's drinking. They agreed to meet with Art once each week to explore in greater depth the reasons for Hal's drinking and what might be done to help him stop. At the end of the session Bev reiterated her insistence that Hal must stop his drinking if he wanted to salvage their marriage.

Hal began attending Alcoholics Anonymous meetings, and both he and Bev continued to meet regularly with Art. It was Art's impression that the McNallys were making good progress. Bev was pleased about Hal's commitment to Alcoholics Anonymous and to sobriety. Hal had begun looking for a new job and was pleased with the prospects available to him. He seemed to be feeling much better about himself and the marriage.

Nearly two months after Art began seeing the McNallys, he attended a conference for marriage and family counselors at a downtown hotel. Following the presentations on the first day of the conference, Art accompanied several colleagues to the hotel's bar for a before-dinner cocktail. The small group approached the bar and ordered their drinks. To Art's surprise, Hal McNally was seated at the end of the bar, drink in hand. Hal caught Art's stare and after a few awkward moments quickly made his way toward Art. Hal stammered and stuttered and tried to assure Art that this was only the third or fourth drink he had had in months, and that he only had a drink when the "guys at work" insisted that he join them at a bar. Hal pleaded with Art not to tell Bev about the drink or his somewhat inebriated condition. He told Art that if Bev found out, she would certainly leave him. Art told Hal that he was taken very much by surprise and that the bar was no place for them to discuss the predicament. He asked Hal to call him at his office the following day to arrange a time for them to discuss the situation.

Art returned home that evening nearly overwhelmed with uncertainty about how to handle the dilemma. Did Bev McNally have a right to know that Hal had been drinking occasionally during the time they had been in therapy? If so, was it Hal's responsibility to tell Bev? What obligation did Art have to honor Hal's request not to tell Bev?

The dilemma facing Art Bulaich is clear: What obligation does he have to respect the wishes of one client that he not share sensitive information with the client's spouse, especially when the information is directly related to the reasons why the couple is in treatment? How tolerant should Art be of Hal's strategy for handling this awkward situation?

A Directive Versus a Nondirective Approach

One of the most enduring debates in social work concerns the extent to which practitioners should actively guide a client toward a course of action, as opposed to supporting, clarifying, and generally assisting a client's efforts to decide for him- or herself the most appropriate approach to a given problem. One side of the debate claims that the social worker's primary responsibility is to help the client think clearly about the advantages and disadvantages of various courses of action. According to this point of view, the worker should facilitate and pose thought-provoking questions rather than provide concrete advice.[19] Others argue that there are instances when practitioners must actively direct the course of a client's life and decisions, either because of the client's lack of competence or because of a threat the client represents to him- or herself or others.[20]

As I argued earlier, it is unrealistic to believe that there are never instances when social workers must deny clients the opportunity to act as they wish. There is little question, for example, that a practitioner is obligated to prevent to the best of his or her ability a client from physically assaulting with malice an acquaintance. Of course, the difficult challenge involves the identification of those circumstances which warrant interference by the social worker contrary, perhaps, to the client's wishes.

We can begin an examination of the circumstances in the McNally case by first asking whose welfare is threatened by Hal's wish to have information concerning his drinking withheld from his wife and in what ways the welfare of each of these individuals is threatened. A simplistic answer to this question is that the welfare of each of the principals in this case—Hal and Bev McNally and Art Bulaich—is to some extent at risk. Hal is afraid that his wife will leave him if she discovers that he has been drinking occasionally. He stands to suffer emotionally as a result. However, if Hal is not forced to confront his drinking problem, he may suffer the debilitating effects which often accompany alcoholism. Bev's welfare is threatened in that she is unaware of important information about her husband's behavior which is directly related to her ability to make a decision about her own future. If she is not informed about her husband's drinking, she may remain committed to a marriage which is destined to continue having serious problems and which is the source of considerable emotional trauma. Bev's ability to fulfill her purposes may be seriously threatened if she is not made aware of Hal's continued drinking. Of course, her welfare may also be threatened somewhat if she is made aware of Hal's drinking and decides to leave him as a result. While such a course of action may in the long run be in her best interests, it is possible that she will also suffer significantly in the process. It is reasonable to assume that the processes of separation and divorce represent at least some threat to her welfare, though the net effect of such a threat is difficult to estimate.

Art's welfare is also threatened in several ways. If he decides to respect Hal's request to withhold information about his drinking from Bev, Art must cope with the discomfort associated with concealing information from a client which seems important to her own well-being. Art must also live with the knowledge that Bev may at some time discover that Art was aware of Hal's drinking and chose not to share this information. In addition to the possibility that Bev will feel betrayed, it is at least possible that Art's professional reputation would suffer as a result. Alternatively, if Art decides that Bev should be informed about Hal's drinking and assumes some responsibility for informing her, he must also live with the knowledge that his actions may result in a separation and divorce.

Thus, the welfare of each of the individuals involved in this case is threatened to some extent, whether Art decides that Bev should or should not be informed about her husband's drinking. Art's responsibility is to consider which of the options available to him seems to best protect the rights to freedom and well-being of the individuals involved.

Options and Consequences

It appears that the least desirable option would be for Art to simply honor Hal's request to withhold details about his drinking from Bev and continue counseling the couple as if this information had not come to his attention. One unfortunate consequence of such a strategy may be that by honoring Hal's request Art reinforces and tacitly condones Hal's use of deception in his relationship with both his wife and his counselor. Not only would Bev be denied information relevant to her own well-being as a result, but reinforcing the use of such deception is likely to severely jeopardize Art's attempt to help the McNallys improve their ability to communicate with each other and, ultimately, to strengthen their relationship. In addition, as I noted above, such a strategy also represents some threat to Art's own peace of mind and the quality of his relationship with both Bev and Hall.

At the same time, however, there appear to be arguments against having Art assume responsibility for informing Bev about Hal's drinking. An immediate consequence of such a course of action may be that Bev will leave Hal, effectively eliminating whatever chance exists for resolving their problems. In addition, Hal may be denied the opportunity to accept responsibility for his problems, to be encouraged to share his problem with his wife, and to introduce the problem as an additional issue to be focused on in their work with Art.

An appropriate strategy in this case would simultaneously enhance the probability that Bev and Hal will continue to work on their marital difficulties, that Bev will not be deliberately misled about Hal's drinking, and that Art will not be expected to be party to a plan to deliberately withhold important information from Bev. Such a strategy would not be a strictly utilitarian one designed to produce "the greatest good"; rather, it would be designed to protect to the greatest extent possible the freedom and well-being of each of the individuals centrally involved in this case and their right to truthful information.

Such a plan could begin with Art explaining to Hal the reasons why he would not feel comfortable continuing to work with him and his wife as long as Hal is deceiving Bev, with Art's knowledge, about his drinking. Art would explain that he cannot tacitly condone the deliberate deception of a client. Art would also explain that the prospects for a marriage founded to some extent on deception are not good and that he is concerned about the threat to his own peace of mind and professional reputation which might result from agreeing to a plan which would conceal important information from Bev. In addition, Art would explain to Hal his belief that it would be best for Hal to inform Bev of his drinking himself and to reiterate his commitment to the marriage and to stop drinking. If Hal has reservations about Art's suggestion that he inform Bev himself about his drinking, Art would explain that it would be difficult for him to continue meeting with them unless Bev is made aware of Hal's problem. Art might offer to meet with Hal for several sessions to help him think about how to share this information with Bev and to discuss Hal's feelings about informing her of his drinking. Thus, Bev's right to well-being would take precedence over Hal's right to freedom, that is, his right to choose to deceive Bev (guideline 2).

Such a strategy would allow Hal an opportunity to continue in treatment and would allow him time to attempt to resolve his feelings about telling his wife about his drinking. It is a strategy designed to allow the McNallys to continue working on their marital problems and to avoid having Art be party to a plan to deliberately withhold important information from Bev. Art would be willing to allow Hal some time to muster his courage and resolve feelings he has about sharing this information with Bev. Handling the case in this manner is justifiable on the grounds that such a plan offers the best prospects for protecting the freedom and well-being of the individuals involved in this case.

The Client's Right to Confidentiality

An important aspect of this case relates to Hal's right to have his drinking kept confidential. One of the most enduring values in the social work profession has been the client's right to have sensitive information treated as confidential.[21] It is commonly believed that if a meaningful, therapeutic relationship is to develop, a client must be able to assume that information shared with a social worker will be kept confidential. It is also commonly believed that it is ethically wrong for a social worker to disclose information shared in confidence by a client with third parties. Thus, not only does a breach of confidence threaten the likelihood that an effective relationship can be sustained between caseworker and client; it is also considered ethically wrong to betray a client's trust by sharing confidential information with others.

However, the client's right to confidentiality represents another important illustration of a prima facie duty which may conflict with other prima facie duties.[22] For example, a client may inform his caseworker in confidence that he plans to kidnap his children from his estranged wife as an act of revenge. In this instance, the client's prima facie right to confidentiality conflicts with his children's prima facie right to basic well-being. One would conclude that the threat to the children's well-being is greater than the threat to the client's (the goods of the children which are threatened, basic freedom and well-being, are more compelling than the goods of the client which are threatened, a wish to seek revenge) and that, consequently, the caseworker's *actual* duty in this case is to report the planned kidnapping to local law enforcement authorities (in accord with guidelines 1 and 2). Thus, while clients generally have a right to confidentiality, there are instances when the rights other individuals have to freedom and basic well-being must take precedence.

The best-known legal precedent establishing professionals' obligation to disclose confidential information in order to protect third parties is found in the 1976 California Supreme Court decision in *Tarasoff v. Board of Regents of the University of California*.[23] In 1969 Prosenjit Poddar, a client at the student health service at the University of California at Berkeley, informed his counselor, a psychologist, that he was planning to kill a young woman upon her return to the university following her summer vacation. Following the counseling session during which Poddar announced his plan, the psychologist telephoned the university police and requested that they observe Poddar for possible hospitalization as an individual who was "dangerous to himself or others." The psychologist followed the phone call with a letter requesting the help of the chief of the university police. The campus police took Poddar into custody temporarily but released him based on evidence that he was "rational." Shortly thereafter, the psychologist's supervisor asked the university police to return the psychologist's letter, ordered that the letter and the psychologist's case notes be destroyed, and directed that no further action be taken to hospitalize

> Poddar. No warning of Poddar's threat was given to the intended victim or her family. Two months later, Poddar killed Tatiana Tarasoff.

Tarasoff's parents sued the Board of Regents of the university, several employees of the student health service, and the chief of the campus police, along with four of his officers, for failing to notify the victim of the threat. A lower court in California dismissed the suit, the parents appealed, and the California Supreme Court upheld the appeal and later reaffirmed the decision that failure to protect the intended victim was irresponsible. The court ultimately held that a therapist who knows, or should have known, that his or her client poses a threat to another has a duty to protect the intended victim.

Since *Tarasoff*, professionals have generally agreed that a therapist has a duty to protect third parties when a client poses a serious and imminent danger to a "foreseeable" victim. A number of court cases since *Tarasoff* has helped to clarify the circumstances when disclosure of confidential information should be made to protect third parties.[24]

Tarasoff and similar precedents have typically been applied to cases where a client threatens to stab, murder, or in some other fashion physically assault a third party. However, with the advent of the AIDS crisis beginning in the early 1980s, the "duty to protect" issue has taken on new —and often unclear—meaning. For example, what should a social worker do if a client who is seropositive refuses to share this fact with his fiancée? Assuming the social worker has done everything possible to convince the client of his duty to inform his fiancée, is he or she obligated to take steps to disclose this information to the client's prospective bride? How should the practitioner balance the client's presumptive right to confidentiality with the duty to protect a potential victim?[25]

> In a recent case, a single father of three adult children contracted AIDS after having a sexual liaison with a man whom he had met at a nearby resort. The positive test result was obtained after a routine blood test prior to major surgery. The father explicitly informed hospital staff that they were not to share this information with his sons; he was terrified that his children might find out that he had a homosexual encounter.
>
> Unfortunately, shortly before his scheduled surgery the client had a psychotic episode and was judged to be incompetent to give informed

consent to surgery. The medical staff summoned the unit's social worker to help obtain informed consent from the client's sons.

Should the staff have informed the sons about the positive AIDS test result? To what extent was this information needed by the sons in order for them to give informed consent to surgery, especially if there was evidence that their father's postsurgery recovery and prognosis may be affected by AIDS? Did the sons have a right to this information in order to protect themselves, assuming they would be involved in their father's care—and may come into contact with body fluids—following surgery? How should this question have been balanced with the client's right to self-determination, especially concerning his explicitly stated wish to conceal information concerning his homosexual relationship?[26]

The possibility that social workers may occasionally have to breach confidentiality and share information with third parties places them in a precarious position. Clients need to believe that information shared with social workers will be held in confidence, and social workers need to believe that it is permissible in extreme circumstances to breach confidentiality. Social workers can avoid placing themselves in this precarious position by not leading clients to believe that information shared by them will *under no circumstances* be disclosed to third parties without their permission. Leaving clients with this impression can be misleading and cannot be defended on ethical grounds. What can be defended is a statement to clients that their counselor intends to treat information shared by them as confidential and that under only extreme circumstances, when the basic well-being of the client or others is seriously threatened, would the social worker even consider disclosing the information to third parties. It is important for social workers to develop trust between themselves and their clients based not on an unrealistic assumption that circumstances will never warrant disclosing confidential information to third parties but on a client's faith in the worker's judgment and ability to decide when such a disclosure might be necessary.

Questions surrounding the issue of confidentiality take many forms. In some instances a client's right to confidentiality is violated inadvertently and inappropriately, such as when clients' names are mentioned in public places or office hallways, when case information is shared with another agency without the client's permission, or when confidential information from case records is left carelessly on desk tops, on a table in an agency's meeting room, on top of a pile in a wastepaper basket, or in a typewriter or on a computer screen that has been left unattended. In other instances we deliberately and with good reason intend to disclose confidential information, as, for example, when a client threatens to harm a third party, as in the Tarasoff case. Thus, in the case of Jan Stanhouse, Jan shared information about Grace's abuse with Rachel Sahlins, and Rachel was faced with a decision about reporting this information to the state Department of Social Services. In the case of the McNallys, Hal McNally asked Art Bulaich not to inform his wife about his drinking. One distinction between these cases is that in the former the client volunteered information to the social worker and assumed it would be held in confidence; in the latter case the social worker accidentally discovered sensitive information about his client's behavior which the client then asked him not to disclose.

It may appear on the surface that a social worker's obligation is significantly different in cases where sensitive information is obtained by accident and cases where such information is willingly shared by a client. It may seem that a social worker has a greater obligation to respect the client's wish for confidentiality in the latter instance than in the former. In the final analysis, however, this distinction is more illusory than real. The social worker's obligation is to assess the extent to which not disclosing the information threatens the welfare of others and to act accordingly. How the information was obtained is of secondary importance.

In the case of Jan Stanhouse, the threat to Grace's welfare may require Rachel Sahlins to report the case against Jan's wishes. In the McNally case, the threat to Bev's welfare was not so severe that Art should have immediately informed Bev of Hal's drinking. However, it would seem important for Art to explain to Hal that information about his drinking can be kept confidential only as long as Hal is attempting to develop the resolve to inform his wife about his continued problem. Art would need to explain to Hal that if Hal were to decide not to tell Bev about his problem, and if Art were to decide as a result that he must terminate treatment because of the deception, Art might feel obligated to inform Bev of the reason for his decision to terminate. It could be wrong for Art to terminate treatment without providing Bev with an explanation of his decision. It would certainly be unfortunate if Bev found out about Hal's drinking from Art. However, it might be even more unfortunate if Bev were not provided with a reason for Art's decision to terminate treatment.

The desire to treat any information shared by a client as confidential runs deep among social workers, and for good reasons. It is important for practitioners to recognize, however, the possibility that extreme circumstances can arise which obligate one to disclose to third parties information shared by a client in confidence. It is thus important for social workers to think carefully about the need to inform clients of this possibility and about the conditions which must be satisfied in order to justify disclosing information against a client's wishes.

The Presence of Coercion

Unfortunately Hal may feel that he is being subtly coerced into telling Bev about his drinking. He may feel that Art has presented him with an ultimatum to inform his wife about his problem. If he chooses not to tell Bev about his drinking, he knows that Art may terminate his relationship with them. A possible consequence is that Art will feel compelled to explain his decision to Bev. Thus, whatever Hal decides, it appears that Bev may become aware of Hal's drinking.

There is an important difference, however, between a strategy which is deliberately designed to be coercive and one which appears to best protect the welfare of the individuals involved in a case but which in fact seems to leave a client with little choice. Art's plan is not constructed with the intention of coercing or forcing Hal to inform Bev about his drinking; rather, it is designed to allow Hal to decide on a course of action and simultaneously to protect Bev's and Art's own legitimate interests. An unfortunate consequence of this strategy is that Hal may feel coerced.

This is not to say that it is never permissible for a social worker to use coercion in his or her work. There certainly are exceptional instances when a practitioner may be required, for example, to physically restrain or report to authorities a client who threatens to seriously injure another individual. But the use of coercion in the McNally case is not justifiable. Forcing Hal to tell Bev about his drinking, if that were possible, could have disastrous consequences for the couple's ability to resolve their problems. A plan designed to allow Hal the opportunity to share this information with his wife and which places limits on Art's willingness to allow treatment to continue while Bev is being deliberately deceived is defensible.

THE PROCESS OF INFORMED CONSENT

CASE 3.6 Sarah and Jack Bumbry had been concerned for months about their seven-year-old son Calvin's behavioral problems. They had received numerous telephone calls from Calvin's school teacher, who was concerned about his short attention span and disruptive behavior in class. The Bumbrys also had some difficulty controlling Calvin's behavior at home.

At the teacher's request, the Bumbrys met with the school's consulting psychologist to discuss Calvin's problems. At the conclusion of the meeting the psychologist encouraged the Bumbrys to arrange for a thorough examination of Calvin by a local pediatrician and social worker who specialize in attention deficit disorder.

The Bumbrys met with the pediatrician, Susan McGregor, and the social worker, Alan Shelby, both of whom work for Behavior Associates. As a result, Calvin was placed on medication, and the family began weekly counseling sessions.

During the course of counseling sessions with their social worker Sarah and Jack began to discuss difficulties they were having in their marriage. The Bumbrys said that they had been experiencing tension between them for some time, particularly after Jack admitted to Sarah that he had been having an affair with another woman. Shortly after Jack's admission Sarah had asked him to leave the house. It was at about this time that Calvin's behavioral problems worsened. Several months ago Sarah and Jack had agreed to try to reconcile their relationship.

About two months after their counseling began, Alan Shelby received a telephone call from the principal of Calvin's school, who wanted to know "how things are going with Calvin and his parents." Because the school department had made the referral to Behavior Associates and had paid for the initial examination of Calvin, Alan prepared a brief written summary of the Bumbrys' progress and forwarded it to the principal.

During a subsequent conversation with the Bumbrys, Calvin's teacher mentioned that recently she had seen the letter sent to the principal by the staff of Behavior Associates. Jack Bumbry became

> very upset, called Alan Shelby, and asked who had given him permission to share information with school officials. Jack said that information about his life and his family's problems was deeply personal and that he was outraged that details had been shared with school personnel. Jack was particularly concerned because one of his wife's relatives also taught at the school and could see the information contained in Calvin's record. Jack said that he was so angry and humiliated that he was going to see an attorney about suing Behavior Associates.
>
> Alan Shelby immediately went to the agency director to let her know about Jack Bumbry's phone call and the threat of a law suit. The agency director asked Alan whether Jack had formally provided consent for the agency to disclose information to the school officials. Alan explained that the Bumbrys' file contained a signed general release of information form, giving the agency permission to use its discretion "to disclose information when, in the agency's judgment, such disclosure is necessary for the proper treatment of the client."

Jack Bumbry's concerns raise questions about clients' right to privacy. Clearly, information shared in confidence by the Bumbrys should not have been shared with school personnel without the Bumbrys' explicit permission. As we shall see below, a general or blanket consent form typically does not provide proper authorization to disclose information to third parties.

In addition to the obvious questions raised about the client's right to privacy, this case also illustrates how agencies can be sued for liability when clients' rights are violated. Liability risks assume a variety of forms in social service. In general, they concern problems with the handling of information about clients or problems with the treatment or delivery of services. For example, agencies and staff may be sued for *misfeasance*—that is, for some form of wrongful conduct, such as sexually harassing a client, defamation of character, terminating treatment prematurely, or breaching confidentiality. They also may be sued for *nonfeasance*—that is, the failure to perform certain duties, such as the failure to protect a third person who has been threatened by a client, consult with a specialist about a client's problems, prevent a suicide, or provide adequate supervision in a residential setting. In this case, the staff of Behavior Associates may be sued for breaching confidentiality and for failure to properly obtain informed consent prior to releasing information to a third party.[27]

The Nature of Informed Consent

A central theme in discussions of client rights is the obligation of practitioners continually to inform clients about plans to intervene in their lives and to obtain client consent to intervention. Consistent with the long-standing commitment of the social work profession to the value of self-determination, social workers traditionally have respected the right of clients to participate fully in efforts to assist the clients.[28]

The historical roots of informed consent have been traced to Plato, who in *The Laws* compares the Greek slave-physician who gives orders "in the brusque fashion of a dictator" with the free physician who "takes the patient and his family into confidence . . . [and] does not give prescriptions until he has won the patient's support."[29] The medieval French surgeon, Henri de Mondeville, also stressed the importance of obtaining patient consent and confidence, although he also urged his colleagues to "compel the obedience of his patients" by selectively slanting information provided to them.[30]

By the late eighteenth century European and American physicians and scientists, such as Condorcet, Mirabeau, Cabanis, Volney, Chaussier, Virey, Rush, Gregory, and Young, had begun to develop a tradition that encouraged professionals to share information and decision-making with their clients.[31] The first major legal ruling in the United States on informed consent is found in the 1914 landmark case of *Schloendorff v. Society of New York Hospital,* in which Justice Cardozo set forth his oft-cited opinion concerning an individual's right to self-determination: "Every human being of adult years and sound mind has a right to determine what shall be done with his own body."[32] To do otherwise, Cardozo argued, is to commit an assault upon the person. Revelations following World War II of medical experiments performed without consent of the subjects and following the civil rights movements of the 1960s helped form the foundation for current informed consent legislation and guidelines.[33] The red-letter event during this era was the 1957 case of *Salgo v. Leland Stanford Jr. University Board of Trustees,* in which the phrase *informed consent* was introduced. The plaintiff in this case, who became a paraplegic following a diagnostic procedure for a circulatory disturbance, alleged that his physician failed to disclose properly ahead of time pertinent information regarding risks associated with the treatment.[34]

Although the concept of informed consent has its origins in medicine and health care, it has recently been applied legislatively, judicially, and administratively to a wide range of other client groups. Social workers regularly provide services to these client groups, and social workers must often serve as advocates of the mentally ill and retarded, minors, medical patients, prisoners, and research subjects. In agencies that provide mental health services, for example, social workers must be familiar with consent requirements related to voluntary and involuntary commitment and the rights of institutionalized and outpatient clients regarding the use of psychotropic drugs, restraints, aversive treatment measures, isolation, sterilization, and psychosurgery.

Social workers in agencies that serve minors must keep pace with rapidly changing standards regarding consent of minors. For example, consent issues arise related to abortion counseling, contraception, treatment of sexually transmitted diseases, mental health services, treatment for substance abuse, and services for children in foster care. Traditionally, minors have not been considered capable of giving consent or entering into contracts; the consent of parents or someone standing in loco parentis has typically been required in other than genuine emergencies.[35] Especially since the 1970s, however, a number of states has begun to recognize the concepts of *mature* or *emancipated* minors, which imply that certain minors are in fact capable of providing their own consent in their relationships with professionals. Mature minors are those who are "judicially recognized as possessing sufficient understanding and appreciation of the nature and consequences of treatment despite their chronological age."[36] Emancipated minors, on the other hand, are those who have obtained the legal capacity of an adult because they are self-supporting, living on their own, married, or in the armed forces.[37]

States vary considerably in the extent to which they grant minors autonomy and the right to consent. For example, with respect to abortion services, substance abuse treatment, dispensing contraceptives, and treatment of sexually transmitted diseases, some states permit professionals to treat minors without obtaining parental consent; some require that parents be notified, that their consent be obtained, or both; and some merely permit agency staff to notify parents, obtain their consent, or both.[38] States also differ in the extent to which parental consent is required to place a child in an inpatient or outpatient mental health program. Missouri and Oregon, for example, require parental consent for commitment of a minor, while

California and Montana permit minors who meet certain conditions to provide their own consent.[39]

Consent issues related to the care of medical patients have received considerable attention recently, especially regarding the care of hospital patients and their right to be informed, refuse treatment on religious grounds, consent to experimental treatment, participate in research, and donate organs. Once again, states vary considerably in the amount of autonomy they grant patients and the procedures health care staff are expected to follow when patients fail to provide consent or request controversial treatment. For instance, in the well-known Quinlan case, the Supreme Court of New Jersey required hospital staff to consult with a hospital ethics committee, rather than a court of law, concerning the decision to remove extraordinary treatment. However, in *Superintendent of Belchertown v. Saikewicz* the Massachusetts Supreme Judicial Court rejected the New Jersey approach, with its reliance on administrative procedures, in favor of court approval of decisions concerning life-prolonging care of incompetent patients.[40]

Debate concerning client consent to participate in research has also received much attention. Discussion has been especially vigorous with respect to clients whose competence to consent is considered questionable or who are considered especially vulnerable. Particular attention has been paid to the right of the mentally ill, elderly, minors, and prisoners to consent to participate in research related to drugs, treatment techniques, and program evaluation.[41]

Obtaining Valid Consent

Although states and local jurisdictions differ in their interpretation and application of informed consent standards, there is general consensus about what constitutes valid consent by clients in light of prevailing legislation and case law. In general, for consent to be considered valid, six standards must be met: An absence of coercion and undue influence must exist; clients must be capable of providing consent; clients must consent to specific procedures; the forms of consent must be valid; clients must have the right to refuse or withdraw consent; and client decisions must be based on adequate information.[42]

Absence of Coercion and Undue Influence. Social workers frequently maintain some degree of control over the lives of their clients. Access to services, money, time, and attention are but a few of the resources social workers control. It is especially important that social workers not take advantage of their positions of authority to coerce a client's consent, subtly or otherwise.[43] Practitioners who want clients to agree to enter or terminate a program, release information to third parties, or take medication, for example, need to be sensitive to the fact that clients may be particularly susceptible to influence and thus jeopardize the validity of their consent.

The inappropriate use of coercion is illustrated in the case of *Reif v. Weinberger,* in which a judge in the District of Columbia ruled that the expenditure of federal funds should be enjoined in some sterilization cases because of the use of coercion. The evidence in this case indicated that a number of public aid clients had been coerced into agreeing to sterilization procedures; they had been told that a portion of their welfare benefits would be withheld unless they agreed to the proposed procedures.[44]

Capacity to Give Consent. Although there is widespread agreement among professionals that only competent clients are capable of giving informed consent, there is much less consensus about the determination of competence. According to Applebaum and Roth, practitioners must consider the ability of the client to make choices, comprehend factual issues, manipulate information rationally, and appreciate his or her current circumstances.[45] Olin and Olin argue for a single standard, the ability to retain information, whereas Owens emphasizes one's ability to "test reality."[46] In contrast, the President's Commission for the Study of Ethical Problems in Medicine and Biomedical and Behavioral Research stated in its 1982 report that competency is determined by the client's possession of a set of values and goals, ability to communicate and understand information, and ability to reason and deliberate.[47]

Despite the unsettled debate about determining competence, practitioners seem to agree that incompetence should not be presumed for any particular client group, such as children, the mentally ill, or mentally retarded, except for those who are unconscious. Rather, some client categories should be considered to have a greater probability of incapacity—perhaps children or profoundly retarded adults. Assessments of client capacity should at least consist of measures such as a mental status exam (accounting for one's orientation to person, place, time, situation, mood and affect, content of thought and perception); ability to comprehend abstract ideas and make reasoned judgments; history of mental illness that might affect current judgment; and the client's recent and remote memory.[48] In instances when clients are judged incompetent, practitioners should be guided by the principle of *substituted,* or *proxy* judgment, in which a surrogate attempts to "replicate faithfully the decision that the incapacitated person would make if he or she were able to make a choice."[49] An important point for social workers to consider is that clients whose competence fluctuates may be capable of giving or withdrawing consent during a lucid phase.[50]

Consent to Specific Procedures. It is not uncommon for social service agencies to have clients sign general consent forms at the first appointment—as apparently occurred with the Bumbrys—or at the time of admission to a program. In a number of cases, however, clients have challenged in court such blanket consent forms, claiming that they lacked specificity and failed to authorize interventions introduced subsequently.[51] Professionals are thus advised not to assume that general consent forms are valid. Rather, consent forms should include specific details that refer to specific activities or interventions. As Fay Rozovsky has observed, "Reliance on a general consent form may be of questionable merit. Courts have been known to examine the circumstances of a specific case to determine whether the general consent was broad enough to permit the treatment in question."[52]

Agency staff especially should be advised to refrain from having clients sign blank consent forms; this is a practice used occasionally to avoid having to contact clients in person for their signatures at a later date. If challenged in court, consent forms might not be considered valid, given the absence of information related to treatment by the agency or intervention at the time client signatures were obtained. In addition, the language and terminology that appear on consent forms must be understandable to clients, and clients should be given ample opportunity to ask questions. Practitioners should avoid as much as possible the use of complex and technical jargon. Particular care must be taken with clients who do not have good command of the English language; social workers should be aware that some clients who are able to speak English reasonably well may not be equally capable of understanding the language. Having access to an interpreter in such instances is important.

Valid Forms of Consent. Many states authorize several forms of consent. Consent may be written or verbal, although some states require written authorization. In general, consent obtained verbally is considered valid, providing that all other criteria for valid consent have been met. In addition, consent may be expressed or implied. *Expressed consent* entails explicit authorization by a client of a specific intervention or activity such as admission to a residential facility or the release of specific information to a third party. *Implied consent,* on the other hand, occurs when consent is inferred from the facts and circumstances surrounding a client. An example is when a client visits a community mental health center and voluntarily requests a regular dose of her psychotropic medication. A reasonable assumption is that the client has consented to the treatment.

Right to Refuse or Withdraw Consent. While it is important for social service staffs to develop sound procedures for obtaining valid consent from clients, it also behooves practitioners to plan for the possibility that clients will refuse or withdraw consent. Of course, such clients also should be considered legally and mentally capable of such a decision, and their decisions need to be informed by details shared by practitioners concerning the risks associated with refusing or withdrawing consent. The fact that clients may be taking psychotropic medication or may be disabled to some degree by mental illness does not by itself provide grounds for denying them the right to refuse or withdraw consent. Rather, client capacity should be judged in terms of the ability of the clients to think clearly, grasp details relevant to their conditions, understand the extent to which their psychiatric history is likely to affect their current judgment, and understand the extent to which they pose a public health risk. Ordinarily, it is in the best interests of an agency to have a client sign a release form absolving staff members of responsibility for any adverse consequences stemming from a decision not to give consent. If a client refuses to sign such a form, detailed notes describing the client's decision and the negotiation should be placed in his or her record.

Client Decisions Based on Adequate Information. Professionals generally agree about the topics that should be covered in discussions with clients before obtaining consent. Commonly cited elements of disclosure include the nature and purpose of the recommended service, treatment, or activity; the advantages and disadvantages of the intervention; substantial, probable, or significant risks to the clients, if any; possible effects on clients' families, jobs, social activities, and other aspects of their lives; possible alternatives to the prospective intervention; and anticipated costs to be borne by clients and their relatives. This information must be presented to clients in understandable language, without coercion or undue influence, and in a manner that encourages clients to ask questions.[53]

Exceptions to Informed Consent

A variety of circumstances exist under which professionals may not be required to obtain informed consent before intervention. In genuine emergencies, for example, professionals may be authorized to act without client consent. According to many state statutes and case laws, an emergency entails a client's being incapacitated and unable to exercise his or her mental ability to make an informed decision. Interference with decision-making ability must be a result of injury or illness, alcohol or drug use, or any other disability. In addition, a need for immediate treatment to preserve a life or health must exist. As Rozovsky has noted, it is important for practitioners not to assume "that a person who has consumed a moderate amount of alcohol or drugs or who has a history of psychiatric problems is automatically incapable of giving consent: the facts and circumstances of individual cases are essential to such determinations."[54] Further, many statutes authorize practitioners to treat clients without their consent to protect them or the community from harm. Cases involving substance abusers, prisoners, and people with venereal disease are examples.[55]

As social workers have come to learn, they may be obligated to disclose information to third parties, even lacking client consent, if there is evidence that serious injury to others or to the state might otherwise result. The case of *Tarasoff v. Regents of the University of California* is cited frequently as an example of circumstances when a mental health worker, because of the danger that a client poses, is expected to share information with third parties which ordinarily would be considered confidential. Cases involving abuse and neglect and where minors request social services also are relevant.

Both statutes and case law have recognized the right of clients to request that they not be informed about the nature of or risks associated with impending treatment or services.[56] In these instances clients may decide that they are better off not knowing what the services or treatment will entail and thus waive their right to give informed consent. Professionals are generally advised to document such a waiver and to consider having clients sign a waiver form.

The most controversial exception to informed consent concerns the concept of *therapeutic privilege*. In several statutes involving the physician-patient relationship, states have permitted practitioners to withhold information if they believe that disclosure would have "a substantially adverse effect" on the welfare of a patient.[57] These statutes allow considerable discretion by professionals and thus have led to extensive debate about possible misuse of the privilege by physicians and other health and mental health professionals. In general practitioners are cautioned to exercise the exception of therapeutic privilege only in extreme circumstances that can be thoroughly documented.[58]

Protection of Clients

The concept of informed consent has done much to protect the rights of clients who are served by professionals. Protection is especially important for social work clients who are vulnerable by virtue of their age, mental or physical capacity, lack of resources, or other forms of dependency. The infamous Tuskegee and Willowbrook cases demonstrate the shocking abuses to which vulnerable clients can be subjected. The Tuskegee experiment, begun in Alabama in the 1930s and concluded in the 1970s, monitored the effects of untreated syphilis in four hundred black men, ending only when an account in the *Washington Star* in 1972 sparked tremendous outrage. At Willowbrook, an institution for the mentally retarded on Staten Island, New York, a research team systematically infected groups of new residents with hepatitis viruses. In both instances vulnerable clients were exposed to extraordinary risks in medical research without adequate protection of their right to consent.[59]

In addition to protecting client rights, it is important to acknowledge other benefits to clients that the process of informed consent can effect. For example, several studies provide evidence that disclosure of detailed information to clients about the nature of impending treatment actually can enhance therapeutic progress.[60] As the President's Commission for the Study of Ethical Problems in Medicine and Biomedical and Behavioral Research concluded in its final report: "Not only is there no evidence of significant negative psychological consequences of receiving information, but on the contrary some strong evidence indicates that disclosure is beneficial."[61] The commission also found that the process of informed consent can provide a useful mechanism for involving family members in the care of a client when a client requests such involvement.

Social workers must also consider that obtaining informed consent entails more than having clients merely sign a form. Consent is a process that includes the systematic disclosure of information to a client over time, along with an opportunity to engage in dialogue with the client about forthcoming treatment and service. As part of this process practitioners must be especially sensitive to clients' cultural and ethnic differences related to the meaning of concepts such as self-determination, autonomy, and consent. Hahn observes that "the individualism central in the doctrine of informed consent is absent in the tradition of Vietnamese thought. Self is not cultivated, but subjugated to cosmic orders. Information, direct communication, and decision may be regarded as arrogant."[62] In contrast, Harwood suggests that mainland Puerto Rican Hispanics expect to be engaged in the therapeutic process and have a strong desire for information and for information given without condescension.[63] It is essential for social workers to be cognizant of such cultural beliefs and preferences if they are to engage in the process of informed consent effectively and sensitively.

The process of informed consent is a key ingredient in the efforts of social workers in attending the rights of clients. As practitioners increase their understanding of this concept, they simultaneously advance the profession's pursuit of its ethical obligations and engage clients as genuine partners in the helping relationship. As with other ethical issues in social work, such as those related to the limits of confidentiality or self-determination, guidelines regarding informed consent leave considerable room for professional discretion, and it is important that such discretion be exercised responsibly. In the end it is the proper exercise of such judgment that characterizes truly professional practice.

The ethical dilemmas which arise in service to individuals and families clearly assume a variety of forms. They include questions about paternalism and the confidentiality of information shared by a client, the social worker's obligation to tell the truth and obey laws, rules, and regulations, informed consent, and ways of resolving conflicts of interest. As we have seen, it is rarely easy to design simple solutions to complex ethical dilemmas. Competing arguments often stand in the way of arguments we develop to support a given point of view. However, we cannot afford to sidestep ethical dillemmas because of the difficulty we often have resolving them. Attempting to understand which questions are important to address and engaging in thoughtful dialogue about them are activities which, by themselves, can take us a long way toward improving the quality of social service.

4

Ethical Dilemmas in Social Planning and Policy

Since the early years of the profession of social work there has been concern about the development and coordination of services for people who have problems. Various theories about social planning have been developed, accompanied by the development of specific techniques and tools for carrying out the relevant tasks. In recent years students of social planning and policy have spent considerable time and effort mastering skills related to problem analysis, decision-making, administration, fostering smooth working relationships between and within organizations, budget analysis, community organization, and program evaluation.

One of the lessons we have learned over time is that policy decisions have many determinants. Policies unfold for a variety of reasons, including the genuine needs of people, economic constraints, and political expediency. It it hard to deny, however, that decisions concerning the merits of particular policies and the means used to implement them frequently reduce to difficult ethical judgments. The effectiveness of various attempts to design and administer social policy certainly depends on the ability of social workers to understand the nature and extent of social problems and on their ability to marry this understanding with technical expertise. And it is certainly the case that social workers need to be sensitive to the economics and politics of policy formation. As we have seen throughout the preceding chapters, however, choices concerning ways of providing assistance to people and choices concerning the specific aid and services to be provided often rest on decisions concerning values and ethics. A decision to develop a public assistance program depends ultimately on a belief that there is an obligation to aid certain individuals in need. A decision concerning the use of certain criteria for distribution public assistance funds also depends on ethical assumptions about what constitutes a just and fair distribution. Whether or not the public assistance program is ultimately approved and commenced may in fact depend on considerations which are primarily economic and political. The extent to which the program is operated in a smooth and efficient manner may depend on the technical expertise of those involved in its design and implementation. However, the decision to endorse the purposes and procedures of the program in principle is fundamentally an ethical one.

It would be difficult to assess in detail the wide variety of ethical dilemmas which arise related to social welfare policy and planning. I will focus on a series of issues which represent a cross section of the dilemmas that practitioners encounter in this area. These issues are: public support for social service programs, distribution of limited resources, the right to welfare, government obligation and private interests, care for extreme needs, and ethical aspects of program design. Solutions we propose for ethical dilemmas in these areas can have important consequences for our ability to carry out our work, whether we engage primarily in direct practice with clients or serve in administrative positions in public or private agencies.

PUBLIC SUPPORT FOR SOCIAL SERVICE

CASE 4.1 The Division of Juvenile Services within the state Department of Corrections had been attempting for twelve months to remove certain juvenile offenders from its training schools and correctional facilities and to place them instead in group homes in various areas within the state. This effort was due in large part to the commitment of the division's recently appointed director, Alan Orsino, to the principle of deinstitutionalization and the belief that many juvenile offenders are incarcerated unnecessarily. Mr. Orsino had appointed one of his staff, Garth Triandos, to coordinate the development of community-based group homes around the state. The group homes were to be designed to house an average of fifteen youths each and were to be located in areas which traditionally had high rates of referral to the Department of Corrections. Mr. Orsino's goal was to arrange for approximately fifteen group homes around the state within eighteen months. The homes would be funded by a variety of sources, including the federal Office of Juvenile Justice and Delinquency Prevention, the state Commission on Delinquency Prevention and Control, and private social service agencies.

Garth Triandos spent several months arranging for a program to be located in a middle-income neighborhood, Lakeview, which was about four miles west of the downtown section of Matson, a city with a population of 183,000. Over the last two years Matson had referred the second largest number of youths to the Department of Corrections of any city in the state. Garth and his staff had contracted with a nonprofit social service agency, Norfolk Social Services, to run the group home. Norfolk Social Services operated three other residential programs for runaway, dependent, and neglected youths and had run a nonresidential counseling program for juvenile delinquents. Garth and the staff of Norfolk Social Services had located a vacant two-story house in a noncommercial, residential section of Lakeview and reached a rental agreement with its owners. The plan was to begin moving youths into the house within nine weeks, after a number of physical modifications were made in the house. The director of Norfolk Social Services also needed some time to hire a staff of counselors, houseparents, child care workers, and a cook and to arrange for a school program with the state Department of Education.

Three weeks before the program was to begin operation a brief article appeared in the local newspaper, the *Daily Journal,* describing the plans for the group home. On the following day Alan Orsino was besieged with telephone calls from residents of Lakeview who were outraged about the plans to move juvenile offenders into their community. Mr. Orsino responded to most of the callers by explaining the reasoning behind the department's deinstitutionalization policy. He assured each caller that the youths referred to the group home were being selected very carefully and would not include anyone who was considered dangerous or a significant threat to the surrounding community. Youths admitted to the program would be limited to status offenders (youths who had been adjudicated for offenses such as running away from home, ungovernability, and truancy) and those who committed relatively nonserious delinquent offenses.

Three days following the appearance of the article in the newspaper, Mr. Orsino was presented with a petition protesting the decision to locate the group home in Lakeview. The petition was delivered by Richard Kitsie, who described himself as the president of the Lakeview Association of Concerned Citizens, and contained 753 signatures. Mr. Kitsie also presented Mr. Orsino with a letter demanding a public hearing on the proposed group home.

This case provides a good example of the clash between public attitudes about a social service program and attempts to implement it. The policy of deinstitutionalization has a relatively recent, though eventful, history and provides an important illustration of the place of ethics in the formulation and implementation of social policy. It is a policy which raises important questions about the community's willingness to support a social service program and about such central values as justice, welfare, and individual freedom. Conclusions we reach about the ethical aspects of this policy thus have important implications for conclusions about ethics and social policy generally.

Beliefs about how juvenile offenders should be treated have changed substantially throughout time. The earliest efforts to remove juveniles from under the wing of the formal criminal justice system can be traced to the nineteenth century, to the founding of the New York House of Refuge in 1825 and the Lyman Reform School in 1846. The introduction of the first state-wide juvenile court in 1899, in Cook County, Illinois, is commonly viewed as the most symbolic effort to distinguish the treatment of juvenile offenders from the treatment of adults. The development of the court enjoyed considerable public support and reflected the widespread opinion of those who worked with troublesome youths that juveniles are less culpable than adults for their mischief and do not deserve to be punished. Instead, juvenile offenders are to be "educated so as to enable them to gain an honest livelihood and to become of use to society instead of an injury to it."[1] According to the Board of Public Charities of the state of Illinois, "the object of reformatory institutions is well stated; it is not punishment for past offenses, but training for future usefulness."[2]

By the 1960s, however, scholars, jurists, and practitioners had begun to raise serious questions about the efficacy and decency of the treatment youths were receiving in correctional institutions. It was becoming more and more clear that despite claims to the contrary juveniles in correctional facilities were generally not receiving benign care. As Francis Allen observed:

> Whatever one's motivation, however elevated one's objectives, if the measures taken result in the compulsory loss of the child's liberty, the involuntary separation of a child from his family or even the supervision of a child's activities by a probation worker, the impact on the affected individual is essentially a punitive one. Good intentions and a flexible vocabulary do not alter this reality. This is particularly so when, as is often the case, the institution to which the child is committed is, in fact, a peno-custodial establishment. We shall escape much confusion here if we are willing to give candid recognition to the fact that the business of the juvenile court inevitably consists, to a considerable degree, in dispensing punishment.[3]

The Shift Toward Noninstitutional Care

Thus, there began in the 1960s a growing concern about the ability of correctional institutions to treat juvenile offenders in a nonpunitive, noncoercive manner, a manner consistent with the humanitarian mission of the juvenile court as originally conceived in the late nineteenth century. A significant consequence of this disillusionment with juvenile corrections was a gradual shift toward policies of diversion and deinstitutionalization. Two significant events were the passage of the federal Juvenile Delinquency Act in 1961 and the publication of the 1967 report of the President's Commission on Law Enforcement and Administration of Justice. Enactment of the 1974 Juvenile Justice and Delinquency Prevention Act foreshadowed a burgeoning of attempts to design and implement diversion and deinstitutionalization programs. As a result, in many jurisdictions around the nation residential and nonresidential programs have been developed as alternatives to formal processing by police, including detention between the time of arrest and appearance in court, intake, and secure correctional facilities.[4]

The gradual shift toward diversion and deinstitutionalization has largely been fueled by an assumption that formal processing of juvenile offenders and confinement in institutions can have damaging effects and deprive many youths unnecessarily of their freedom. Critics of the juvenile court and of traditional methods of treating juvenile offenders have long argued that both youths and the community at large suffer when institutional care is preferred to community-based care. Youths committed to institutions become stigmatized and suffer experiences which frequently leave them more embittered and alienated following release than before arrest.[5]

The move toward the use of noninstitutional care for juvenile offenders has not, however, been without its detractors. Alongside the substantial efforts in recent years to develop diversion and deinstitutionalization programs has been a series of attempts to introduce legislation which would enable law enforcement personnel in many jurisdictions to increase the severity and certainty of penalties imposed upon juvenile offenders and to bind youths charged with particularly serious offenses to criminal courts for trial as adults. These attempts to "get tough" with juveniles are largely a function of public anxiety about apparent increases in the frequency and seriousness of offenses committed by juveniles. Arguments concerning the treatment of juvenile offenders, between those who favor the principles of diversion and deinstitutionalization and those who lobby for stricter sanctions and less liberal responses, represent one of the most controversial and compelling debates concerning the translation of beliefs in certain values—such as justice, freedom, retribution, and punishment—into social policy and social service programs.

Values, Empiricism, and Policy

As I noted earlier, the juvenile court was originally conceived as a benevolent institution whose mission was to rescue and "save" wayward children rather than to punish them for their misdeeds. The court was guided by the English doctrine of *parens patriae,* under which juveniles were not considered culpable for violations of the law. It is clear that the earliest proponents of the juvenile court adhered not to punishment as a primary value but, instead, to rehabilitation. The court's justification for intervention was a deep-seated belief that the community's obligation was to assist and bolster these youths whose early deprivation had led them into the nether world of delinquency. As concern about increases in offense rates grew, however, concern about public safety also increased, resulting in time in the glaring clash between those whose actions were guided by a fundamental belief that institutional care was often unnecessary and evil and those guided by a belief in the need to protect the public and punish offenders.

This debate cannot be settled easily by turning to ethical formulae for a determination of which values should take precedence. The essential conflict is between the youths' right to freedom and the community residents' right to well-being. According to the guidelines derived earlier, in cases of conflict an individual's right to basic well-being takes precedence over another individual's right to freedom. The difficult task, of course, is to determine whether the well-being of community residents in Lakeview is in fact threatened by the youths' freedom. If so, there would be good reasons to conclude that the group home should not be located there; if not, there would not be good reasons to reject the plan to open the group home.

The question concerning the extent to which the well-being of the residents of Lakeview is threatened is largely an empirical one. It is, of course, not possible to predict with certainty whether the prospective residents of the group home would in the future threaten the safety of community residents. The best information available concerning the likelihood that residents of Lakeview would be threatened comes from studies of juvenile offenders who in the past have been provided with community-based care. In 1976, for example, the federal Office of Juvenile Justice and Delinquency Prevention sponsored an evaluation of an eight-state project which included programs designed as alternatives to detention for status offenders between the time of arrest by police and appearance in court.[6] The programs generally provided supervision of the youths in their own homes, foster homes, and group or shelter homes in place of secure detention. The results of the study indicated that over a twelve-month follow-up period there were no significant differences in the recidivism rates of youths who had been placed in secure detention and those placed in alternatives to detention. Community-based care and secure confinement had similar effects on subsequent offense rates regardless of the youths' offense histories —that is, regardless of whether they had no prior offenses, marginal involvement in status offense behavior, a history of a series of status offenses, or a history of a substantial number of both delinquent and status offenses.

A collection of evaluations comparing the effects on recidivism rates of long-term confinement in correctional institutions following adjudication and community-based alternatives also fails to demonstrate significant differences. In an evaluation of California's Community Treatment Project, Ted Palmer found that community-based, intensive supervision and counseling appear to be more effective than institutional care with some categories of youths, but not with others.[7] Empey and Erickson report some reduction in recidivism as a result of a community-based "guided-group interaction" program which included supervised employment and assistance with school-related problems.[8] In their detailed summary of the effects of the abrupt closing of all large juvenile correctional institutions in Massachusetts, Coates, Miller, and Ohlin conclude that community-based alternatives resulted in recidivism rates little different from those of youths confined in institutions.[9] The results reported in a group of additional evaluations are also equivocal.[10]

Other studies indicate the difficulty involved in attempting to predict which youths represent a risk to the community and are likely to engage in illegal behavior in the future. In a study of a birth cohort of 9,945 Philadelphia youths, Wolfgang, Figlio, and Sellin found that 46 percent of all youths who had been arrested had committed only one offense as a juvenile (as indicated by police records), and that an additional 35 percent had a record of only two arrests.[11] (Eighteen percent of the total group had five or more contacts with the police.) The authors did not find evidence to suggest that the seriousness of youths' offenses escalated as they committed subsequent offenses. A similar result is reported in a study of juvenile court records in three New York and New Jersey counties[12] and in a study of a cohort of youths in Columbus, Ohio.[13] Following their study of 4,000 California youths who had been placed on parole, Wenk, Robison, and Smith concluded that "There have been no successful attempts to identify within . . . offender groups a subclass whose members have a greater than even chance of engaging in an assaultive act."[14]

The empirical data regarding the benefits and risks of institutional and noninstitutional care thus do not provide any evidence that one intervention is superior to the other or that the likelihood that a youth will in fact threaten the welfare of the community can be predicted. In fact, the results of these various studies lend themselves to conflicting interpretations. On the one hand, the data suggest that there is no clear benefit as a result of community-based programs over and above institutional programs. Those who feel strongly that the community ought to at least express its outrage and condemn youths who violate its laws might argue that institutional care, with its punitive connotation, is to be preferred. The primary consideration according to this point of view is the community's right to reprehend and censure juvenile nuisances; as the eighteenth century essayist John Foster observed, "Retribution is one of the grand principles in the divine administration of human affairs." On the other hand, however, these data might be interpreted as evidence that there is no justification for incarcerating juveniles in secure institutions. In light of evidence that institutional care and community-based programs are equally effective, confining youths in correctional facilities represents nothing more than a vengeful response and gratuitous interference in the lives of juveniles. Secure custody is especially inappropriate for status offenders, who generally represent a lesser threat to the welfare of the community than do delinquent youths, who commit offenses that would be crimes if committed by adults.

This case thus provides us with a clear example of what David Hume referred to as the "is-ought" problem, according to which normative or evaluative conclusions cannot be deduced directly from descriptive statements of fact. The descriptive evidence that there are no significant differences in the recidivism rates of youths who have been provided with institutional care and community-based programs does not lead us directly to an undebatable conclusion about which of these interventions *ought* to be preferred. Such a conclusion reduces, therefore, to an ethical choice between values such as freedom and punishment. This is not to say that empirical evidence from research cannot contribute to the decision. Empirical evidence certainly helps us in many cases to anticipate the likely consequences of certain policies, their costs, or the success we may have in our attempts to implement them, and in this respect it may inform our ethical decisions. However, evidence from research cannot be translated directly into policy. There is no logical connection, in the formal sense of the canons of deductive logic, between descriptive statements of fact and ethical judgments. As Martin Rein has eloquently stated: "Social policy is all about social objectives and the values that embody the choice of social programs. These are precisely the problems that touch the limits of social science and raise the spectre of that ancient but still inadequately explored terrain where facts and values merge."[15]

The Morality of Outcome and Process

Earlier I concluded that in cases of conflict an individual's right to basic well-being takes precedence over another individual's right to freedom (guideline 2) and that an ethical defense of the policy of deinstitutionalization must be sensitive to the possible clash between the youths' freedom and the well-being of the residents of Lakeview. Our review of the empirical evidence available concerning the effects of community-based programs indicates that caring for youths in noninstitutional settings does not, on the average, pose any greater risk to the safety and well-being of the public than does institutional care. (There is also the additional fact that many noninstitutional programs are considerably less expensive to operate per youth than secure institutions.) It thus appears that in light of this evidence the policy of deinstitutionalization is defensible because of the greater degree of freedom it affords youths without increasing, on the average, the risk to the community. In addition, there is at least partial evidence that lower recidivism rates can result when youths participate in community-based programs which emphasize their relationships with family, friends, and community organizations.[16] This is not to fully discount the community's desire to express its deeply felt resentment of youths' misbehavior. The communication of such resentment is to be expected and is not necessarily undesirable. But there is no evidence available to suggest that secure confinement in an institution is necessary in order to carry this message to juvenile offenders. There is, to the contrary, reason to believe that most youths can be served humanely in noninstitutional settings which attempt to establish meaningful ties between each youth and his or her community while simultaneously communicating to the youths that the community-at-large is not willing to tolerate their mischief.

The conclusion that a policy of deinstitutionalization is defensible on ethical grounds and that the establishment of group homes by the Department of Corrections is justifiable does not necessarily lead to the conclusion that the procedures followed in the department's attempt to locate the group home in Lakeview are defensible. In fact, several questions can be raised about the ethical aspects of these procedures. For example, it appears from the details provided that the staff of the Department of Corrections made a unilateral decision to place in community-based programs certain youths currently being cared for in correctional institutions. There was no deliberate attempt to consult with residents of Lakeview about the plan to locate a group home in their community. This strategy in effect denied these residents the opportunity to participate in the development of a program which could to some extent affect their well-being. Like Bev McNally, they were not made aware of information which may have an important bearing on their ability to carry out their plans and fulfill their own purposes, and this cannot be defended on ethical grounds. The residents of Lakeview have the right to protest the proposed group home and to have information which will enable them to make an informed decision about moving from or remaining in the neighborhood. Not sharing information about the group home with community residents in effect violates aspects of their right to freedom. This is not to say that their right to freedom must be respected to the extent that their protest should be allowed to prevent locating the group home in their neighborhood; the youths' right to freedom from unnecessary institutionalization takes precedence over the residents' right to freedom in this particular respect. Rather, the residents' right to information which will enable them to carry out their own plans short of sabotaging the group home program should be upheld. Staff of the Department of Corrections should have made a deliberate effort to acquaint Lakeview residents with their plans for the group home and to consult with them about its particular location, youths served, services provided, and so on.

There is an additional reason why the staff of the department should have invited community residents to learn about and participate in plans for the group home. Research concerning the effects of community-based programs suggests that lower recidivism rates tend to be associated with those programs which systematically attempt to gain community support and establish ties between youths and local schools, employers, businesses, churches, and residents.[17] There is some evidence that enhancing the quality of these relationships and the community's support of the program in general can have an important effect upon a youth's ability and willingness to cease engaging in illegal behavior and to pursue instead a style of life which does not threaten the welfare of the community. Attempts by staff of the Department of Corrections to cultivate community support and meaningful ties between youths and the community should have been included from the very beginning.

The conclusion that the principle of deinstitutionalization is justifiable on ethical grounds while the procedures used to locate the group home in Lakeview are not suggests that there is an important distinction between the majority of outcomes and the morality of process. As the old adage goes, the ends do not necessarily justify the means. This, of course, is one of the principal difficulties with classic utilitarianism; according to its doctrine, the ends can and often should justify the means if the result is the greatest possible good. As we have seen, however, such a guideline can trample upon the rights of individuals, and this we must seek to avoid.

The difficulties encountered in the attempt by the Department of Corrections to locate a group home in Lakeview are not unlike those frequently encountered when efforts are made to establish public support of programs for other populations of clients, such as the poor, aged, mentally ill, and retarded. Attempts to establish services for these clients are often met with vehement protests from citizens who view the presence of these people as annoying or as a serious threat to the safety of the community. The ethical questions related to noninstitutional care of juvenile offenders are equally germane to controversies related to publicly supported care for other client groups.

DISTRIBUTION OF LIMITED RESOURCES

CASE 4.2 Violet Roenicke had lived in the Fairview Nursing Home for nearly twelve years. She was seventy-nine years old and her care was paid for by state and federal funds. Violet moved into Fairview following surgery for a rare eye disease. She was both partially blind and deaf and had arthritis. Violet was able to care for herself to a considerable extent; she was able to partially dress herself and had little difficulty feeding herself. She was also able to bathe herself, requiring only slight assistance getting in and out of the bathtub.

The secretary of the state Department of Disabilities, Alfred Lowenstein, had appointed a committee to review various aspects of the service being provided to disabled people whose care was supported by government funds. The committee had been charged with reviewing the characteristics of the patients who had been placed in nursing homes, their average length of stay, the quality of care being provided, the characteristics of the staff providing the care, and the costs of care. Mr. Lowenstein had been concerned for some time that many patients who required primarily custodial care were being provided with expensive medical care in nursing homes and that public funds were, as a result, being spent unwisely. Decisions about where disabled individuals should be placed were made primarily by referring physicians with only scant screening conducted by staff of the nursing homes. In addition, decisions to discharge patients from nursing homes also tended to be left to attending physicians.

The committee appointed by Alfred Lowenstein spent several months gathering information about referral and admission procedures, patient and staff characteristics, and costs. They selected a random sample of nursing homes from around the state—stratified according to size—and sent pairs of their office staff to each home to gather the needed information. Patient records were reviewed and the extent of patients' disability was rated, staff were interviewed, and accounting procedures were used to record information about capital costs, operating costs, and other costs which influenced per diem rates.

The committee's final report contained a series of rather startling findings. Documentation was presented that in most instances nursing homes were not carefully screening patients before admitting them. Many nursing homes had no intake criteria whatsoever. In addition, many nursing homes did not have procedures for regularly reviewing the status of patients in order to determine whether nursing home care was still required. Among the most disturbing findings was that many patients with very similar degrees of disability were being provided with care in nursing homes whose quality and cost varied considerably. Some were in nursing homes which provided primarily custodial care, while others were in homes which employed the services of several physicians and billed the state government for expensive medical care. The report presented information demonstrating that the per diem rates for patients with similar disabilities varied substantially among nursing homes and in many instances within nursing homes as well.

The committee recommended a massive revision of the procedures used to refer, admit, care for, and discharge disabled patients who seemed to require nursing home care. Among the recommendations was a proposal to construct a grading system which would allow staff of the state Department of Disabilities to rate the disability of each patient currently placed in nursing homes. Points would be assigned for patients' ability to feed, clothe, toilet, bathe themselves, and so on. Patients who received less than 40 points out of 100 would be placed in nursing homes which provided relatively intensive and costly medical care. Patients who received at least 85 points would be transferred to facilities which provided adequate custodial care meeting state-regulated standards but which did not provide unnecessary medical services. Those who received between 40 and 85 points would be served by nursing homes which provided a moderate amount of medical care.

After several months, staff of the Department of Disabilities began grading residents of the Fairview Nursing Home. Violet Roenicke received a total of 92 points. Within two weeks she received a notice—read to her by one of the nurses at Fairview—informing her that in approximately three weeks she would be transferred to the Allendale Nursing Home, a facility designated by the department to serve patients who required relatively little medical care. The notice also explained the reasons for the transfer.

Violet was very upset about the move. She said that she did not want to leave the only home she had known for the past twelve years and that she did not want to leave her friends. But her protests were to no avail. Staff at Fairview did their best to explain the reasoning behind the transfer, but Violet failed to be persuaded by their arguments. The weeks passed, and Violet was moved to the Allendale Nursing Home against her wishes.

This case, like the preceding case concerning the location of a group home in a residential neighborhood, contains important questions about the ethical nature of both procedures and outcome. Let us first consider the outcome. Violet Roenicke had spent the last twelve years of her life in a nursing home and rather suddenly was uprooted and transferred to another facility as a result of an administrative decision concerning the extent and cost of nursing home care provided to disabled patients. She lost the security of her familiar surroundings and the comfort of the friendships she had established at Fairview. She was an elderly woman—seventy-nine years old—whose home was taken away from her against her wishes. Is it possible that Violet's transfer was justifiable? What are the implications of the conclusion we reach concerning this question for the policy which the Department of Disabilities has developed regarding the placement and care of individuals eligible for nursing home care?

Several points must be considered in our attempt to untangle the various dilemmas involved in this case. Certainly we are obliged to consider the effects of the department's policy on the well-being of the individuals affected by it. But we cannot afford to restrict our consideration to only those disabled individuals who are or are about to become residents of nursing homes. The reason is that the welfare of other individuals is also affected by this policy and must be taken into account.

The Place of Sentiment

It is hard to imagine that most of us do not feel deep regret when we learn of the plight of someone like Violet Roenicke who, late in life, is faced with a serious disruption of her living arrangements. Circumstances such as those faced by Violet are of the sort that we do our best to avoid creating. They are unpleasant, sad, and they tug at our hearts. But life is filled with lamentable circumstances, and it is important for us to consider what place our sentiments about unfortunate circumstances should have in our ethical deliberations.

Many people stand to be affected by the policy developed by the Department of Disabilities. If Violet Roenicke is provided with care which is more intense, sophisticated, and expensive that her condition requires, it is quite possible that someone whose condition is more serious and who requires extensive care will not be able to receive it. Or a portion of the funds being used to provide Violet with a degree of care which her condition does not require could perhaps have been spent purchasing medicine to save or prolong another individual's life or to pay the salary of an additional social worker in a facility where staff are overwhelmed. While it may be very painful for Violet to have to face a sudden upheaval in her life, it cannot be argued that for this reason alone her transfer is unjustifiable and wrong. While it may not be permissible to transfer her to a facility which provides less costly care in order to save funds to purchase new fish tanks, it does seem permissible to transfer her to a facility which provides decent, humane care if the savings are to be used to provide more sophisticated care for other individuals who have greater disabilities, and if it can be demonstrated that a transfer would not seriously threaten Violet's basic well-being. To deprive other individuals of needed care only to avoid upsetting Violet cannot be justified. The state Department of Disabilities has a legitimate interest in spending its funds in a manner which is designed to result in the greatest and most effective degree of care possible for patients. Given the limited funds available to it, the department is justified in its attempts to relocate and place patients in facilities which provide care commensurate with their degree of need. It is indeed unfortunate that certain individuals may have been allowed to remain in facilities for long periods of time only to be told that they must be transferred to new and foreign settings. But to avoid relocating individuals because of the sadness we feel about the threat to their welfare is to participate in an action which may threaten to an even greater extent the welfare of other disabled patients. This we cannot condone.

This conclusion does not mean, however, that the sentiments we have about our actions should not figure into ethical decisions. Sentiments we have about the distress experienced by people are what frequently move us to be concerned in the first place about social work and welfare, and they often provide important clues and guides to the needs of individuals. But sentiments themselves cannot be substituted for a systematic and impartial assessment of people's needs and of ways of responding to them. Sentiments can lead to and encourage our efforts toward right action, but they do not guarantee right action.

Procedural Considerations

There seems to be little question about the legitimacy of the policy designed to match disabled patients with particular facilities which provide care and services commensurate with their needs. It is justifiable for the state to assume responsibility for providing care for uninsured disabled individuals and to arrange for care in a manner which is financially efficient (guideline 6). But we cannot confine our analysis of the ethical aspects of this policy to the legitimacy of the goal it is designed to pursue. As I observed in discussing the location of a group home in the community of Lakeview, it is important to consider the ethical aspects of the procedures used to implement a policy as well.

Several aspects of the procedures used to implement the policy concerning the transfer of disabled individuals merit attention. It appears from the details provided above that virtually no attempt was made to acquaint disabled residents of nursing homes with the plan to rate them according to their degree of disability and to move them to facilities which provide services commensurate with their needs. Each patient who had been selected for transfer simply received a letter announcing the impending move. The letter provided a brief explanation of the policy and provided details concerning the date of transfer and the name and location of the new facility. There was little forewarning.

It is unfortunate that Violet Roenicke and her fellow patients were not acquainted with the department's policy well in advance of the anticipated transfers. This is so for several reasons. First and perhaps foremost, being provided with advance notice of the transfer would have given the patients time to adjust to the idea of moving to a new location and to plan for changes in routine, relationships, and services which were likely to accompany a move to a new facility. A large number of the patients designated for transfer had spent many years in their respective nursing homes, and the prospect of a sudden change of location was no doubt very upsetting and frightening. These patients were denied information to which they were entitled. Not having this information affected their ability to plan their futures (a form of positive liberty) and represented a threat to their emotional well-being.

It also appears that very little effort was made by staff to help those patients who were notified of a transfer to adjust to the prospect of moving. Certainly the timing of the notice left staff with little opportunity to spend time talking with patients and their families and friends about the transfer. This too is an unfortunate consequence of the department's failure to notify the patients far in advance of the transfer. It is possible that the efforts of social workers and other staff to talk with patients about their transfers would have helped ease some of the anguish associated with being moved.

It would also have been appropriate for the patients to have been given an opportunity to indicate whether they had a preference among the nursing homes for which they were eligible. It is possible that a sufficient number of nursing homes were not available to enable patients to have the opportunity to choose among them. However, given the disruption which many of the patients were destined to experience as a result of the transfer, staff of the Department of Disabilities should have attempted, to the extent possible, to provide patients with an opportunity to learn of the location and the characteristics of the services provided by each of the facilities for which they were eligible. This information may have helped the patients decide whether to attempt to arrange for some alternative form of care, for example, from a relative or in a facility not subsidized by the department.

In addition to providing the disabled patients with advance notice of the plans to transfer them, it would also have been appropriate for the Department of Disabilities to provide them with an opportunity to appeal these decisions. A patient's appeal might concern, for example, the validity of the criteria used to rate the degree of disability or the choice of the facility to which the patient was scheduled to be transferred. Reasonable steps should have been taken to provide each patient with due process. This does not mean that a full complement of legal proceedings and defense attorneys should have been imported. Sound administrative procedures which would have permitted a patient to present his or her concerns and arguments to an individual or committee charged with hearing appeals would have sufficed. Advocates (for example, an attorney or physician) should, however, have been provided for patients who were not able to present their own cases clearly and cogently.

It is evident that an analysis of ethical aspects of a social welfare policy designed to distribute limited resources must pay close attention to the morality of both the goals of the policy and the procedures used to implement them. The morality of goals is a necessary condition for the morality of a particular policy. It is not, however, a sufficient condition. Contrary to a strictly utilitarian point of view, the ends do not necessarily justify the means. If a policy is to be defended on ethical grounds, compelling evidence must be amassed to demonstrate the morality of both its goals and the procedures used to implement it.

THE RIGHT TO WELFARE

CASE 4.3 The debate in the state legislature's senate Subcommittee on Welfare had become quite heated. Senator Hendricks was willing to make several minor revisions in his proposal for a statewide "workfare" program, but he was determined not to succumb to the arguments of several of his colleagues who vehemently opposed the bill. Senator Hendricks had been arguing for weeks in subcommittee hearings that something needed to be done to stem the tide of growing numbers of general assistance recipients. He claimed that hundreds and perhaps thousands of able-bodied recipients throughout the state were taking advantage of the overly generous general assistance program and that many people who were capable of working were not actively seeking employment because of the availability of welfare benefits.

Senator Hendricks' proposal would require welfare recipients who were able to work to accept employment in a government agency or in a nonprofit organization at the prevailing minimum wage. The wages earned by the recipient would be credited against the amount of welfare the individual received. Under the guidelines specified in the proposal, any recipient who refused to accept work in a setting arranged by the Department of Public Aid's Bureau of Social Services would have his or her benefits terminated.

Senator Hendricks' proposal had been supported by nearly two-thirds of the Subcommittee on Welfare. There was considerable agreement among the supporters that able-bodied recipients of general assistance should not be allowed to receive benefits over long periods of time without "reimbursing" the community. Several proponents of Senator Hendricks' bill argued that incentives needed to be built into the current welfare legislation to encourage recipients to seek employment in the private sector and to discourage recipients from accepting handouts and from taking advantage of taxpayers' largesse. As Senator Ripken stated: "We have tolerated for too long the healthy individuals who simply lack the self-respect, pride, and determination to find employment. We have no obligation to maintain these individuals on welfare indefinitely. If they are not willing to put in an honest day's work, then we should feel no obligation to rescue them from their financial plight. Enough is enough."

The bill introduced by Senator Hendricks also had a small group of vocal opponents. Senator Wilhelm argued, for example, that to terminate welfare benefits because a recipient "does not want to work as a janitor" is unfair and punitive. Yes, Senator Wilhelm agreed, recipients should be helped to find employment, but to threaten them with the termination of benefits because they refuse to engage in menial labor would be unconscionable. He also argued that the costs required to administer a workfare program could very well exceed the savings realized by the state. Senator Hendricks' proposal called for twenty-two counselors who would work with an initial group of approximately one thousand general assistance recipients who were considered eligible to participate in a workfare program. In addition, these counselors would have to be supervised by four administrators and a director and provided with secretarial and clerical support. The creation of this program would also place new demands on other state and local agencies, for example, the Bureau of the Budget and local units of government which monitored payments and services provided to welfare recipients.

Other arguments against the proposed workfare program were presented as well. Senator Stoddard complained that he had received several telephone calls from representatives of two local trade unions who were concerned that the workfare program would provide jobs to recipients which would otherwise go to union members. The callers argued that it would be unfair to penalize hard-working, tax-paying citizens in order to provide jobs to "lazy welfare cheats." Senator Stoddard also speculated that individuals participating in a workfare program would lose their incentive for seeking employment in the private sector, and that this would run counter to one of the principal goals of welfare programs.

Debate concerning Senator Hendricks' proposals persisted for several weeks. A series of compromises were proposed and debated. By the time of the Christmas recess, however, a number of serious disagreements remained among the members of the subcommittee. In response to a newspaper reporter's question about the bill's prospects, Senator Hendricks responded, "I wouldn't bet any money on this one. We are as divided on this proposal as we've ever been. There are lots of very strong feelings about the merits of this program."

Debate concerning welfare benefits and the extent to which individuals have a right to them represents one of the most persistent themes in social welfare history, dating back at least to the Elizabethan Poor Law of 1601. Funds to administer the original Poor Law were raised through taxes and administered by local parishes. The law was designed to provide aid to three categories of individuals who were dependent and had no relatives to support them: those who were involuntarily unemployed, helpless adults (the old, the sick, and the handicapped), and dependent children. Work was to be provided by the community for individuals who were involuntarily unemployed, and helpless adults were to be cared for in private homes or almshouses. Dependent children were to be apprenticed.

Deserving and Undeserving Poor

It is clear that as early as the seventeenth century sharp distinctions were made between individuals who, through no particular fault of their own, required assistance (such as those who suffered unemployment because of unstable market conditions, the old, and the infirm), and those who were considered to be largely responsible for their destitute state. These so-called undeserving poor generally included beggars, vagrants, and other able-bodied individuals who were not willing to work. Jailing and physical punishment were not uncommon treatments for them.

Distinctions between the deserving and undeserving poor have persisted ever since the Elizabethan era. They were evident in debate around the English Poor Law reforms of 1834, the development of the first Charity Organization Society, the settlement house movement, the social insurance programs proposed in the early twentieth century, the creation of the first state department of public welfare in 1917, and the spate of social security, public assistance, and welfare programs created following the tragic era of the Great Depression of the 1930s. The debate which surrounded Senator Hendricks' workfare proposal was thus part of a legacy of controversy which has descended from at least the time of Elizabeth I. The central issue has been remarkably steadfast over these many years: What is the nature of society's obligation to aid the poor?

Rights and Privileges

The heart of the debate concerning welfare has been the issue of whether benefits should be regarded as a right or as a privilege. The concept of welfare benefits as a right suggests that there is a duty or obligation to assist those who are destitute. The concept of welfare benefits as a privilege, however, has a significantly different meaning; it suggests that individuals receive benefits because of the community's generosity and willingness to provide them, not because poor people have a right to them. This distinction may appear subtle; in fact, it has shaped significantly the extent of aid which has been provided to the poor throughout history. For example, those who believe that indigent individuals have a right to welfare benefits generally do not claim that recipients "owe" the community anything in return for whatever aid is provided. It is unlikely, for example, that someone who believes in welfare benefits as a right would support the proposal for a workfare program on the grounds that recipients should be expected to reimburse the community by providing some form of public service. However, individuals who believe that the poor receive welfare benefits as a privilege may be more inclined to support the idea of a workfare program.

The extent to which individuals regard welfare benefits as a right or as a privilege seems to depend on a variety of factors, including political and religious beliefs, and beliefs about the causes and magnitude of poverty. It is commonly believed that poverty is largely a result of a lack of willingness and determination to work hard and steadily, and that welfare rolls are primarily made up of lazy, shiftless individuals. In fact, it may be the popularity of this belief more than any other which explains the widespread conviction that welfare benefits should be regarded as a privilege rather than as a right. But is the common perception of the poor as indolent and dronish warranted? To what extent are the welfare rolls made up of slothful individuals who are in fact capable of earning a livelihood?

Contrary to popular myth, there is considerable evidence to suggest that the poor are not a permanent group of able-bodied, employable people.[18] In 1986, for example, 10.7 percent of those living in poverty, according to the federal poverty index, were sixty-five years of age or older, and 39.8 percent were younger than eighteen years of age.[19] Thus, one-half of those living in poverty in 1986 were individuals who are not ordinarily expected to support themselves through employment, simply because of their age.[20] In addition, a substantial number of the poor between the ages of eighteen and sixty-four were either employed (often at low-paying jobs) or had left the work force because of layoffs, illness, or disability. According to Joseph Califano, Jr., Secretary of the former federal Department of Health, Education, and Welfare under President Carter:

> 71 percent of the poor in this country, many of whom are on welfare, are people a civilized society does not normally ask to work—children and young people under 16, the aged, the severely disabled, students and mothers with children under six. Nearly a fifth of the poor work either full- or part-time, but do not earn enough to take themselves out of poverty. Some eight percent are women with family responsibilities. Only two percent even resemble the stereotype—able-bodied males under 65 who do not work. Census figures indicate that most of this group is between 62 and 64 and is ill or looking for work.[21]

What these data suggest is that most of the unemployed poor are not in fact employable, either because of personal handicaps, family circumstances and responsibilities, age or because of labor market conditions. This is a fact which has been demonstrated repeatedly.

Additional evidence not only indicates that the number of employable poor is relatively low but challenges the myth that the poor are comprised of a permanent, intractable group of individuals. Morgan (et al.) followed the economic life of a representative sample of five thousand American families for a decade.[22] The authors found that only one person in five who was poor in 1975 had also been poor in each of the previous nine years. On the other hand, one out of three Americans fell below the poverty line once during the decade. Thus, only a very small percentage of the population can be considered permanently poor according to the official poverty index. These individuals are most likely to be members of families headed by a person who is old, or black, or female, or disabled, or poorly educated.[23]

Culpability and Welfare

One of the primary arguments made by proponents of workfare programs is that measures must be taken to reduce the numbers of "undeserving," able-bodied poor who receive welfare benefits. The empirical evidence indicates, however, that any such program will, at best, affect only a very small proportion of those individuals who receive welfare benefits. The vast majority of recipients is not in a position—because of disability or family status—to assume employment in exchange for benefits. It is simply not possible that programs such as workfare would result in a substantial increase in the proportion of recipients who worked in exchange for benefits. The widespread belief that individuals capable of participating in such programs exist in large numbers is based more on figment than fact. The argument that workfare programs are justifiable because of the significant inroads they would make into the problem of parasitic welfare recipients is not tenable. This conclusion does not necessarily mean that workfare programs cannot be defended on any grounds; it simply means that they cannot be defended on the grounds that they stand to substantially diminish the number of able-bodied poor who receive benefits while contributing nothing to the community in return. A question which remains for us to consider, then, is whether workfare programs can be justified on other grounds for the relatively small proportion of welfare recipients who are physically able to work in exchange for benefits.

Workfare programs have been designed to achieve a variety of goals in addition to that of discouraging the able-bodied poor from applying for public aid. Another goal has been to save taxpayers' money by, in effect, having welfare recipients perform public service jobs which would otherwise be carried out by civil service employees, for example, maintenance of public facilities such as office buildings, streets, and parks. It has been claimed by some that another useful consequence of participation in workfare programs is the development of vocational skills, for example, by young men or women who learn about automobile mechanics as a result of their work assignment in a county motor pool. An additional goal of workfare programs has been retribution, that is, an attempt to communicate to the recipient that the community is not willing to unconditionally support able-bodied individuals and expects to be compensated for its largesse. The primary goal in this respect is to ensure that the recipient of welfare benefits is not allowed to "get away with" living off the dole without paying a substantial penalty; that the able-bodied client be made to suffer for accepting public support. This goal is related to a final goal, which assumes that requiring welfare recipients to work in exchange for benefits will discourage many of them from remaining on the rolls and encourage them to pursue gainful employment more closely aligned with their interests. Thus, some of the goals of workfare programs spring from practical concerns about the cost of welfare and represent attempts to reduce the extent to which the public is required to support those in need. Other goals, however, relate much more closely to taxpayers' resentment of able-bodied individuals who are willing to accept welfare. It is from this resentment that the desire for restitution and retribution, as represented by programs which require recipients to work in exchange for their benefits, has grown.

On the face of it, these various goals may seem riddled with malice. However, it does not seem unreasonable for taxpayers to administer a welfare program in a manner designed to minimize costs, encourage the development of vocational skills, and discourage dependency. One might even go so far as to argue that it is acceptable to design a program such as workfare in a way that communicates to genuinely able-bodied participants the public's resentment of their idleness, though this seems more debatable. In fact, it can be argued that it would be wrong for able-bodied clients to receive welfare without attempting to repay the community in one form or another. To do otherwise would result in an imbalance to the extent that taxpayers are required to donate funds to support able-bodied individuals, funds they would prefer to spend in other ways. To expect taxpayers to provide such support to individuals who technically are not in need (that is, lacking the wherewithal to support themselves) is, strictly speaking, a violation of taxpayers' right to freedom, that is, to spend their assets as they wish, beyond what is required to support the truly needy. There is little question that citizens are obligated to pay taxes to provide aid to those who are in genuine need, such as many elderly and disabled people. This is justified by the guideline I presented earlier to the effect that the obligation to prevent basic harms such as starvation and to promote public goods such as housing, education, and public assistance overrides the right to retain one's property (guideline 6). But there is an important distinction between the right to aid when one is in dire need and the right to aid when one is indeed capable of helping oneself. As Alan Gewirth has observed, "to prevent other persons from losing basic, nonsubtractive, or additive well-being or to assist them to have these is not the same as to increase their stock of additive goods to the point where the persons become blissful. Persons in general have no strict right to be made blissful by others, although, of course, to try to produce such bliss is permissible and even praiseworthy."[24]

It appears, then, that workfare programs are not unacceptable on ethical grounds simply because they require able-bodied recipients to work in exchange for their benefits. To the contrary, there are reasons to believe that requiring the relatively few individuals on public assistance who are genuinely able-bodied to work is permissible and to be encouraged. But we must be very clear about the conditions under which workfare is permissible and the reasons which render it justifiable.

The Importance of Intent

Workfare may be permissible in selected cases primarily because able-bodied individuals do not have a right to be supported by others ad infinitum. We must make an assumption here that able-bodied individuals do not qualify as needy in the strict sense with which I have used this term; by definition, the relatively few able-bodied welfare recipients are capable of supporting themselves, providing that jobs are available (it is important to specify that able-bodied implies both the physical and mental wherewithal to engage in work). To expect taxpayers to support these individuals is to interfere to some extent with the freedom of taxpayers to decide how to spend their assets, beyond what is required to provide assistance to people who are in fact needy.

Several conditions must, however, be attached to this conclusion. First, there is not necessarily a sharp line of demarcation between the able-bodied and disabled. There is only a small percentage of welfare recipients who are truly able-bodied. Many recipients are disabled, though possessing to various degrees at least some ability to work. We must be careful to distinguish as best we can between those individuals who are entirely able-bodied and those who are able-bodied only in part. The former do not have a right to unconditional support, and there is nothing ethically wrong with expecting them to work in return for whatever assistance is made available to them; the latter have a right to assistance commensurate with their degree of disability. It is not permissible to require these individuals to work beyond their capacity. As was established earlier, they have a right to assistance and the community has an obligation to provide them with it.

The difficult problem enters, of course, when one attempts to measure the extent of each individual's disability, both physical and mental. Obviously, there are no sophisticated formulae that determine with considerable precision the degree of an individual's disability. As always, these decisions must rest on the soundest professional judgment available, accompanied by a healthy acknowledgment of the room for disagreement which such assessments permit. In general, though, this guideline would prohibit the use of workfare programs for the majority of welfare recipients, who are either disabled or whose family responsibilities do not allow time to work.[25]

It is also important that workfare programs not serve to discourage individuals who participate in them from seeking employment in the private sector. In fact, it may be difficult to design workfare programs in a way which encourages participants to seek ordinary employment. On the one hand, it is important to try to assign participants work which trains them in a skill which may enable them to secure regular employment, as opposed to assigning participants to menial labor. The appeal of such workfare jobs may be such that participants would not have an incentive to seek regular employment; however, to assign participants to menial labor, which would perhaps serve as an incentive for them to seek more challenging employment in the private sector, would be to contradict the obligation to help able-bodied individuals develop marketable skills. A reasonable compromise would be to attempt to place able-bodied recipients in jobs which help them prepare for positions in the private sector, to monitor their progress regularly, and to encourage them to seek employment. A primary purpose of workfare programs would thus be training for future employment, in addition to rendering a service to the community in exchange for benefits. In effect, then, workfare programs would closely resemble job training programs for poor people who lack vocational skills.

This line of reasoning suggests that the primary justification of workfare programs should be not vindictive retribution but training for future gainful employment with careful attention paid to the degree of a recipient's disability. Such a justification respects the public's right to avoid unconditional support of truly able-bodied individuals who have chosen not to work and attempts to compensate for whatever shortcomings recipients may have which discourage or prevent them from seeking employment. Justifying workfare programs primarily as a retributive gesture designed to penalize recipients cannot be defended on ethical grounds.

GOVERNMENT OBLIGATION AND PRIVATE INTERESTS

CASE 4.4 Bolton Park was not unlike many urban neighborhoods which had undergone steady change in recent years. Most of the Italian and Polish residents of the neighborhood had moved north, replaced by, for the most part, Puerto Ricans. Property values gradually dropped over time, and buildings were being repaired less and less frequently. Several shopkeepers who had been mainstays in the neighborhood for over twenty years either closed their doors or sold their businesses. Despite the physical deterioration in Bolton Park, however, the neighborhood still bustled with activity. It had by no means been abandoned.

Bolton Park was one of six communities in the city which had been earmarked by the Commercial District Development Commission for rehabilitation. As a rule, the commission's strategy was to work with consultants in developing a plan designed to attract private enterprise —both large business concerns and smaller entrepreneurs—to areas of the city considered to be in the midst of a significant economic decline. The commission's ordinary strategy involved coordinating federal funding, city government funding, and private investments in an effort to revitalize an area. One of the more successful strategies used by the commission in recent years involved making public property available to private developers (for nominal rent or with tax exemptions) who agreed to upgrade a commercial area. According to Donald Shula, the director of the commission, such partnerships between government and private business had proven to be the most efficient approach to neighborhood rehabilitation; neither private business nor government-sponsored programs had been successful on their own over the years. Private businesses were ordinarily attracted to deteriorating communities only when certain financial incentives existed to draw them there, either in the form of favorable lease agreements or tax exemptions.

The Commercial District Development Commission had contracted with a consulting firm to develop a plan for the rehabilitation of Bolton Park. After three months' work the project manager, Earl Weaver, submitted a plan to Commissioner Shula which proposed that the city develop an eleven-acre shopping area. The project would include the creation of a "Latino-flavored" mini-mall of shops and offices in an abandoned, 300,000-square-foot warehouse which had been considered an eyesore in the neighborhood for years. Many other existing buildings would be renovated, and approximately eight new stores would be built, including a large supermarket and pharmacy. In order for the plan to succeed, the proposal stated, the city would need to buy and clear away thirty-six multifamily buildings. Most of the homes would need to be demolished, although the proposal encouraged the city to explore the possibility of relocating some of the residences to nearby vacant lots.

After reviewing the report, Commissioner Shula asked his assistant, Jackie Brandt, to organize a meeting with community leaders in Bolton Park in order to assess their reactions to the rehabilitation plan. Ms. Brandt conducted a meeting with ten leaders identified by the pastor of the major church in the neighborhood and reported back to Commissioner Shula that only two members of the group were opposed to the plan. Commissioner Shula made several minor revisions in the plan, concerning the timetable and financing arrangements, and then approved the project. He had Ms. Brandt contact a reporter from the *Evening Gazette* in order to have a newspaper article written about the city's plans. The article was published in the *Gazette* and announced that a public meeting, sponsored by the Commercial District Development Commission, would be held to answer community residents' questions about the project. Ms. Brandt conducted the meeting and reported back to Commissioner Shula that the overwhelming majority of the 150 residents in attendance spoke in favor of the project: "They want a better place to shop, even if it means a few homes must be cleared." Ms. Brandt said that at least 70 percent of the group voted to endorse the plan.

A group of residents, however, was strongly opposed to the plan. One of the leaders of the group, Paul Blair, requested and was granted a meeting with Commissioner Shula. Mr. Blair argued that community opinion about the project had not been accurately gauged and that the meeting held in Bolton Park had been overrepresented by precinct captains and city workers. He also argued that "there was no vote to endorse this plan. I should know—I helped chair the meeting. The people were not the people you normally see at community meetings. These were the garbage truck drivers and the city workers under orders by their supervisors to be there. I know most of these people. And I also know what they really want. This project is being pushed because it's a way to begin to drive Latinos out of the community and bring more white, middle-class people in. That's what they really want, and that's what they mean when they talk about revitalizing the area and bringing new people in."

Commissioner Shula acknowledged that "it's not the greatest plan in the world. We are losing some housing units and it's understandable that some of these people are upset. But what the community and city will gain is far greater. This plan would recycle an abandoned warehouse, revitalize an already existing shopping area, and put in a badly needed grocery store. Commercial developers are interested in this city again, but their idea of a shopping center is based on the sterile, suburban shopping mall—a sea of asphalt placed near an expressway. We need this development to show them what commercial developers should do if they want the city's cooperation. I am also convinced that the community as a whole wants this project. Those who now live on the site naturally don't want to move and be inconvenienced. But these people are not the community; they are merely a small part of it. We have to consider the community as a whole."

Throughout history governments have assumed the right to make improvements within their boundaries at the expense of property rights of individual citizens. In fact, the power of government to appropriate private property for public use has been exercised at least since Greco-Roman days. The justification of the practice has always been straightforward: the government's responsibility to improve and maintain public facilities for the common good requires on occasion that private citizens forfeit title to their property.[26]

The relatively modern idea of eminent domain, which gives government the right to take private property for public use, can be attributed to such seventeenth-century European jurists as Hugo Grotius and Samuel Pufendorf. The principle was of little importance in the United States prior to the nineteenth century. Until then the government's right of eminent domain was exercised primarily for the construction of roads and grist mills. The right of eminent domain began to be invoked much more frequently, however, as the nation began to industrialize and open up previously untraveled lands.[27] Eventually the Fifth Amendment to the Constitution of the United States included a clause which prohibited the federal government from taking private property without "just compensation."

Over the years Congress and state legislatures have delegated the power of eminent domain to government commissions and agencies, political subdivisions, and on occasion to private individuals and corporations. The practice has generally been restricted to the acquisition of land for the development of facilities for public use, such as highways, railroads, and flood control projects; however, the principle of eminent domain has periodically been used to authorize the acquisition of property for private use.

The Justification of Eminent Domain

The principle of eminent domain provides a compelling example of a practice which throughout its history has been justified almost exclusively on utilitarian grounds. It has been accepted for centuries that "the greatest good for the greatest number" will result only if governments enjoy the right to acquire private property when "public necessity or advantage is involved."[28]

The principle that individuals do not always have a right to retain their property is hard to debate. On utilitarian grounds it would be quite reasonable to assume that instances arise when the public interest must take precedence over the right individual citizens have to their own property and their right to acquire and dispose of it as they wish. For example, the community's right to well-being would certainly take precedence over an individual's right to purchase hand guns to be used to wantonly assault, maim, and kill innocent neighbors. As we have discovered repeatedly, however, classic utilitarianism permits too much room for the justification of abhorrent acts on the grounds that the greatest good for the greatest number will result. A strict utilitarian might, for instance, justify the seizure of the homes of a small group of individuals in order to finance the construction of a liquor store. It is entirely possible that the happiness of the people who are affected by such a move would outweigh the unhappiness of the families who would be displaced, but the result is not one we could possibly accept. There is little question that the homeowners' right to private property takes precedence over the right of another individual citizen to seize property in order to make alcoholic beverages available to the consuming public (in accord with guideline 2). However, it is one thing to assert that this conclusion is self-evident; it is quite another to defend it on philosophical grounds.

Property Rights and the Public Good

We have discovered in our review of ethical dilemmas that some are more troublesome than others. There is little doubt, for example, that a social worker should not lie to prospective clients about his or her academic and professional credentials in order to attract business. There is also little question that social workers who anticipate the termination or interruption of service to clients have a responsibility to notify clients as soon as possible. Ordinarily, these are not hard cases. However, we know that others are not settled so easily. We have reviewed a number of cases which seem to resist easy solutions; with these it is only after considerable debate and contemplation that we even begin to see a glimmer of resolution. The predicament in Bolton Park and the issue of eminent domain seem to present just such a case. Many good reasons can be argued for and against the right of government to force people to abandon their homes in order to rehabilitate a community. On the one hand, some relocation may be necessary in order to save a declining community. On the other hand, one wonders if the threat to a community could ever be so great as to justify the forced removal of people from their homes. Let us consider these conflicting points of view in light of the guidelines developed earlier for examining ethical dilemmas.

Several of the guidelines are relevant. First, I have concluded that individuals ordinarily have a prima facie duty to obey rules to which they have voluntarily and freely consented (guideline 4). The Fifth Amendment to the Constitution includes a clause which authorizes the federal government to acquire property in exchange for "just compensation"; similar authority is vested by the state government in the city's Commercial District Development Commission. It can be argued that the residents of Bolton Park, by virtue of their citizenship in their state and in the United States, have voluntarily agreed to abide by the laws of these respective bodies of government. I also concluded that the obligation to prevent basic harms and to promote public goods such as housing, education, and public assistance overrides the right to retain one's property (guideline 6). These two guidelines taken together suggest that the government's authority to exercise the power of eminent domain may be justifiable. However, another guideline—that individuals' rights to basic well-being override social rules in cases of conflict (guideline 5)—suggests that there may be instances when the government's right of eminent domain should not prevail because of the threat it represents to individuals' welfare. Once again, then, we must reconcile several prima facie duties in order to settle on our actual duty.

Distinctions Among Goods

It would be difficult to argue that the government either always has or never has the right to acquire property in order to promote public goods. It would not be permissible for a unit of government to seize property no matter what its purpose, and it would be equally impermissible for government never to have the right to acquire property in order to promote public welfare. As is so often the case, the difficult task is attempting to specify the conditions under which the acquisition of property is justifiable.

The guidelines presented earlier suggest that units of government have the right to acquire property in order to prevent basic harms and to promote public goods and that citizens have an obligation to act in accord with this right *except* when the rules concerning this right threaten individuals' basic well-being. The key term here is *basic*. The extent to which a unit of government does in fact have the right to acquire private property for public use against the will of its owners depends on whether such action is necessary either to prevent *basic* harms or to enable others to have access to *basic* goods.

Earlier I described distinctions among what Gewirth has labeled *basic, additive,* and *nonsubtractive* goods. Basic goods are those aspects of well-being which are the necessary preconditions of the performance of any and all action, such as life, health, shelter, and mental equilibrium. Additive goods are those which enhance one's ability to engage in purposive action, such as education, knowledge, income, and self-esteem, beyond those included under basic goods. Nonsubtractive goods are goods the loss of which would diminish one's ability to fulfill one's purposes, for instance, as a result of being lied to, cheated, stolen from, or being subjected to inferior living conditions or harsh labor.[29] It is important to consider the relationship of these goods to one another, since actions which may be justifiable in order to prevent a threat to basic goods (such as life itself) may not be justifiable if they are intended to promote additive goods (such as the pursuit of wealth). As Gewirth has observed:

> Although every agent regards his whole well-being as a necessary good because of its relation to his purpose-fulfillments, its components fall into a hierarchy determined by the degree of their indispensability for purposive action. The *basic* capabilities of action, whereby the agent has basic goods, are the most necessary of all, since without these he would be able to act either not at all or only in certain very restricted ways. Among these basic goods there is also a hierarchy, headed by life and then including various other physical and mental goods, some more indispensable than others for action and purpose-fulfillment. Of the other two kinds of capabilities, the nonsubtractive rank higher than the additive because to be able to retain the goods one has is usually a necessary condition of being able to increase one's stock of goods.[30]

In order to determine the justifiability of the plans to purchase and clear thirty-six multifamily buildings, two questions must be addressed. First, is such an action necessary in order to prevent basic harm to the residents of the Bolton Park community or to enable them to have access to basic goods? Second, does such action threaten the basic well-being of the residents and owners of the buildings which the city plans to clear?

The city would be acting within its rights if, for example, it moved to acquire this property in order to construct a dam which would contain threatening flood waters. Under such circumstances the residents of the thirty-six buildings could not have a right to jeopardize the basic well-being of other community residents whose personal safety and homes were threatened because of high waters. But is the plan of the Commercial District Development Commission necessary to protect the basic well-being of the residents of Bolton Park in a comparable way? This, of course, is a debatable question. The proponents of the project would likely argue that the proposed rehabilitation is necessary in order to revitalize the economic life of a desperate community. They might argue that jobs, the ability to own and maintain homes, and the resources needed to support families in a decent fashion depend on such rehabilitation and that a failure to implement the plan would threaten the basic goods of the community. Opponents of the project, however, would likely argue that harms to basic goods would not be prevented by the project. To them it may appear that the project would actually threaten the basic and nonsubtractive goods of the residents of the buildings targeted for clearance, promote additive goods of middle-income individuals who would benefit from upgraded shopping facilities, and threaten the basic and nonsubtractive goods of low-income individuals who might eventually be driven from the community because of attempts to enhance the quality of housing in the community generally.

It is difficult to know from the details provided above whether the basic and nonsubtractive goods of the residents of Bolton Park actually depend on the success of the city's rehabilitation plan. What we can say, however, is that the burden of proof falls on the Commercial District Development Commission to make a very strong case that the acquisition of property is necessary to prevent harms to the basic goods of the community residents or to enable them to have access to basic goods. It might be difficult to muster evidence to support such a case. It is clear that basic and nonsubtractive goods of the residents of the targeted buildings are threatened by the city's plan and that many current and prospective residents of Bolton Park might benefit from a revitalized commercial district because of enhanced access to additive goods. Given the hierarchy of goods I outlined earlier, the argument could then be made that the city's plan would not be justifiable if a very strong case could not be made that the protection of basic and nonsubtractive goods of the residents of Bolton Park depended upon the clearance of the buildings and the subsequent rehabilitation.

Developing Assessment Procedures

At a minimum, any attempt to assess the extent to which the economic survival of a community depends on the acquisition of private property for commercial development should include a systematic survey of the opinions of community residents, especially the residents of the buildings targeted for clearance. An impromptu or lightly publicized meeting of residents cannot suffice; an attempt would have to be made to invite all interested community residents to share their views about a proposed rehabilitation project. Deliberate attempts to canvas opinions and advertise meetings with community officials would be required. Such procedures would be consistent with the conclusion reached earlier that rules which permit occasional coercion (which would be present at least to some extent in any plan to revitalize a community at the expense of a minority of property owners) must be imposed to the extent possible by the procedures of the method of consent.[31]

It is important to stress that soliciting the opinions of interested community residents would be required *as a minimum*. It would be a necessary but not a sufficient condition for a decision to proceed with the contested acquisition of private property. Consent, in the form of majority opinion or some other standard, does not by itself necessarily determine the morality of an action. Consent is often necessary in order to respect individuals' rights to freedom of choice and to determine their own destinies, but it is not always a sufficient condition. For example, consensus among a majority of community residents to prohibit members of a certain religious, ethnic, or racial group from moving into their neighborhood would not render such a policy moral; no group of residents in any community has such a right. The right individuals have to choose a community of residence takes precedence over the right other residents have to decide, according to the method of consent, to prohibit or interfere with such choice. Similarly, it would not be permissible for residents of a community to force the relocation of certain of their neighbors in order to construct a liquor store. History has shown that human beings can at times have the unfortunate capacity to agree among themselves to commit unconscionable acts which plainly violate the rights of others to freedom and well-being. A decision to force the relocation of residents whose property stands in the path of commercial revitalization is only justifiable if it meets the conditions of both necessity and sufficiency —that is, if it is based to the extent possible on the method of consent *and* on evidence that the protection of the basic and nonsubtractive goods of community residents (and not their additive goods or the additive goods of commercial developers) depends on such revitalization. It would be necessary to establish in addition that an alternative rehabilitation plan could not be developed which would avoid forcing individuals to relinquish their property and residence. In many cases these conditions, as a group, are difficult to satisfy.

Government intervention in the lives of citizens is often controversial.

Sometimes it is necessary. It is important, however, that government programs be designed to avoid treading unnecessarily on the freedom of individuals.

CARE FOR EXTREME NEEDS

CASE 4.5 The Commissioner of Public Welfare, Dave Belanger, received a phone call from a newspaper reporter who was inquiring about a rumor that twenty to twenty-five juveniles were being held in Bridgetown Institute, the state's prison for the adult criminally insane, where they were periodically subjected to both emotional and physical abuse. Commissioner Belanger had been appointed to his position only five weeks earlier and admitted to the reporter that he simply had not had the time to become familiar with the population being held at Bridgetown. He explained that he was trying to learn as quickly as possible the characteristics of the individuals being cared for in all of the institutions for which he had responsibility, including the state mental hospitals, adult prisons, and the institution for the adult criminally insane. He promised the reporter that he would assign one of his deputy commissioners the task of gathering detailed information about the population at Bridgetown.

Commissioner Belanger met briefly with Suzanne Aparicio, the deputy commissioner in charge of institutions. Mr. Belanger asked Ms. Aparicio if in fact juveniles were being held in Bridgetown. Suzanne reported that there was a relatively small group of juveniles at Bridgetown, though she was not certain of the exact number. Her impression was that the reporter's estimate of twenty to twenty-five was reasonably accurate. Ms. Aparicio explained that for years the state had had a difficult time knowing how to handle severely disturbed juvenile offenders. These were youths who had been diagnosed as psychotic, very often schizophrenic, and who had been arrested for serious offenses, frequently including armed robbery, rape, assault with a deadly weapon, or arson. Many of these youths had a history of mental illness and seemed prone to thought disorders, impaired judgment, and delusions. Ms. Aparicio described the difficulty the state's juvenile correctional institutions had been having working with these youths. Staff of these facilities frequently complained that these youths were "very sick," disruptive, and simply not compatible with the majority of youths who populated the juvenile correctional facilities. She also explained that adolescent units in the state's mental hospitals had traditionally been unwilling to accept youths who had been arrested for serious or violent offenses because of the danger which they apparently represented to the safety of staff and other patients. Because of the inability and unwillingness of the state's juvenile corrections facilities and state mental hospitals to handle these severely disturbed offenders, many of them had been sent by default over the years to the Bridgetown Institute for criminally insane adults.

Commissioner Belanger asked Ms. Aparicio to look into the possibility of developing a program specifically for these youths. After two months' work, many meetings, and consultation with professionals around the country, she outlined a program which seemed to her to represent the only reasonable way of treating the severely disturbed juvenile offenders in the state. The program would require a large number of professional mental health staff for relatively few youths and would thus be expensive to operate. Clinical social workers and psychologists would need to be hired, and they would command much higher salaries than would child care workers who ordinarily staff programs which serve delinquents. Ms. Aparicio's estimate, based on a review of the costs of programs currently operated by the Department of Public Welfare's Juvenile Corrections Division and the costs of several programs around the country designed specifically for severely disturbed juvenile offenders, was that the annual cost of such a program per youth would be nearly twice the cost of care provided these youths in Bridgetown Institute. She suggested that the Department could save a considerable amount of money by using an abandoned cottage on the grounds of the Midtown State Hospital, which could accommodate a twelve-bed program.

Commissioner Belanger decided to convene a meeting of the directors of the Adult and Juvenile Corrections divisions, the Division of Mental Health, and the administrator of Bridgetown Institute. Everyone at the meeting agreed that severely disturbed juvenile offenders represented a serious problem and supported the idea of establishing a program for them, despite the substantial expense. They agreed that the severity of the youths' disturbance merited sophisticated clinical treatment and that the state should be willing to meet the necessary expense. Fred Miller, the administrator of Bridgetown Institute, shared with the others who were present at the meeting several stories of youths who had been sexually assaulted and regularly intimidated by the adults in his institution. He urged Commissioner Belanger to move as quickly as possible on the development of the program.

Commissioner Belanger explained to those present at the meeting that in order to fund such a program, he would need to transfer funds from an unexpended balance in the capital improvement portion of his budget. In order to do so, he needed to obtain the approval of the legislature's budget review subcommittee, which was responsible for authorizing any transfer in excess of 25 percent of the funds from one category of a department's budget to another.

Commissioner Belanger submitted his proposal to the subcommittee and attended a hearing in order to respond to questions of its members. Much to his surprise, three of the five members of the subcommittee were opposed to approving the transfer of funds for establishment of the program. They argued that the state could not afford a program for these youths that would cost nearly twice as much as care provided in Bridgetown Institute. They argued that the youths being held in Bridgetown had committed particularly heinous offenses and should be in a prison for the criminally insane rather than in an expensive treatment program. Commissioner Belanger argued that these youths were being held in Bridgetown only because no other facility was willing to accept them, not because Bridgetown had treatment programs which were particularly well suited for them. Most important, he argued, these youths were frequently abused in Bridgetown and, if for no other reason, an alternative program was needed to remove them from a setting in which their safety was constantly at risk.

Debate among the subcommittee members continued without resolution. At the conclusion of the hearing they agreed that it would be helpful to have a more detailed report on the proposed program—its goals, treatment plans, staffing and security needs—and on the dangers the youths in Bridgetown were subjected to. Commissioner Belanger left the hearing perplexed by the subcommittee's lack of support, but determined to present a report to them which would convince them of the dire need for the program.

This case raises important questions about the kind and extent of care we are willing to provide to a group of individuals with extreme needs. Conclusions we reach in this case have important implications for decisions regarding any group of clients whose care seems to require a disproportionate expenditure of public funds.

The problem of the emotionally disturbed offender is not new. Throughout the history of penology and corrections it has been commonly believed that a substantial proportion of offenders—both juveniles and adults—suffer from some form of mental illness. The term *mental illness* has, of course, been defined in many different ways, including, on the one hand, extreme manifestations of psychotic behavior (for example, characterized by hallucinations, paranoia, or delusions) and, on the other hand, the more common forms of dysfunctional behavior.

It has long been assumed by correctional workers that a small but inordinately troublesome percentage of youths in secure facilities or training schools are severely disturbed, requiring intensive psychiatric treatment. These youths are frequently described as psychotic and subject to severe regression to early levels of development, interpersonal withdrawal, hallucinations, paranoid ideation, and self-destruction.[32] They have traditionally been considered by both mental health and corrections personnel to be among the most difficult youths to handle. Corrections personnel routinely complain that a group of severely disturbed youths are disruptive when mixed with a general population of juvenile offenders and demand an inordinate amount of staff time and expertise. These staff also argue that such youths require sophisticated psychotherapy which ordinarily cannot be provided in secure correctional facilities. Mental health personnel, conversely, contend that severely disturbed juvenile offenders represent serious security risks and cannot be cared for in mental health programs because of the threat they pose to other residents. As a result, severely disturbed juvenile offenders have for decades been "the kids nobody wants." As the findings from a survey conducted by the Pennsylvania Youth Development Center indicate, "the numbers of youths who manifest both deviant behavior and psychosis have been shown to be increasing in the population,"[33] thus resulting in "a group of youth who 'fall between the cracks,' too delinquent to be treated in a hospital setting and too psychotic to be rehabilitated in a correctional setting."[34]

Falling Between the Service Cracks

As a result of the reluctance of departments of corrections and departments of mental health to assume responsibility for severely disturbed juvenile offenders, these youths have been frequently relegated by default to programs and settings which as a rule have afforded them little help. This unfortunate predicament raises several important ethical questions. What obligation is there to design programs specifically for this population which has extreme needs? To what extent should the costs of such programs influence whether or not they are established? Finally, what goals should characterize programs for severely disturbed juvenile offenders?

There is considerable evidence to indicate that juvenile offenders who are severely disturbed are frequently treated in a manner which represents a serious threat to their well-being. Youths who are placed in conventional correctional facilities and in facilities for the adult criminally insane are frequently abused and are rarely provided with genuine attempts to treat their mental illness.[35] The threat to the youths' well-being is clear, and for this reason alone there appears to be an obligation to design program which would remove them from these intimidating and all too frequently dangerous environments. This is especially so because of the commonly accepted principle that psychotic individuals are technically not responsible for violations of the law and have a right to treatment which supersedes the community's right to punish lawbreakers. Thus, severely disturbed juvenile offenders not only have a right to avoid serious threats to their well-being as a result of confinement in a correctional institution but have in addition a right not to be punished for their misbehavior.

The Limits of Benevolent Care

It is one thing to conclude that severely disturbed juvenile offenders have a right to avoid the threatening environments of conventional correctional facilities and prisons for the adult criminally insane; it is quite another to identify what form or forms of treatment should be preferred as alternatives. Two related considerations must enter into decisions about the type of care which should be provided for these youths. One is the cost of various forms of treatment and the community's willingness to provide funds. The second is the goals such care should be designed to pursue. Is it enough to provide these youths with a reasonably safe environment in a secure setting, or is it incumbent upon us to provide them with sophisticated and intensive forms of psychotherapy or milieu therapy? The answer to this question will depend on beliefs about what severely disturbed juvenile offenders deserve and about what we, the public, are willing to afford them. The choice is essentially between programs which emphasize custodial care in a safe environment and those which emphasize intensive clinical treatment. In principle it is hard to argue against providing these youths with sophisticated forms of clinical treatment. We have an ethical obligation to assist those who suffer from serious mental illness and who are not fully capable of helping themselves. Alan Donogan refers to such an obligation as the principle of beneficence: "If a man respects other men as rational creatures, not only will he not injure them, he will necessarily also take satisfaction in their achieving the well-being they seek, and will further their efforts as far as he prudently can."[36]

It is clear, however, that whatever obligation we have to assist those in need—in this case severely disturbed juvenile offenders—has limits. These limits follow from our obligation to balance the pursuit of well-being for one group of individuals with the needs of others. As I concluded in the previous chapter, while the physician attending to Sharlene Thomas had an obligation to do whatever he could to provide her with humane care, it would have been wrong to devote thousands and thousands of dollars worth of resources on this one patient if the likelihood that she would recover were virtually nil. Given limited resources, we are obligated to distribute them in a manner designed to protect, to the greatest extent possible, individuals' well-being; expending inordinate resources on cases with extremely poor prognoses is not consistent with this principle.

A Question of Prudence

Donagan's principle of beneficence states that each individual should provide assistance to those in need (for example, those who have suffered from injury, illness, desertion, senility, and so on) "inasmuch as one can do so without proportionate inconvenience."[37] The difficulty, of course, is deciding when assistance to others constitutes proportionate inconvenience to oneself and in addition disproportionately threatens the well-being of others. We know from centuries of experience that it is difficult to calculate precisely the point at which the provision of aid in one direction (to one individual or group of individuals) begins to have diminishing returns and, as a result, represents a disproportionate expense of either funds or effort. As I observed earlier, this has been one of the most obstinate difficulties with which utilitarians have had to contend. But we also know that decisions about the relative merits and effectiveness of various intervention and social welfare programs must nevertheless be made and that our only choice is to recognize the limits of our ability to be precise and do our best to identify the factors which should influence our decisions.

A decision about the extent of care which should be provided to severely disturbed juvenile offenders should be influenced by several relatively pragmatic factors. One is the likelihood that intensive clinical treatment (and the funds required to support it) will in fact improve the quality of these youths' lives, affect the severity of their mental illness, and enable them to live in the free community without representing a serious threat to the safety of others. But the sad fact of the matter is that the results of efforts to clinically treat severely disturbed juvenile offenders have been mixed and frequently disappointing.[38] In many cases massive amounts of treatment have apparently had little effect on the behavior and functioning of many of these youths. Yet nearly every program designed to treat severely disturbed juvenile offenders has had its share of success stories. It is frequently hard to know if the changes some youths have experienced have in fact been the result of the care they have received, but it is reasonable to assume that these changes have in some instances been direct consequences of professional help. In the end, however, the expectations of staff who work with severely disturbed juvenile offenders tend to be modest.

A second practical consideration, then, is whether the number of so-called successes merits the vast resources apparently required to bring them about. The relatively few programs which have been designed specifically for severely disturbed juvenile offenders have been, on the average, almost twice as expensive to operate as conventional correctional facilities.[39] This is because programs for severely disturbed youths tend to employ a larger number of staff who have greater amounts of professional training (for example, social workers, psychologists, or psychiatrists). The annual cost of care per youth is thus considerably higher for these programs than for correctional programs which typically have both fewer staff and staff who have had less professional training.

A realistic estimate of the amount of funds required to support programs for these youths must thus be based on an estimate of the number of juvenile offenders in any given state who can be judged to be severely disturbed. The fact that programs specifically designed for these youths can be nearly twice as expensive as programs which rely on more conventional custodial care in correctional institutions will be more or less significant depending upon the number of youths who may be eligible for them. This is an example of how empirical evidence can help inform ethical judgments.

The Incidence of the Problem

There is little information on the actual prevalence of severely disturbed juvenile offenders. National indicators do not exist. Rather, the literature on delinquency contains numerous statements to the effect that many juvenile offenders suffer more from various forms of psychosis than from neurotic and other personality disorders.[40] Only a handful of studies have addressed the problem of estimating the incidence of severely disturbed juvenile offenders. Acknowledging that a precise estimate of "the number of delinquents who may be mentally disordered is unknown," a District of Columbia Department of Public Health report estimated, for example, that "the behavior of over 10 percent of the delinquents has been considered sufficiently disturbing to warrant serious evaluation."[41] In a study of five California counties approximately 3 percent of the 651 juveniles sampled in detention centers were judged to be psychotic.[42] Perhaps the best estimate of the prevalance of severely disturbed juvenile offenders is from a carefully conducted study by the Massachusetts Department of Youth Services in 1977 based on a random sample of youths then in custody. A panel of knowledgeable professionals from the fields of child welfare, law enforcement, probation, and social service research carefully reviewed the files of the youths in the sample to determine the number who required secure care and, in addition, the number who required secure care in a program operated by the Department of Mental Health because of the severity of their emotional disturbance, considering factors such as offense history, commitment and placement histories, clinical diagnoses, and caseworkers' treatment plans. The findings indicated that a maximum of 11.2 percent of the youths required secure care and that 23 percent of this group needed to be placed in programs operated by the Department of Mental Health because of the extent of their emotional disturbance. Thus, a total of only 3 percent of the (1,500) youths in the custody of the Department of Youth Services were considered to need placement in programs designed specifically for severely disturbed offenders.[43]

The expense required to support the care of severely disturbed juvenile offenders in such special programs seems justifiable given the threats to their basic well-being known to exist in the correctional facilities and adult prisons for the criminally insane which now house many of them (in accord with guideline 6). In addition, there is some evidence that at least some of these youths have benefited from intensive clinical treatment.[44] Realistic limits must, of course, be placed on the amount of funds allocated for such programs; it is important to recognize that at some point the addition of well-trained professionals to the staff of these programs cannot be justified. Other groups of disabled and needy individuals also have legitimate claims to public funds earmarked for welfare programs. One can only exhort those responsible for the design and administration of these programs to attempt to locate the fine line between spending resources required to provide competent, professional treatment in a safe environment and spending resources in excess of what is required to provide such care.

Severely disturbed juvenile offenders represent a group of clients who have extreme needs. The debate concerning the extent and quality of care the public is willing to provide these youths raises many important questions about our willingness to help individuals whose conditions are serious, whose needs are great, and whose prognoses are in many cases poor. In these respects the questions about care for these youths are similar to questions concerning the amount of aid which should be provided to terminally ill patients. An important difference, of course, is that severely disturbed juvenile offenders have engaged in behavior many of us deeply resent.

Life is full of cases where individuals who have serious problems engage in behavior which we find repugnant. In the end, however, we must come to grips with the fact that many people who have profoundly serious problems have little capacity, for whatever reason, to do anything about them without a considerable amount of help. Massive amounts of aid do not guarantee success and at times seem entirely futile. But extreme circumstances frequently require extreme (and expensive) responses. When people appear to need such aid, we should be willing to provide it, being mindful of our obligation to balance their needs with the needs of others and of their rights to due process.

ETHICAL ASPECTS OF PROGRAM DESIGN

CASE 4.6 Burt Unitas received a notice in his morning mail that the federal Administration on Aging was planning to award $325,000 to fund a demonstration project designed to help disabled elderly individuals avoid referral to and placement in institutions. The funds were to be awarded to a local unit of government in order to provide services which would enable these people to remain in their own homes. Burt Unitas was the director of the Warren County Office of Senior Citizens and had a long-standing interest in devising ways of avoiding unnecessary placements in institutions.

Burt arranged a meeting with his associate director, Jerry Logan, to discuss how they might respond to the "request for proposal." Both Jerry and Burt were excited about the possibility of receiving federal funds to help them purchase in-home services for some of the disabled elderly in their county. They agreed that Jerry would spend three weeks gathering information about existing programs for such in-home services and would prepare a brief discussion paper which would include a series of recommendations concerning a program which the Warren County Office of Senior Citizens might propose to the Administration on Aging. Burt Unitas would then circulate the discussion paper among staff of the office for their review and comments.

Jerry spent nearly a week and a half contacting colleagues in various regions of the country who worked with the disabled elderly. He also located several journal articles and unpublished documents which discussed programs designed to maintain disabled elderly individuals in their homes. It became clear to Jerry that most such programs relied on case managers who worked with disabled elderly people and their families. The case managers had responsibility for consulting with each family to determine the degree of the elderly member's disability and the need for and likely benefit from in-home services. In addition, case managers authorized specific services and monitored their delivery. Most of the programs seemed to provide homemaker services (cooking, laundry, shopping, and housecleaning), personal care services (nursing care and physical or speech therapy), transportation, meals, and equipment needed to enable an individual to remain at home (a wheelchair or telephone designed for the disabled). In most programs the case managers had the authority both to determine eligibility for service and to approve the assignment of services.

Many of the colleagues Jerry had contacted believed that they were having reasonable success preventing, or at least postponing, institutionalization of many of their clients. Several, however, expressed some concern about the amount of discretion case managers were delegated under their programs. These colleagues complained that clients were occasionally forced to accept services which they did not want but which were convenient for a case manager to arrange. Several of Jerry's contacts suggested that he devise some way to increase the clients' participation in the decisions about service assignment.

Jerry drafted a discussion paper which described the various programs and included an outline of a possible program he believed would both enhance client participation in decisions about services and avoid some of the abuses plaguing other programs. The core of Jerry's proposal was a voucher system, under which eligible clients would be able to decide to a large extent which services they wanted to purchase. The program would be designed for elderly individuals who applied for institutional care through the state Medicaid program. To be eligible for the program an individual would have to be sixty-five years of age or older, a resident of Warren County, and have specific physical, mental, or emotional impairment. Each applicant would be administered a standardized measure of impairment which focused on learning ability, vision, speech, hand and arm movements, mental state, mobility, and bowel and bladder control. Those who scored moderately, seriously, or severely impaired would be accepted into the voucher program. Each participant would then receive a voucher to be used to purchase a specific range of services up to a maximum dollar value. The maximum amounts of the vouchers would be based on the degree of impairment identified during the screening procedure; these values would be determined by estimating the cost of typical services required by individuals with specific levels of impairment.

Jerry submitted his brief proposal to Burt, who then circulated it to the five administrators in the Office of Senior Citizens and arranged a meeting with them. Each staff member was asked to come to the meeting prepared to discuss Jerry's recommendations.

Emily Bellamy began the meeting by supporting Jerry's proposed voucher system. She agreed that it was important to allow participants to make decisions about services that would be provided to them. She acknowledged that some people might oppose any plan that would allow disabled elderly clients to decide on their own how public money should be spent on services, but that a closely monitored voucher plan which enhanced client discretion was preferable to a program where case managers had full authority to select and assign services. Joe Cuozzo and Amy Lyles strongly disagreed. They argued that it would be a mistake to allow the clients to select their own services, even if they were limited by a maximum dollar amount. They claimed that in their experience people served by the Office of Senior Citizens frequently showed poor judgment and could not be trusted to make wise decisions about the best use of the funds made available to them. As a rule, they argued, experienced case managers were much better able to make informed judgments about the services disabled elderly people need. Joe and Amy also pointed out that if decisions about services were left to the clients, instances might arise where individuals failed to receive critical services and suffered substantially as a result. Criticism for such neglect would ultimately be directed toward staff of the Office of Senior Citizens.

Burt Unitas and his staff debated Jerry's proposal for an entire afternoon. They were as sharply divided at the conclusion of their meeting as they had been at its beginning. The central disagreement was between those who favored the voucher program because of the degree of choice it would permit participants and those who opposed it because of their lack of confidence in the ability of the disabled elderly clients to make sound judgments. Burt Unitas explained to the group that in order to meet the federal agency's deadline for submitting applications, he would need to make a decision within a week about the basic design of the program which the Warren County Office of Senior Citizens would propose. He asked each member of his staff to prepare a brief position paper in response to Jerry's recommendations, outlining their respective reasons for supporting or opposing his proposal. Burt then informed the group that he would carefully review each of their statements and settle on a program plan which would serve as the foundation for the office's proposal.

There is little question that the goal of preventing or postponing institutionalization of disabled elderly is a noble one. Few would question the aim of providing services to people which would allow them to remain in their own homes. As this case illustrates, however, there can be considerable disagreement about the most appropriate way to organize a program designed to provide such in-home care. On the surface it may appear that the debate among the staff of the Warren County Office of Senior Citizens is primarily concerned with issues related to the efficiency and effectiveness of program design, not with issues of ethics. However, embedded within this case are a number of important ethical questions which are germane to the controversy surrounding the proposal to be submitted to the Administration on Aging. An examination of this case will provide a useful illustration of the ways in which the design of social service programs can, and frequently should, depend on the answers we provide to questions of ethics.

The Sides of the Debate

The debate among staff of the Office of Senior Citizens seems to have several themes. One is the clients' right to choose services which might enable them to remain in their homes. Jerry Logan argued that it is important to encourage clients to participate in decisions about services available to them. In short, he placed primary emphasis on the value of client choice, an extension of the client's prima facie right to freedom. Joe Cuozzo and Amy Lyles seemed less concerned with the client's right to freedom of choice; their primary concern was the soundness of clients' judgments and their ability to make informed choices among services. Joe's and Amy's concerns seem to have several bases. On the one hand, they considered the clients' well-being; that is, they are concerned that if decisions about services are left to the disabled elderly, individuals who in fact need certain forms of care in order to maintain their health might go without them because of their poor judgment. Thus, Joe and Amy argued, it would be in the clients' own interests to have services assigned by experienced case managers who have a good knowledge of the range of available services. Joe and Amy also made the point that the staff might be vulnerable to criticism if clients were allowed to choose their own services and if, as a result, they did not receive adequate care.

The ethical issues involved in this case therefore have several sides. First, do the clients have the right to choose which services will be provided to them even if their choices conflict with those of professional caregivers? Second, does this right supersede whatever obligation the staff of the Warren County Office of Senior Citizens has to help elderly people choose services which will enable them to remain in their own homes? Does the Office of Senior Citizens have a responsibility to select services for its clients in order to ensure that the public funds which support the program are efficiently used? Finally, do staff have a right to assign services in order to protect themselves from charges that they allowed the clients to select services which were not in their best interest? As we shall see below, the answers to these questions have important implications for the design of the program.

The Idea of Case Management

Programs operated according to a case management approach typically employ professionals who have responsibility for diagnosing need and prescribing service. Case managers have traditionally had considerable discretion and the authority to assign services to clients based on their professional judgment. An underlying assumption has been that trained professionals are in the best position to make these decisions, a form of paternalism.[48]

Case management has not, however, been without its critics. It has been argued, for example, that case management which vests the authority to select and assign services with professionals has contributed considerably to escalating costs of care because case managers have assigned services which clients have not requested or needed.[49] In addition, allowing professionals to make decisions about service assignment has allowed service providers who are not meeting client needs in an efficient and conscientious manner to ignore market conditions and the preferences of the "consumers" of the services. As a result, there has at times been little pressure to weed out the least competent or desirable service providers; in the long run, it has been argued, this can threaten the well-being of impaired elderly people.[50]

The most common criticism raised concerning the use of case managers to make decisions about service assignment has been related to the possibility that clients may be subjected to some degree of coercion.[51] This coercion may take a variety of forms. The clearest is denying clients the opportunity to choose for themselves the services which seem most appropriate. An individual case manager might conclude that the services of a physical therapist who would help the client learn to walk again should be secured, while the client might prefer a homemaker who would help prepare meals, clean house, and serve as a companion. In addition, because of the lack of uniformity in the criteria case managers use to diagnose conditions and assign services, individuals who have similar degrees of impairment may receive very different benefits and services. In effect, case manager discretion can be used to withhold or distribute goods and resources clients may desire and need and thus has the potential to serve as a means of social control.[52]

A related problem with the use of the traditional case management approach is that professionals whose positions permit the use of considerable discretion have an opportunity to select and concentrate on clients who appear to make the least demands on their time, who appear to be gratifying clients to work with, or who seem least likely to be troublesome. This phenomenon is referred to as "creaming" or "skimming" and sometimes results in the neglect of certain clients who are genuinely in need of assistance.[53]

Alternatives to Traditional Case Management

Unwanted consequences are encountered with any program which depends on worker judgment, and programs which rely on case managers are certainly no exception. Any program which requires decisions about the allocation of benefits necessarily depends to some extent on human discretion. No matter how ambitious attempts might be to specify detailed criteria for distributing resources, some room for judgment will remain. As Dwight Frankfather has noted, "the replacement of all aspects of individualized assessment and the elimination of flexibility in regulation appears to be an untenable proposition. If public program regulations attempt to cover every human condition or life circumstance, the immense volume of directives would be difficult to implement. The possibility would always remain that response to some special circumstances was not clearly prescribed by the regulation."[54]

Any program designed to provide services to enable disabled elderly individuals to remain in their homes should have several goals in order to provide appropriate care and to minimize undesirable consequences. First, it should enhance to the greatest extent possible the clients' freedom to choose services. This is consistent with the ethical obligation to respect each individual's right to freedom. Second, it should be designed to protect each client's right to well-being. A client's well-being may be threatened by his or her inability to make sound judgments about needed services or by case managers who use their discretion to withhold services or assign inappropriate services. Third, the program should be designed so that staff are not expected to follow procedures which are likely to invite allegations of wrongdoing, incompetence, or neglect on their part. Finally, the program should be designed to minimize the opportunity for misappropriation of public funds, as a result of poor judgments and decisions made by either clients or staff.

In principle, a program designed to provide in-home services to disabled elderly can be administered in one of three ways: with services assigned by case managers who are not required to act in accord with client preferences, selected by program clients who are not required to obtain case manager approval, or selected by clients who are expected to consult with and obtain the approval of case managers who are in turn responsible for helping clients make informed decisions. Recognizing the possible threats to the freedom and well-being of the clients, case managers, and taxpayers that may result from programs which place the exclusive authority for the assignment of services with either clients or case managers, the most reasonable design on ethical grounds would appear to be one that conforms to the third option, where the assignment of services is based on a consideration of clients' preferences which have been informed by consultation with case managers. Under this arrangement the right clients have to freedom of choice would be respected, case managers would be expected to monitor clients' decisions and thus protect the clients' and their own well-being, and taxpayers would be provided with some assurance that public funds were being spent appropriately.

Program Features

How might these ethical considerations be built into a program design? Such a program might have the following characteristics. In accord with the recommendations developed by Jerry Logan, the program would serve individuals applying for institutional care through the state Medicaid program. In order to be eligible for the program, an individual would have to be a resident of Warren County and have serious impairment. It would be important to have standard criteria for identifying impairment so that individuals with similar degrees of disability were not treated differently. An instrument such as the *Activities of Daily Living Index* might be used for this purpose.[55] This scale measures the extent of an individual's disability with respect to hand and arm movements, learning, vision, transfer, mobility, bowel and bladder control, speech, and mental status. The program would employ staff whose primary responsibility would be to administer this instrument. Ratings on the scale would be used to classify individuals into various categories of impairment, ranging from severely impaired to minimally impaired. (Individuals who fall into the category "minimally impaired" may not be in need of long-term care and should perhaps not be considered eligible for services.)

Following admission, each applicant would receive a copy of the assessment of his or her impairment. In instances where an applicant disagreed with the findings and classification, an evaluation of the client's condition could be obtained from his or her attending physician. Any client who did not have an attending physician would be assigned a physician consultant who was not affiliated with the program and who could be expected to provide an objective review of the findings from the original assessment. The assessment of each individual's impairment would be reviewed every six months (or after some other specified period of time), unless a client requested an earlier review because of a substantial change in disability level. An attempt would be made to have only one staff member (or as few as possible) conduct the assessments in order to enhance the consistency and reliability of the results. This specialist (a nurse or other allied health professional) would receive extensive training in the administration of the *Activities of Daily Living Index* and would be expected to consult with a physician when appropriate.

As Jerry Logan's proposal stipulated, each client would be assigned a voucher which could be used to purchase from among a specified range of services. The amount of each client's voucher (that is, the maximum dollar amount) would be based on the category of impairment assigned to each individual and the cash value of a "typical" package of services considered appropriate for each category. This procedure would be consistent with the obligation to provide the greatest amount of assistance to those individuals who were most in need and whose well-being was most threatened. (The content of a typical package of services would be determined by a group of professionals—physicians, nurses, physical therapists, social workers, speech therapists, occupational therapists, and other allied health personnel—familiar with the care needed by individuals with various degrees of impairment. The corresponding cash values would need to be reviewed periodically in order to adjust for rates of inflation, and so on. Consideration would also need to be given to whether or not the value of a client's voucher should be reduced based on his or her income and assets and the income and assets of his or her spouse.)

Available Services

The program would make available to each impaired elderly person all of the services necessary to remain in his or her home (or some other noninstitutional setting). They would include home maintenance services and health care services. Home maintenance services would include a homemaker who would assist with activities such as cooking, shopping, cleaning, bathing, toileting, feeding, medication, and walking. Certain equipment and other supplies which enhance the safety and independence of the client would also be available (for example, a walker or wheelchair). In addition, clients would also be able to avail themselves of various means of transportation—for example, in vehicles specially equipped for the handicapped, taxis, and other forms of public transportation. Adult day care, home-delivered meals, and the opportunity to arrange for heavy-duty cleaning and home maintenance might also be considered available services. Health care services would include nursing care and physical, speech, and occupational therapy.

I concluded earlier that it would not be permissible for clients in such a program to have the authority to purchase services of their choice without any consultation with or approval of a case manager; it cannot be assumed that all clients would be competent to choose services that are in their best interests. There would be an obligation to monitor and guide the selection of services for some clients. The extent of monitoring required would, of course, depend on the extent of a client's competence. In addition, some degree of monitoring is justifiable in order to protect program staff from allegations that they neglected the needs of certain clients.

In order to protect against possible abuses of their authority, it is important to specify in detail the nature of the monitoring activities it would be permissible for case managers to perform. First, an initial plan would be agreed upon by a client and case manager. The plan would specify the goals of the care to be provided for each client (for example, to have the house cleaned weekly and two meals prepared daily, or to learn to walk again) and the services which would be necessary in order to reach those goals. The goals themselves would ordinarily be those specified by the client, though the case manager may be relied on for advice and consultation. The case manager would provide the client with information on where the various services could be obtained and on the costs of services delivered by various providers. A special effort would have to be made to train case managers to understand the distinction between providing consultation in an effort to help clients clarify their preferences and deliberately steering clients toward services preferred by the case manager.

After agreement has been reached between the client and case manager, the case manager would sign off on the care plan. This is to ensure that the client has not proposed a plan which threatens his or her basic well-being and to ensure that the client is planning to spend within the monetary limits of the voucher. The requirement that case managers approve a client's plan in this manner provides a mechanism for ensuring a balance between a client's freedom of choice and the protection of well-being (the client's, staff members', and that of taxpayers as well). If a client were so impaired as to be unable to make arrangements with service providers directly, the case manager would be available to help arrange, at the request of the client or his or her family, the delivery of the services. This would entail communicating to the provider the amount, content, and duration of service the client prefers and the client's specific needs. The case manager would also be responsible for helping the client arrange services or other benefits which were not available through the voucher account (for example, legal counsel or inpatient hospital care). Arrangements would be made for the case manager to regularly monitor each case by home visit and telephone contact. Adjustments could be made in the service plan depending on changes in a client's health or on the suitability and effectiveness of the various services. An important feature of this program would be the opportunity for a client to appeal any decisions made by a case manager—for example, when a case manager unilaterally assigns specific services or denies a client's request. Appeals would be made to the program administrator, who would also be responsible for reviewing a decision by a case manager to require services rejected by a client or to deny services which a client has requested.[56]

The case manager would thus have a variety of responsibilities, some of which resemble those assumed by case managers in more conventional programs, where they have the authority to assign services to clients. The principal difference would be that a voucher program would vest considerable responsibility with each client (or the client's family) for the selection and purchase of services. This is a strategy which can be defended on ethical grounds and which would be designed to protect to the greatest extent possible the client's and the public's rights to freedom and well-being. It is also a strategy which demonstrates how the design of a social service program can be informed by ethical considerations.

The range of ethical issues which emerge in social policy and planning is obviously wide. I have touched upon a variety of issues practitioners have encountered and will likely encounter in the future, whether they work directly with individuals and families or occupy administrative positions. They include questions about the role of government in the provision of social services, the community's willingness to provide care to those in need, clients' rights to freedom of choice, welfare rights, and the relationship between ethics and program design.

One of the important lessons to learn from these cases is that ethical dilemmas in social policy and planning are not always readily apparent. Some, such as dilemmas involving the sudden transfer of elderly people in nursing homes or the acquisition of private property in order to revive a community, are not too difficult to identify. Others, such as those involving the relationship between ethics and program design, are more subtle and less readily apparent. An important skill for practitioners to develop is the ability to recognize ethical issues, whether they linger beneath the surface or float more visibly on top.

5

Ethical Dilemmas in Relationships Among Practitioners

Ethical dilemmas encountered by social workers are not limited to the relationships they have with individual clients or to the morality of social welfare policies. Another important class of ethical dilemmas involves social workers' relationships with other practitioners, in particular their colleagues and employers. Many of us would prefer to think of our relationships with our colleagues and employers as ones where we are like-minded professionals united in a common effort to improve the lot of our clients' lives. In fact, though, we know that these relationships are sometimes laden with difficult ethical choices.

The range of ethical choices social workers face in their relationships with colleagues and employers is wide. These dilemmas fall generally into two categories. One includes what is sometimes referred to as *whistle-blowing,* exposing questionable practices among colleagues. Examples include reporting to administrative authorities a practitioner's apparently unprofessional behavior and engaging in furtive activities in order to uncover wrongdoing among agency staff. The second category includes instances when a practitioner must decide whether to violate an agency regulation or administrative policy in order to safeguard the welfare of a client, a colleague, or oneself. As has been typical of the cases we have examined thus far, practitioners who face these dilemmas must inevitably choose from among a series of compelling but competing values. As we shall see below, these choices are often difficult.

QUESTIONING PROFESSIONAL COMPETENCE

CASE 5.1 Donna Shinnick and Roberta Boyd had been working together at the Fallstaff Center, a residential psychiatric facility for children, for a little over a year. Donna had been on the staff of Fallstaff as a clinical social worker for three years. Roberta had been a full-time clinical social worker on the staff for three months, after having served as a student intern at the center during the previous nine months while completing her final year of graduate school. Roberta and Donna spent quite a bit of time together at Fallstaff. Roberta frequently consulted with Donna about some of the children on her caseload, and Donna occasionally asked Roberta to help her develop treatment plans for several children who had been diagnosed as borderline schizophrenic; Roberta had studied childhood schizophrenia in graduate school and had concentrated on these cases during her field placement at Fallstaff.

Over time Roberta and Donna became close friends. During the year that they had worked together Donna had separated from her husband of eight years and had filed for divorce. She and Roberta spent many hours talking about Donna's troubled marriage and the difficulty she was having adjusting to life on her own.

It seemed to Roberta that Donna had been drinking frequently during the weeks following her separation. The two women had begun spending quite a bit of their free time together, and Roberta had noticed that Donna was ordering drinks at restaurants and fixing her own drinks at home more often than she had before her separation. Roberta was somewhat concerned, though not alarmed; she had no reason to think that Donna had a serious drinking problem and assumed that Donna's increased drinking would stop as she began to adjust to her new lifestyle as a single woman.

A month passed, however, and Roberta had not noticed much of a decline in Donna's drinking. Roberta began to wonder whether she should share her concern with Donna. Before she had a chance to decide, she received a phone call from Donna who said she was very depressed and needed to talk; she was crying and asked Roberta if she would come to her apartment. Roberta left immediately and drove to Donna's apartment; she knocked on the door, and after waiting several minutes for Donna to open the door, let herself in. Roberta found Donna slumped over the kitchen table with a half-empty bottle of liquor. Roberta tried to talk to Donna but quickly discovered that Donna was too inebriated to talk clearly. Roberta convinced Donna to simply go to bed and assured her that they would talk at length the following morning.

Roberta met Donna at her apartment the next morning. Donna seemed very tired and worn and confessed to Roberta that she was having trouble controlling her drinking and that she knew she needed to do something about it. She also told Roberta that she was concerned about the effect her problems and her drinking were having on her performance at work. Roberta mentioned to her that their supervisor, Lou Michaels, had asked Roberta if Donna was under any special stress; he had noticed Donna being uncharacteristically curt with several children and wondered if anything in particular was wrong. Donna was not surprised; Mr. Michaels had asked her the same question the day before. The two women agreed that it was important for Donna to get some help with her problems, both for herself and for the sake of the children at Fallstaff.

Donna began seeing a private therapist. For several weeks Roberta was encouraged by the changes she saw in Donna; Donna was more calm and cheery than she had been in months, and she seemed to be drinking only at social gatherings. One morning following a meeting with her husband, however, Donna came to work with a strong smell of alcohol on her breath. Roberta tried to speak with her but was brushed off. Several days that week Donna came to work clearly inebriated, and Roberta was very distressed to see how Donna was treating the children in Fallstaff. Donna was unusually impatient and screamed and cursed at several children who failed to listen to her instructions. On one occasion Roberta was horrified to see Donna slap a child who would not sit still.

Later that week Roberta stopped by Donna's apartment. Roberta told Donna that she was very concerned about her and was frightened by the way she was treating the children. Roberta told Donna that she had seen her slap the one child. Donna shook her head and told Roberta that she did not know what was happening to her, that her life seemed to be falling apart. Roberta left the apartment feeling very dejected; she had little confidence that Donna was going to be able to resolve her problems quickly and wondered about Donna's ability to work competently with the children at Fallstaff. As she drove home, Roberta recalled Lou Michaels' concern about Donna's behavior on the job and wondered if she should share her concern about Donna's condition with him. Roberta was worried, however, that Donna might lose her job as a result. She was also worried that she would lose Donna as a friend.

Roberta's dilemma has several faces. Does she have an obligation to share what she knows about Donna's problems with Lou Michaels so that he can act in the children's best interest? But suppose Michaels decides to release Donna from her position at the agency. How would Donna react? Would she be able to bear losing her job and her husband at the same time? How would a decision to talk with Mr. Michaels about Donna's problems affect Roberta's relationship with her? Should she keep Donna's problems to herself in order to keep the relationship intact?

The Nature of Culpability

Roberta has three options. First, she can tell Lou Michaels about Donna's problems on the grounds that the children at the Fallstaff Center have a right to be protected from a staff member who is not providing competent care. Second, she can encourage Donna to talk with Lou Michaels herself, to share with him some of the problems she is experiencing and to speak with him about her own needs in relation to those of the children and the center itself. Third, Roberta can decide that it is not her responsibility to become involved in Donna's affairs. Donna is free to approach Mr. Michaels in order to discuss her problems, and he is free to confront Donna based on his own observations of her recent behavior. For Roberta to intercede might constitute unwarranted meddling which could have harmful consequences for Donna and for Roberta's relationship with her.

The major choice Roberta must make is between taking a course of action directed toward having Lou Michaels become aware of Donna's problems (which would entail encouraging Donna to share her problems with him or bypassing Donna and going directly to Mr. Michaels herself) and not taking any such action. That is, Roberta must decide between doing something and doing nothing.

The choice between doing something (intervening) and not doing something (not intervening) is one we have encountered before. Michael Bunker was faced with a decision between allowing Helen to live in the alley as she wished and attempting to coerce her into accepting a variety of social services. Similarly, Art Bulaich had to decide whether to take matters into his own hands and tell Bev McNally about her husband Hal's drinking, or to permit Hal to handle the predicament however he wished. To what extent could Roberta be held responsible if she failed to share information about Donna's problems with Lou Michaels and one of the children in Donna's care were seriously injured because of Donna's unprofessional behavior? We ordinarily consider ourselves responsible for actions we actively carry out. Is it possible that we can also be held responsible for actions we fail to carry out?

The Idea of Negative Responsibility

The Cambridge philosopher Bernard Williams has presented a provocative example of a dilemma which forces us to think about the extent to which individuals are morally responsible for their inaction as well as their actions:

> Jim finds himself in the central square of a small South American town. Tied up against the wall are a row of twenty Indians, most terrified, a few defiant, in front of them several armed men in uniform. A heavy man in a sweat-stained khaki shirt turns out to be the captain in charge and, after a good deal of questioning of Jim which establishes that he got there by accident while on a botanical expedition, explains that the Indians are a random group of the inhabitants who, after recent acts of protest against the government, are just about to be killed to remind other possible protestors of the advantages of not protesting. However, since Jim is an honoured visitor from another land, the captain is happy to offer him a guest's privilege of killing one of the Indians himself. If Jim accepts, then as a special mark of the occasion, the other Indians will be let off. Of course, if Jim refuses, then there is no special occasion, and Pedro here will do what he was about to do when Jim arrived, and kill them all. Jim, with some desperate recollection of schoolboy fiction, wonders whether if he got hold of a gun, he could hold the captain, Pedro and the rest of the soldiers to threat, but it is quite clear from the set-up that

> nothing of that kind is going to work: any attempt at that sort of thing will mean that all the Indians will be killed, and himself. The men against the wall, and the other villagers, understand the situation, and are obviously begging him to accept. What should he do?[1]

As Williams notes, there are several possible answers to this question. A strict utilitarian would no doubt conclude that Jim should shoot one of the Indians in order to save the lives of nineteen of the group; the calculus is straightforward and persuasive. For the utilitarian it is not necessarily important to ask whether Jim would be morally responsible for the lives of the twenty Indians if he refused to shoot one of them. The outcome of his decision to shoot or not shoot determines the morality of his action; a utilitarian would likely not be interested in Jim's culpability per se but, rather, in the morality of the *consequences* of his action.

Such an approach to Jim's dilemma would probably not be very satisfying to a deontologist, who would be more interested in judging the inherent morality of Jim's actions (that is, the act of killing a defenseless human being) than in the consequences. For example, a popular view among deontologists is that it is morally wrong to intentionally kill an innocent human being regardless of the consequences. Thus, it would be wrong for Jim to kill an innocent Indian regardless of the number of lives that would be saved as a result. This point of view is consistent with the view of St. Paul, who stated that it is impermissible to do evil that good may come of it (Romans 3:8). However, this conclusion runs counter to the utilitarian position and to the idea of *negative responsibility,* according to which one *can* be held morally responsible for failing to engage in an action which could have prevented harm or suffering. As Bernard Williams states: "It is because consequentialism attaches value ultimately to states of affairs, and its concern is with what states of affairs the world contains, that it essentially involves the notion of *negative responsibility*: that if I am ever responsible for anything, then I must be just as much responsible for things that I allow or fail to prevent, as I am for things that I myself, in the more everyday restricted sense, bring about."[2]

These contrasting points of view suggest important questions about Roberta Boyd's dilemma and the extent to which she would be morally responsible if she failed to share information about Donna's problems with Mr. Michaels and if, subsequently, children in Donna's care were harmed. I argued earlier that strict utilitarian and deontological approaches to ethical dilemmas will not suffice. Utilitarian interpretations do not necessarily take into account the means used to bring about a certain end, and deontological interpretations can at times reduce to what J. J. C. Smart has referred to as "rule worship." I have repeatedly argued that a systematic approach to ethical dilemmas in social service must depend instead on a series of principles or guidelines which contain both teleological (or utilitarian) *and* deontological criteria, such that our instinct to act in a manner which results in the greatest good for the greatest number is influenced and constrained by a respect for individuals' rights to freedom and well-being. This is necessary in order to avoid engaging in actions which result in the greatest aggregate good while sacrificing the rights of a minority of individuals in the process.

The Limits of Professional Immunity

It seems clear that Roberta Boyd's primary concern is to safeguard the welfare of the children for whom Donna is responsible. As a first step, Roberta should encourage Donna to talk with their supervisor herself. If, however, Donna does not bring her problems to their supervisor's attention and if, according to her best professional judgment, Roberta believes that Donna's condition and behavior represent a serious threat to the children, she has a responsibility to bring her impressions to the attention of a supervisor who is in a position to respond humanely and authoritatively to Donna. Because of their close friendship, Roberta would probably find it very, very difficult to "betray" Donna in this fashion. It is not easy to place one's professional obligations above a close personal relationship. However, if it in fact appears that the children's welfare is likely to suffer if Donna continues to work with them while in her present condition, Roberta's first priority is to do what she can to prevent harm. The right of the children to basic well-being must take precedence over Roberta's concern about her relationship with Donna (in accord with guideline 1) and over her concern about Donna's right to freedom from interference (guideline 2). This is certainly a difficult choice for Roberta to make, yet it is one she must make. Ideally, Roberta would explain the predicament she is in and her decision to Donna. If Roberta has done her best to be patient with Donna and to help Donna resolve her difficult problems and if Donna's behavior has not changed and does not seem likely to change substantially, it is Roberta's responsibility to share her opinion with a supervisor. It would be wrong for her not to inform a supervisor of Donna's problems. Roberta would then be free to do what she could to help Donna weather her problems, if the quality of their relationship would permit such aid. As difficult as it may be, however, the welfare of the children, because of their vulnerability and the threat to their well-being, must take precedence over the possible loss of Donna's job and of her personal relationship with Roberta.

This conclusion suggests that it could be wrong for Roberta to fail to share her impressions of Donna's problems with Lou Michaels (or some other appropriate agency official). If she failed to bring Donna's problems to his attention and the children were harmed by Donna, one could conclude that Roberta failed to help prevent harm which she was in a position to help prevent. This is not to say that Roberta *caused* the children to be harmed, any more than we could say that Jim caused the murder of the twenty Indians by refusing to kill one of them; Roberta did not directly harm the children herself, just as Jim did not shoot the Indians. Yet Roberta was in a position to help prevent a greater harm (to the children) at the expense of a lesser, though serious, harm (the possible loss of Donna's job and her relationship with Roberta). Thus, the principle of negative responsibility pertains.

Boundless Obligation

The conclusion that Roberta has a responsibility to talk with a supervisor about Donna's problems is based on an assumption that social workers must act in order to prevent injuries and harm to individuals in need. Taken to an extreme, however, this conclusion suggests that social workers are obligated to help others ad infinitum and selflessly, allowing no time for nonaltruistic activities. This would seem to be a particular problem for utilitarians. As the philosopher Charles Fried has said: "For utilitarians there is always only one right thing to do, and that is to promote in all possible ways at every moment the greatest happiness of the greatest number. To stop even for a moment or to rest content with a second best is a failure of duty."[3] It seems obvious that limits need to somehow be placed on social workers' obligation to assist others. But what is the nature of these limits, and on what grounds can they be justified?

Consider for a moment an individual, Sam, whose small sailboat has capsized in placid waters and who is about to drown. Adam, who is an award-winning swimmer and lifeguard, is standing on a ledge very near where Sam plunged into the water. Adam searches around for a life preserver or rope but finds none. He quickly ponders whether or not he should try to rescue Sam himself. He remembers that he is scheduled to participate in a gymnastics event that evening and will need to conserve his energy. Adam decides not to rescue Sam, who subsequently drowns.

Was it morally wrong for Adam to fail to intervene? It seems quite clear that it was. The reason is that he failed to respect another individual's right to basic well-being when he could have done so without seriously risking his own well-being. As Alan Gewirth has observed, a responsible individual should "not only refrain from interfering with his recipients' freedom and well-being," but should also "assist them to have these necessary goods when they cannot have them by their own efforts and when he can give such assistance at no comparable cost to himself."[4] Thus, like Roberta Boyd, it would be wrong for Adam to stand idly by while Sam drowns when he could have used his life-saving skills to prevent Sam's death. People are at times responsible for the consequences of their inaction.

But if this is so, would it not also be the case that Adam (or Roberta) is likewise obligated to personally commit his life to preventing mining accidents in Poland or political murders in South America? Isn't it possible that such acts could be prevented by diligent efforts on Adam's part? In order to answer this question we must recall our earlier conclusion that responsible individuals are obligated to respect the rights others have to freedom and well-being *as well as* their own right to freedom and well-being. We can say first of all that any individual who feels compelled to assist others without respite, wherever the objects of his concern may be located, is a person whose own well-being is very likely to suffer as a result. We know that the most benevolent among us reach a point when both the body and mind are ready to collapse from fatigue. To travel the globe without taking time off to rest is to interfere with one's own right to well-being. It may be permissible to push oneself to the point of physical and emotional exhaustion, if such a decision is made voluntarily and with knowledge of the likely consequences, but there certainly is no obligation to behave in such a manner. It is simply not possible to save a drowning person, prevent mining accidents in Poland, and interfere with political murders in South America all in one day. We are obligated to do what we can to assist those in dire need who are around us and who fall within our realm of influence. We are responsible for some things, but not everything, especially not at the price of our own well-being. Charles Fried has stated it well in his *Right and Wrong:*

> If, as consequentialism holds, we were indeed equally morally responsible for an infinite radiation of concentric circles originating from the center point of some action, then while it might look as if we were enlarging the scope of human responsibility and thus the significance of personality, the enlargement would be greater than we could support. For to be responsible equally for every thing is to have the moral possibility of choice, of discretion, of creative concretization of one's free self wholly preempted by the potential radiations of all the infinite alternatives for choice. Total undifferentiated responsibility is the correlative of the morally overwhelming, undifferentiated plasma of happiness or pleasure.[5]

Our choices about the extent of our obligation to assist others in need must be guided by several criteria in order to be consistent with the guidelines I have developed along the way for approaching ethical dilemmas. First, one must consider both the kind and degree of harm which threatens another person. Threats to basic goods, such as life itself or serious physical injury, are more important than threats to the acquisition of additive goods, such as vacation homes or fine paintings. Thus, it would be important for Adam to rescue Sam from drowning, though Adam should not feel obligated to give Sam money to purchase a yacht which would enable him to enjoy the water safely. Similarly, if the basic goods of the children under Donna's care are threatened by her behavior and general condition, Roberta has an obligation to do what she can to prevent injury to them. Roberta does not, however, have an obligation to personally subsidize a trip for the children to the local amusement park, though such a gesture on her part would be quite commendable.

Second, we must consider the extent to which individuals in need are able to help themselves. Our obligations to aid others are greater for those who are not able, because of physical or emotional disabilities, to care for themselves and resolve their own problems. Sam was apparently not in a position to help himself and required assistance. The children in Donna's charge, because of their age and vulnerability, are also not likely to be able to avoid harm on their own and consequently have a right to assistance, which Roberta is in a position to provide, at least indirectly.

Finally, we must consider the extent to which providing assistance to others threatens our own well-being. If Adam were a poor swimmer, he would certainly not be obligated to attempt to rescue Sam by himself. Adam's own well-being is as important as Sam's, and it would be reasonable, though unfortunate, for Adam to decide not to risk his own life in order to save Sam's. It is conceivable that both of the men would die if Adam did make such an attempt. If Adam were in fact a poor swimmer, he should have done everything he could—for example, shouting for help or throwing a floatable object to Sam—short of risking his own life by diving in. In Donna Shinnick's case, however, it does not appear that an effort on Roberta's part to protect the children by sharing her observations with a supervisor would represent a serious threat to her own basic well-being. This is not to deny that Roberta might suffer deeply because of her actions; she may lose a close friend in the process and may feel very guilty if Donna loses her job at the Fallstaff Center. However, if the children's welfare appears to be in jeopardy because of Donna's behavior, Roberta cannot fail to intervene on the grounds that the costs for her own well-being are too great. The threat to her welfare in this case is not comparable to the threat to the welfare of a poor swimmer who encounters a drowning person.

The distinction between positive and negative responsibility—between being responsible for acts one engages in and for acts one fails to engage in—is an important one in social service. We are not always responsible for an action simply because we have engaged in it (such as when someone is forced by someone with a gun to be an unwilling accomplice in a crime); conversely, we are at times responsible for the consequences which follow a decision not to act (such as when an air traffic controller is held responsible for failing to warn the pilot of a departing aircraft about another aircraft arriving in its path). Deciding not to act is itself an act, and it is sometimes necessary to hold people accountable for such decisions.

COMPLYING WITH AGENCY POLICY

CASE 5.2. Dick Hall was a supervisor on the staff of the local Big Brothers organization. The organization served 180 young boys with 165 Big Brothers. Dick was one of seven supervisors who matched young boys with Big Brothers and consulted with Big Brothers about problems that arose in their work. Dick also had responsibility for screening young boys and their families once they had applied for a Big Brother and for recruiting and training Big Brothers.

Steve Barber was one of the Big Brothers under Dick's supervision. Steve had been a Big Brother for nearly seven months and, in Dick's eyes, had developed into one of the organization's most valuable volunteers. Steve had been matched with an eleven-year-old boy, Jeffrey, whose father had deserted his family shortly after Jeffrey's second birthday. During the first interview with Steve, Jeffrey's mother, Suzanne, described her son as very lonely, quiet, and withdrawn. He had no close friends and spent most of his free time playing alone with his dog or watching television. Though his teachers thought Jeffrey had the potential to be a very good student, his school performance was consistently mediocre. Suzanne speculated that Jeffrey had never recovered from being abandoned by his father and had missed having an adult male in his life.

Steve spent almost one day each week with Jeffrey. They frequently went to ballgames together, and to movies and museums. On occasion they went on overnight hikes. According to Suzanne, the time Steve spent with Jeffrey was doing wonders for her son. Jeffrey was gradually becoming more outgoing and was smiling and laughing more than ever. His school teacher also reported to Suzanne that Jeffrey was much more sociable in school and that the quality of his work was gradually improving.

Steve called Dick Hall one afternoon and asked for an appointment to discuss his relationship with Jeffrey. Steve and Dick talked at length about Jeffrey's progress and about the activities Steve might arrange which would encourage Jeffrey to spend even more time with boys and girls his own age. Toward the end of the conversation Steve mentioned that there was one other problem he wanted to speak with Dick about. Steve explained that it was a very personal and sensitive matter and asked Dick if he could talk with him in confidence. Dick assured Steve that whatever he shared would be kept confidential.

Steve began by telling Dick that he was aware of the Big Brother organization's formal policy against accepting homosexual volunteers. Steve explained that he had been a homosexual for five years, but that he had originally been unaware of the organization's policy.

"When I did learn about the policy—after my first interview with you—I had already gotten so excited about working with Jeffrey that I decided not to say anything about my homosexuality. I knew that it would not get in the way of my work with Jeffrey. I knew that I could be just as effective as any Big Brother you had ever had. But recently I've begun to feel guilty about not telling you that I'm a homosexual. I still don't think there's a thing for you to worry about—I mean I'm not, you know, at all interested in Jeffrey. I've done a lot for him and I can do more. But I don't like the fact that I didn't tell you the truth."

Dick told Steve that he was pleased that Steve was so committed to telling the truth after originally concealing the fact that he was a homosexual. "I imagine that it was very difficult for you to come in here and tell me what you've just shared with me. And I have no reason not to believe you when you say that your homosexuality will not get in the way of your relationship with Jeffrey. But the truth is, I'm now in a real predicament because of what you've told me. You're right—Big Brothers does have a strict policy against accepting homosexual volunteers. It's not that we discriminate; unfortunately, several years ago there were a couple of incidents where mothers complained that their sons were molested by their Big Brothers. There was a scandal of sorts, and ever since then there has been a firm rule about accepting homosexuals; our Board of Directors believed that the policy was necessary in order for us to protect our public image. I frankly don't think prohibiting all homosexuals from being volunteers is right. But according to regulations I'm supposed to share what you've told me with my supervisor. What makes it so difficult is that I know you've done a very good job with Jeffrey, and I suspect that you would continue to be very helpful to him. I really don't know what to do."

Two related but distinct questions are raised by this case. First, does Dick have an obligation to act in accord with his organization's policy and report Steve's self-disclosed homosexuality to Dick's supervisor, even though he feels strongly that Steve has been doing a good job with Jeffrey? Is it possible that it would be permissible for Dick to ignore the policy which prohibits homosexual Big Brothers, for Jeffrey's sake, especially when he questions the policy's legitimacy? Second, is Dick obligated to keep confidential the information Steve has shared with him? Prior to telling Dick that he was a homosexual, Steve asked Dick if he could share information with him in confidence. Dick assured Steve that whatever information he shared would be kept confidential. What obligation does Dick have to honor his promise of confidentiality given the organization's explicit policy against accepting homosexual staff?

Obeying Agency Policy

From childhood we are taught to obey rules and laws. We generally believe that without rules and laws great disorganization and chaos would prevail or, as Thomas Hobbes observed in the *Leviathan,* without *laws* of nature, the *state* of nature would overwhelm us with a world where life would be "solitary, poor, nasty, brutish, and short." Few of us would disagree with the assertion that rules and laws are necessary to maintain relatively smooth working and personal relationships among people. Similarly, few of us would argue that social service organizations should not have policies designed to enhance the quality and efficiency of services provided to clients, such as policies related to personnel practices, intake criteria, service assignment, or decisions concerning discharge.

Many of us are tempted to believe that there are certain instances when it is permissible to violate rules, laws, and policies, despite the good consequences which generally result from acting in accord with them. For example, virtually no one would question the importance of obeying the law which requires the driver of an automobile to halt at a red light. We recognize that it is in our own interest and in the interest of the safety of others to stop at red lights. But it is also widely believed that it is permissible to break this law in an emergency, such as when a driver is carrying a critically ill passenger to a hospital for emergency treatment. Similarly, few of us would question violating a rule which prohibits seeing clients for more than fifty minutes when a client threatens suicide at the conclusion of a session. However, there are many instances when the legitimacy of violating a rule, law, or policy is not clear. For example, it has long been debated whether civil disobedience is justifiable when individuals complain of being subjected to harsh political regimes. One popular point of view has been expressed by John Rawls: "We are not required to acquiesce in the crushing of fundamental liberties by democratic majorities which have shown themselves blind to the principles of justice upon which justification of the constitution depends."[6] An alternative point of view holds that, to the contrary, such violations are not permissible. As Richard Wasserstrom has observed, "given what we know of the possibilities of human error and the actualities of human frailty, and given the tendency of democratic societies to make illegal only those actions which would, even in the absence of law, be unjustified, we can confidently conclude that the consequences will on the whole and in the long run be best if no one ever takes it upon himself to 'second-guess' the laws and to conclude that in his case his disobedience is justified."[7]

The view that it is at times permissible to violate laws or policies is essentially teleological; that is, it is consistent with the line of reasoning which holds that actions which violate established laws or policies are justifiable when they result in greater good than would result from acting in accord with the laws or policies. To teleologists it does not make sense to adhere to laws or policies when a greater good would result from violating them. To do otherwise, they claim, is to commit the naive error of "rule worship." This point of view is of course directly opposed to the strict deontological position that it is never right to violate laws or policies.

It is important to note, however, that not all teleologists subscribe to the view that it is permissible to violate laws and policies when the consequences which would follow are preferable to those which would follow strict adherence to the laws and policies. In fact, some teleologists take a position which is quite opposite, one which asserts that we have an obligation to *always* obey laws and policies because in the long run the greatest good will result, even though there may be isolated cases where disobeying a law or policy would not lead to the best consequences. This argument is consistent with Wasserstrom's and is characteristic of philosophers known as *rule utilitarians.* Rule utilitarians hold that one is obligated to obey rules because of the importance rules have in the maintenance of honesty, order, and so on, even when in *individual cases* better consequences would result from a violation of a rule. This is in contrast to the view of *act utilitarians,* who hold that it is not justifiable to obey a rule in a specific instance when violating it would result in better consequences.

Dick Hall might agree, for example, that it is justifiable for him to ignore, and hence violate, the policy of the Big Brothers organization regarding homosexual staff on the grounds that a greater good would result (with respect to Jeffrey's welfare) than if he were to obey the organization's policy and were to seek to have Steve dismissed. This position would be consistent with the *act utilitarian* point of view. Or Dick might argue that he has a fundamental obligation to obey his organization's policy, regardless of the immediate consequences for Jeffrey. This position would be consistent both with the *deontological* point of view that rules, policies, and laws always ought to be obeyed for their own sake and with the *rule utilitarian* point of view, which holds that rules, policies, and laws always ought to be obeyed because in the long run such obedience will result in the greatest good (though in the short run it may not).

The Obligation to Obey

According to the guidelines I developed earlier, an individual ordinarily has an obligation to obey rules to which he or she has voluntarily and freely consented (guideline 4). In this respect, Dick Hall has at least a prima facie obligation to act in accord with the rules or policies of the Big Brothers organization, unless he can demonstrate that in doing so he would seriously threaten the basic well-being of others (see guideline 5). On the face of it, Dick has an obligation to report to his supervisor the fact that Steve Barber is a homosexual. Dick was made aware of the organization's policy when he joined its staff and is therefore committed to acting in accord with the policy. He voluntarily chose to join a professional organization and is thus obligated to obey its rules. As Gewirth has concluded, "if there are to be groups or associations regulated by rules that persons are morally obligated to obey, then these persons must freely consent to belong to the associations and to accept their rules."[8] Gewirth argues further, in defense of the obligation to obey rules voluntarily agreed upon unless they conflict with the right to well-being, that

> if any participant refuses to accept an adverse impact of procedurally justified rules on himself or on others, or if he violates any of the rules, then he contradicts himself. For in agreeing to participate in the activity, he has accepted the need for obeying the rules: 'I and all the other participants ought to obey the rules.' But in violating one of the rules he says, in effect: 'I have a right not to obey the rule,' or 'It is not the case that I ought to obey the rule.' This point applies not only to the direct participants but also to such persons as umpires or other officials who are charged with applying the rules to the participants in particular cases.[9]

Thus, Dick could be held responsible if he failed to comply with the organization's policy regarding homosexuals. Acting in accord with the policy would therefore be consistent not only with the obligation to obey agency guidelines but with Dick's obligation to respect his own right to well-being as it relates to job security.

It is perhaps tempting to think that it would be permissible for Dick to disobey the organization's policy on the grounds that Jeffrey's right to basic well-being would be threatened otherwise (in accord with guideline 5). It would be difficult to establish, however, that Jeffrey's *basic* well-being would necessarily be threatened. It is certainly possible that harmful effects might result if Dick informs his supervisor of Steve's homosexuality. But it is true that if the agency were no longer to authorize Steve to work with Jeffrey, Steve would be free to continue working with Jeffrey on his own. If Steve were not interested in continuing to work with Jeffrey without the sanction of Big Brothers, Dick could assign another volunteer to work with Jeffrey. This would not necessarily be an ideal solution, of course; it is quite possible that Jeffrey would suffer because of enforcement of the organization's policy.

It is reasonable to ask whether the legitimacy of the organization's policy regarding homosexuals should affect Dick's decision to act in accord with it. There are certainly instances when policies represent such severe threats to individuals' rights to well-being that they should be violated. The policies of the Nazi regime provide a compelling example. But the legitimacy of the Big Brothers' policy regarding homosexuals is less clear. The organization had difficulty in the past when two homosexual volunteers were accused of molesting young boys, and it seems reasonable for the organization to be concerned about its public image. It is questionable, however, whether it was appropriate for the organization to prohibit all homosexuals from becoming Big Brothers. A more suitable alternative would be to screen prospective volunteers more closely so that any applicant who appeared to pose no threat to the boys could be employed as a Big Brother. Questions concerning the legitimacy of this policy would not, however, justify a decision by Dick Hall to entirely disregard it. The severity of the threat to the *basic* well-being of children and staff is not so great in this case that disobedience would be justifiable. A more appropriate strategy on Dick's part would entail attempting to have the organization's policy changed to allow homosexuals to become Big Brothers and to encourage the establishment of more careful screening procedures. Dick might also consider informing his supervisor that he does not feel that he can in good conscience comply with the agency's policy; agency officials would then need to decide if they were willing to permit Dick to continue working for the agency. Though it may not be an appealing option, Dick also has the option of resigning from the organization if he is not satisfied with its policies. It would not, however, be appropriate for Dick to simply violate the agency's policy without informing agency officials of his intentions.

The Issue of Confidentiality

We must also consider Dick's obligation to keep confidential the information Steve Barber shared with him. Does Dick's promise of confidentiality obligate him to withhold information about Steve's homosexuality from a supervisor? Is it ever permissible to breach a promise of confidentiality?

As I observed earlier, debate concerning the need to honor promises of confidentiality has persisted throughout the history of the social service professions.[10] The most common assumption is that practitioners should hold in confidence any information shared by a client or colleague in the context of a professional relationship. For example, according to the NASW Code of Ethics, "the social worker should respect the privacy of clients and hold in confidence all information obtained in the course of professional service." However, this general prescription is qualified with the statement that "the social worker should share with others confidences revealed by clients, without their consent, only for compelling professional reasons."

There is little doubt that under special circumstances it may be necessary for practitioners to reveal to others information shared in confidence by a client, colleague, or some other third party. But what is the nature of these special circumstances? There are primarily two sets of circumstances under which it may be justifiable to reveal information shared in confidence. In the first, confidential information must be released in order to protect another individual whose safety is threatened. For example, if a client who has been promised confidentiality informs his social worker that he intends to violently harm his estranged wife, the worker would have an obligation to protect the client's wife. The worker should of course initially treat the threat of assault as a clinical issue which requires attention in therapy sessions. However, if the client were to persist in his threat to the point where it appeared that he would carry it out, the worker would be obligated to breach his or her promise of confidentiality. The right of the client's wife to well-being supersedes the client's right to confidentiality (guideline 1) and his right to freedom from interference (guideline 2).

There is not much question that it is permissible to reveal confidential information in order to save someone's life or to protect an individual from serious bodily harm. However, cases where the risk is to an individual's *mental* health are less clear. For example, it may be that Steve Barber's homosexuality does not represent a threat to Jeffrey's physical safety. Given the details provided above, there is no reason to believe that such a danger exists. However, how should we respond to someone who argues that Steve's homosexuality represents a threat to Jeffrey's mental health? Jeffrey is a young boy without a father figure in his life, and Steve's homosexuality may be viewed by some as detrimental to Jeffrey's emotional equilibrium.

Generally it would be wrong to reveal confidential information simply because one thinks that doing so might protect another individual's mental health. There may be extreme circumstances where it seems that only the revelation of confidential information will save someone from deep emotional trauma, and such disclosure may in fact be justifiable. These cases are rare, however. Thus, it would not be permissible for Dick to share information with a supervisor about Steve's homosexuality primarily in order to protect Jeffrey's mental health. There is no compelling evidence that Jeffrey's mental health was seriously threatened because of Steve's sexual preferences.

On what grounds, then, can Dick justify sharing confidential information about Steve's homosexuality with a supervisor? This brings us to the second set of circumstances under which it is permissible to breach a promise of confidentiality. I concluded earlier that it is permissible to lie to a potential killer in order to prevent him or her from endangering another person's life. I argued that a lie under these circumstances is justifiable because the threatened individual's right to well-being (in the form of life itself) takes precedence over the assailant's right to freedom (the right to assault the prospective victim). There is, however, another important reason why it is technically permissible to lie to the assailant, one which is relevant to our concern about confidentiality. Individuals ordinarily have the right to be told the truth, in that truthful information is necessary in order to pursue one's purposes. However, an individual who threatens the safety of another individual interferes with that individual's right to freedom from interference and to well-being and should not be allowed to pursue his or her purposes in this regard. For this reason—because of the proposed interference with the right of another individual to freedom and well-being—the assailant forfeits his right to be told the truth. Hence, it is permissible to lie to the assailant about the target's whereabouts.[11] Similarly, Steve Barber, by failing to tell the truth about his homosexuality at the time of his initial interview, interfered with the organization's attempt (questionable though the policy may have been) to screen applicants who appeared to threaten the welfare of its clients. By failing to respond truthfully, Steve may have forfeited his right to have the fact that he presented false information held in confidence. He obtained his position with Big Brothers under false pretenses and therefore does not necessarily enjoy the right to have the false information he presented about himself kept confidential, despite earlier promises. Similarly, a client who presents false information in order to obtain services does not have a right to assume that a worker who later discovers the deception will keep it confidential. The client may be depriving another individual of needed service because of his misrepresentation, and the worker may have to reveal the substance of a client's confidential disclosure as a result.

One of the important lessons to be learned from this case is that practitioners should avoid providing clients, colleagues, and employers with blanket guarantees of confidentiality. We know from experience that instances can arise which require workers to breach a promise of confidentiality in order to protect another individual's welfare or to act in accord with an agency policy. These instances may occur only rarely, but they do occur, and for this reason practitioners should judiciously avoid giving a client, colleague, or staff member the impression that information shared in the context of a professional relationship will be kept confidential without exception. Such a promise may be difficult to keep at times, and the individuals with whom we work should be made aware of this possibility. This is not to suggest that a worker should, during the beginning stages of each professional relationship, make a formal pronouncement concerning the limits of confidentiality. Introducing such caveats routinely can be both awkward and inappropriate. However, when occasions arise which invite promises of confidentiality, practitioners should be careful to qualify any assurance given. Apprising clients, colleagues, and staff members of the limits of our ability to keep information confidential respects their right to truthful, accurate information and respects the rights of others whose welfare may depend on the disclosure of confidential information.

PRIVILEGED COMMUNICATION

CASE 5.3 Leonard and Audrey Moore had been divorced for about two years. The couple had been married for eight years before separating. Leonard and Audrey's marriage was a strained one from the beginning. The couple decided to get married after Audrey became pregnant with their only child. By the time of the wedding, Audrey and Leonard had known each other for only three months.

Leonard had been employed only sporadically during the first year of the marriage. He eventually found a steady job as a maintenance man for a large apartment complex. According to Audrey, "Things began to settle down after the first year. Leonard was working regularly and we were so excited about our new baby. Even though we had had a rough start, we were beginning to feel like things would work out."

In time, however, Leonard and Audrey's relationship deteriorated. Audrey filed for a divorce, charging that Leonard subjected her to mental cruelty and, on occasion, physical abuse. When the couple divorced, Audrey was given custody of their child, Richie. About a year after the divorce Audrey began seeing a private social worker, Stephanie Haymond, for counseling. Audrey originally explained to Stephanie that she was "nervous a lot of the time" and got "upset much too easily over little things."

Audrey and Stephanie met weekly for about nine months and discussed a range of issues, including Audrey's reaction to the divorce, difficulties she was having raising Richie by herself, and her loneliness. Audrey was especially concerned about her short temper, and she spent quite a bit of time talking with Stephanie about various ways of handling her feelings of frustration.

Nearly nine months after Audrey had begun seeing Stephanie, she received a phone call from Leonard, who said that he wanted custody of Richie, who by then was nine years old. Leonard told Audrey that he did not think she was capable of raising Richie properly. He accused Audrey of being too lenient with their son and of providing inadequate supervision. Leonard told Audrey that he was planning to see a lawyer in order to request a custody hearing.

Several weeks later Audrey received a phone call from a woman, Michelle Curtis, who identified herself as a social worker employed by the county's Family Court to mediate custody disputes. Ms. Curtis explained to Audrey that, as a matter of routine, the court tried to settle custody disputes without having to resort to formal court hearings. She asked Audrey if she would be willing to meet to discuss Leonard's allegations. Ms. Curtis explained that eventually she would probably want to meet with Leonard and Audrey together.

Audrey met with Ms. Curtis and explained in detail why she believed she would be a better parent for Richie than would her former husband. At the conclusion of their conversation, Ms. Curtis told Audrey that after she spoke again with Leonard and after she gathered as much information as she could about the case, she would bring the couple together for a conference.

During the week following her conference with Audrey and Leonard, Ms. Curtis phoned Stephanie Haymond and told her that she was preparing a summary of the case for the court record. Ms. Curtis explained that Leonard had filed some rather serious allegations about Audrey's inability to adequately care for Richie and that it was important for the court to have as much information as possible about Audrey. Ms. Curtis asked Stephanie to meet with her so they could discuss the Moores' problems and the custody dispute. Stephanie told her that she would not feel comfortable meeting unless Audrey approved. Stephanie explained that she considered information shared by Audrey to be confidential and would share it only with Audrey's permission.

Stephanie told Audrey about the conversation she had had and asked Audrey how she felt about Ms. Curtis' request. Audrey became very upset and told Stephanie that she did not want her "to tell that woman at the court what we've talked about here. That's my personal business." Stephanie told Ms. Curtis that she was not willing to discuss information Audrey had revealed in their sessions together, explaining that it was important for her to respect her client's wish for confidentiality. Ms. Curtis responded by telling Stephanie that if she refused to consult with her about Audrey, it would probably be necessary to file a request with a judge to subpoena Stephanie's statement about Audrey's competence as a parent.

It is not uncommon for social workers to have occasion to share with professional colleagues information about a client. In many settings it is accepted practice, and in many instances such sharing seems entirely benign and appropriate. For example, few of us would raise questions about a hospital social worker who spoke in detail with a school social worker about a child who, having been hospitalized for months with a serious illness, is planning to return to school. In such a case we would consider the hospital social worker's professional responsibility to include attempts to provide, with the parent or guardian's permission, information to other professionals who are in a position to help the child make a smooth transfer back to school. Similarly, we would approve of the actions of a social worker in a family service agency who shared information about a client with a supervisor. In general, our convictions about enhancing the continuity and quality of service to clients entail an obligation for social workers to occasionally share information about a client with another worker.

However, we know from experience that in many instances the appropriateness of sharing information about clients with other practitioners is not so clear. Is it appropriate for a social worker in a correctional facility to share details about an inmate's behavior and habits with a practitioner or personnel officer who works for an employer who is considering offering the inmate a job following his or her release? Should a private practitioner who is seeing a client who is having marital difficulties share information with a colleague who is seeing the client's spouse? More particularly, should Stephanie Haymond agree to reveal information about Audrey's abilities as a parent to Michelle Curtis?

Answers to questions about the extent of social workers' obligations to share information with professional colleagues necessarily depend on a careful consideration of the principles of confidentiality and privileged communication and of their place in social work. In general there is a prohibition against releasing to other persons information which has been shared by a client in confidence. As I noted earlier, the NASW Code of Ethics contains the statement "the social worker should respect the privacy of clients and hold in confidence all information obtained in the course of professional service." I also noted, however, that the code recognizes that there may be instances when it is necessary to share information with others, without a client's consent, for "compelling professional reasons." The obvious challenge, of course, is to decide what constitutes compelling professional reasons and what circumstances justify the release of sensitive information to other parties without a client's permission. The criteria we establish in this regard will have important consequences for the nature of social workers' relationships with their professional colleagues (as well as with their clients).

The Right of Privileged Communication

The right of privileged communication has its origins in British common law, under which no gentleman could be required to testify against another in a court of law. Among professionals the attorney-client relationship was the first to be accorded the right of privileged communication. Eventually, other groups of professionals, such as physicians, psychiatrists, psychologists, and even clergymen sought legislation to provide them with this right.[12] Social work is one of the most recent of the professions to pursue such legislation.

The arguments professionals have presented regarding the need for privileged communication have traditionally been based on the assertion that in order for relationships with clients to be effective, clients must be assured that information shared by them will be kept confidential. This is a theme I have touched upon repeatedly. Professionals have argued that they must be protected by statutes from requests to reveal confidential information. In line with this reasoning many states have enacted legislation which permits practitioners to withhold from the courts information shared by a client in confidence. Four conditions, originally proposed by the jurist John Henry Wigmore, are commonly accepted as necessary in order for information to be considered privileged: (1) The communication must originate in a confidence that it will not be disclosed; (2) this element of confidentiality must be essential to the full and satisfactory maintenance of the relationship between the parties; (3) the relation must be one which in the opinion of the community ought to be sedulously fostered; and (4) the injury that would inure to the relation by the disclosure of the communication must be greater than the benefit thereby gained for the correct disposal of litigation.[13]

Regarding the first condition, it is reasonable to assume that most clients expect that information they share with social workers will be kept confidential. As Gordon Hamilton has observed:

> It is part of the attributes of a profession that the nature of the confidential relationship assumes significance. In lay intercourse intimate things are told at the teller's own risk. Under authoritative external pressures or prosecution it is assumed that a person is not obliged to incriminate himself, but in law, medicine, and religion it is imperative for successful treatment that the person put himself unreservedly into the hands of his counselor or practitioner or priest. In a general way this is true of social work, and as profes-

sional competence has increasingly developed skill in the interviewing process, the client tends to yield himself fully, trusting in the worker's understanding and skill to help him.[14]

It is a central tenet in social work practice that effective casework depends on a client's willingness to trust the worker with the most personal details of his or her life and that such trust is necessary for, as Wigmore's second condition states, "the full and satisfactory maintenance of the relationship between the parties." It has long been assumed among psychiatrists, psychologists, family counselors, and social workers that unless clients are able to assume that information shared with practitioners will be held in confidence, the effectiveness of the therapeutic relationship will necessarily be inhibited. Further, the assumption that relations between clients and practitioners are important and valuable is generally accepted by the community at large, thus meeting Wigmore's third criterion. The fourth condition, that the injury caused by disclosure of confidential information is greater than the benefit gained from disclosure, is ordinarily the most difficult to satisfy and stimulates the greatest debate.

Over the years, courts have identified a number of exceptions to the client's right of privileged communication. A number of these exceptions pertains to judicial proceedings, such as when a client introduces in court the fact that he or she has received counseling for emotional problems resulting from an accident that has led to a suit for damages, or when a social worker's testimony about a client is required in order to defend him- or herself against a suit filed by the client. Disclosure of privileged information may also be appropriate in cases where a client threatens to violently injure an identifiable third party (or the therapist), when a client threatens to commit suicide, when information is shared in the presence of a third person, or when a minor is the subject of a custody dispute, is involved in criminal activity, or has apparently been abused or neglected. Because statutes differ from state to state and because case law sometimes is inconsistent, social workers would be wise to consult with an attorney to determine the status of a particular client's right to privileged communication.[15]

Benefits and Costs

Our beliefs about the relative benefits and costs of disclosure of confidential information ultimately determine decisions we reach about revealing this information. As I noted earlier, the need to reveal confidential information is quite clear in some cases, and ambiguous in others:

> Against these facts and speculation as to the harm that results from forced disclosure and the frequency with which disclosure occurs, society's interest in the correct disposal of litigation must be balanced. That interest is obviously great, but does not seem to have a constant value, i.e., society as a whole has a greater interest in the correct disposal of a charge of murder than it has in a charge of peace disturbance arising from a marital quarrel. Thus the answer to Wigmore's fourth requirement can be viewed as depending upon the facts of the particular case rather than a predetermined evaluation. For example, the correct disposal of the murder charge probably outweighs any injury that would inure to the social worker-client relation. But the desirability of preserving a marriage of thirty years seems to override the benefit which would be gained by the correct disposal of the charge of peace disturbance.[16]

It may be that many of us would agree with this conclusion. The importance of resolving a charge of murder does seem to take precedence over resolving a charge of peace disturbance, considering the threats to basic well-being each charge entails. But what of the case involving Audrey Moore and Stephanie Haymond? Is it clear whether the importance of the court proceeding involving custody of Richie requires that Stephanie honor Michelle Curtis' request for information which Audrey insists be kept confidential?

The interests of several individuals must be taken into account as we consider the extent of Stephanie's obligation to keep the information Audrey has shared with her confidential. First, there are Audrey's interests. If Stephanie discloses personal information about Audrey to the court, Audrey may suffer embarrassment and may lose custody of her child, depending upon how the information is interpreted. Second, Audrey's husband, Leonard, has interests which need to be considered. Leonard has claimed that Richie is being raised improperly; from his point of view it is essential that information about Audrey's abilities as a parent be revealed by Stephanie. Third, Stephanie may be affected by a decision to disclose information about a client. If knowledge of her disclosure becomes known, her relationships with her current and future clients may suffer, and she may have difficulty attracting new clients. The individual whose interests are most relevant in this case, however, are clearly Richie's. By virtue of his age and his status as a minor, his rights to freedom and well-being are the most vulnerable. It may be that his mother's actions and abilities as a parent are not at all questionable. However, allegations—though they are perhaps without foundation—have been raised about Audrey's abilities as a parent and must be considered diligently. For this reason any conclusion we reach about Stephanie's obligation to reveal confidential information shared by Audrey must be based *primarily* on consideration of the likely consequences for Richie.

Judicial Discretion

The primary—and by all means legitimate—interest of the court in this case is to investigate and judge the validity of Leonard Moore's claim that Audrey is not an adequate parent for their son. Ms. Curtis opened the case appropriately by interviewing both parents in order to obtain information about their respective backgrounds and the history of their relationship. During the course of her interview with Audrey, she learned that Audrey had been seeing a therapist during the preceding nine months. Ms. Curtis realized that Stephanie Haymond, a professional colleague, might be able to provide relevant information about Audrey's abilities as a parent.

In principle there is nothing objectionable about Ms. Curtis' efforts to gather as much information as she possibly can about Audrey Moore's activities as a mother. It appears, however, that in asking Stephanie Haymond to disclose information Audrey shared with her in confidence during the course of their professional relationship, Ms. Curtis may have acted inappropriately. This suggests that the analysis of this case must take into account not only the extent of Stephanie's obligation to withhold or disclose confidential information but also the legitimacy of Ms. Curtis' initial request.

I have observed repeatedly that in rare instances it may be necessary for social workers to violate a client's right to confidentiality in order to protect another individual's right to basic well-being. This is consistent with the conclusion that one duty takes precedence over another if the good that is related to the former duty (protecting someone's life or basic well-being) is more necessary for the possibility of action and if the right to that good cannot be protected without violating the latter duty (withholding confidential information). In this respect, Stephanie certainly would have had an obligation to inform the court about Audrey's abilities as a parent *if* she had substantial evidence to indicate that Richie's life or health were threatened by Audrey's care or lack of care (guideline 1). It was not the case, however, that Stephanie had any such evidence, and she was therefore under no obligation to disclose the content of her meetings with Audrey or any other information about her client to Michelle Curtis. It would have been appropriate for Stephanie to explain to Ms. Curtis that she was aware of her obligation as a social worker to reveal confidential information under extreme circumstances, but that there was no evidence that the circumstances in the case involving the Moore family were extreme.

Ms. Curtis, on the other hand, should not have asked Stephanie to disclose confidential information about a client during the course of her routine investigation, unless she had evidence that Richie's basic well-being was seriously threatened. If she did in fact have reason to believe that Richie's basic welfare was at stake, it would have been appropriate for her to have sought a court order requesting such information. Without such evidence, however, her request invites violation of Audrey's right to confidentiality and to privileged communication.

It is conceivable that Ms. Curtis' assessment of the threat to Richie's welfare conflicted with Stephanie's assessment. From Ms. Curtis' point of view it may have seemed necessary for Stephanie to disclose information about Audrey; from Stephanie's vantage point such disclosure may have seemed both unnecessary and inappropriate. Under such circumstances, where the professional opinions of two colleagues conflict about the need to disclose confidential information, it may be necessary to submit the relevant facts to a judge who is authorized to rule on the disagreement. Such a ruling could be obtained, for example, during the course of the custody hearing.

Responding to Court Orders

A social worker in Stephanie Haymond's position might face an additional dilemma if she were subpoenaed or if the court were to rule that information about a client should be disclosed. If the social worker practices in a state where laws grant the right of privileged communication, he or she may be able to avoid complying with the subpoena. Contrary to common belief, it is possible to respond to a subpoena with arguments that the requested information should not be disclosed.[17] A subpoena itself does not require a practitioner to disclose information. It is essentially a request for information, frequently lacking compelling justification. According to Maurice Grossman: "If the recipient knew how easy it was to have a subpoena issued; if he knew how readily the subpoena could demand information when there actually was no legal right to command the disclosure of information; if he knew how often an individual releases information that legally he had no right to release because of intimidation—he would view the threat of the subpoena with less fear and greater skepticism."[18]

It is possible, however, that despite a practitioner's attempts to resist disclosure of confidential information, a court of law will formally order the social worker to reveal this information. This may occur even in states which accord the clients of social workers the right of privileged communication. For example, in New York State a social worker whose client was presumably protected by the right of privileged communication was ordered to testify in a paternity suit after the court ruled that "disclosure of evidence relevant to a correct determination of paternity was of greater importance than any injury which might inure to relationship between social worker and his clients if such admission was disclosed."[19] This case clearly demonstrates the difficulty of arriving at unequivocal interpretations of Wigmore's fourth condition for considering information privileged.[20]

If it should evolve that a social worker in Stephanie Haymond's position were ordered to testify in court and reveal confidential information, the practitioner would have to make a difficult choice between complying with the order and being held in contempt of court. A worker is not obliged to face contempt charges and possible incarceration in lieu of testifying in court, and each practitioner does have the option to decide not to testify. It is important to recognize, however, that a worker who agrees to testify in court is not necessarily required to disclose any and all information revealed by a client during the course of their professional relationship. A practitioner can still do his or her best to convince the court that certain requested information is not sufficiently relevant to warrant disclosure. Stephanie, for example, could argue that she is aware of no evidence based on her relationship with Audrey which indicates that Richie's basic well-being is threatened because of Audrey's behavior as a parent. The court may not accept her judgment and may press for additional information. However, it is permissible for Stephanie to try to withhold information she firmly believes to be irrelevant to the custody dispute.

An important additional point is that a social worker in Michelle Curtis' position should do her best to gather information about cases assigned to her without requesting professional colleagues to reveal confidential information. On occasion valuable and relevant information can be obtained from third parties. The extent of a practitioner's obligation to reveal confidential information may in fact be viewed by the court as a function of the availability of information from other sources. According to Suanna Wilson: "When data sought by the court can be obtained through some other source, a professional who has been subpoenaed may not have to disclose his confidential data. If the practitioner freely relinquishes his confidential though non-privileged data with little or no objection, the courts may not even check to see if the information can be obtained elsewhere. If the professional resists disclosure, however, the court may investigate to see if it can get the data from some other source."[21]

The temptation to share information about clients with professional colleagues is often strong. In many instances it is entirely appropriate to exchange such information with colleagues. Attempts to maintain continuity and quality of service frequently require a social worker to transfer information about a client to another practitioner who is planning to become involved in the client's life. Social workers also need to be able to share information with supervisors who are providing consultation on cases. These are instances when there is little question about the legitimacy of sharing relevant information. But it is important to realize that there are limits on the extent to which practitioners should permit themselves the freedom to share information about clients with others. Under other than extreme circumstances (such as when serious harm or life itself is threatened or when a court of law orders certain information to be revealed) disclosure of confidential information should be made only with the client's informed consent. The principle of privileged communication is important to uphold in order to enhance the quality of the social worker-client relationship; clients must be able to trust that social workers will not indiscriminately share sensitive information about them with others. The client's right to confidentiality is also important to uphold because clients have at least a prima facie right (though perhaps not always an actual right) to it.

THE USE OF DECEPTION

CASE 5.4 The Committee for the Improvement of Government had been operating in the city for approximately five years. Its primary mission was to serve as a watchdog of local government practices and procedures. During the life of the organization the CIG had carried out a number of major investigations which had uncovered a considerable amount of abuse of public funds, fraud, and other illegal practices. One of the investigations documented the fact that a number of the city's building inspectors were overlooking serious fire code violations in exchange for substantial payoffs. In another investigation CIG staff exposed rampant violations of standard medical practice in a group of private, profit-making abortion clinics throughout the city.

In each of these investigations the CIG was able to arrange to have members of its own staff employed undercover by the agency or firms under investigation or placed in other strategic positions which allowed for the gathering of evidence that would otherwise be unavailable. In the investigation of bribe-taking by city building inspectors, for example, the CIG placed several of its staff undercover in establishments which were required to be inspected, such as newly renovated restaurants. In several instances CIG staff actually negotiated bribes with city inspectors and recorded the transactions on film. In the investigation of the medical practices carried out in the private abortion clinics several CIG staff were hired as nurse's aides, without informing their employers of their affiliation with the CIG. In their capacity as staff of the abortion clinics the CIG staff witnessed and documented substantial mistreatment and abuse of patients.

The results of these CIG investigations were well publicized and widely applauded. Many of the city building inspectors who took part in bribes were fired or disciplined. Agency administrators throughout the city began to monitor licensing and other activities much more closely. The abortion clinics found to be in violation of state law were closed, and state licensing procedures for such private clinics were revised and made more stringent. It was generally believed that the CIG investigations had done much to expose serious abuses being carried out unchallenged throughout the city.

Ruth Arnsparger was a social worker employed by the CIG. She had not been directly involved in any of the earlier undercover investigations. Most of her time was spent researching state and local legislation relevant to ongoing investigations. One afternoon Ruth was asked to meet with the associate director of the CIG, Miriam Flanagan, to discuss plans for a new investigation which was in the early stages of development. Ms. Flanagan explained to Ruth that in recent months the CIG staff had obtained information which suggested that there were serious problems with the treatment of clients by staff of the state Department of Social Services, the agency responsible for handling reported cases of dependency and neglect. It was well-known around the state that the department had for years been having difficulty managing its caseload. There were frequent allegations that cases of abuse were reported to the department but never responded to, that children were being placed in unlicensed group and foster homes, that records for a number of children in foster care could not be located, and that the department was reimbursing private service providers for services which were never rendered. A new commissioner had been hired to run the department a year earlier but, according to Ms. Flanagan, there was still substantial evidence of widespread problems.

Ms. Flanagan explained to Ruth that the CIG had recently received a grant from a private foundation to conduct a study of the quality of care provided to the clients of the Department of Social Services. She explained that the CIG administrative staff had decided that for the investigation to be successful, it would be necessary to place a staff member in the department in a capacity that would allow him or her to gather information relevant to department practices. She told Ruth that a CIG employee who formerly worked for the Department of Social Services had been able to arrange to have a CIG staff member hired as an administrative aide in the office of the assistant commissioner for programs. No one in the Department of Social Services would be aware of the employee's affiliation with the CIG. Ms. Flanagan explained that after considerable thought she and the director of the CIG had decided that Ruth should fill the position in the department.

Ruth responded that she had never really thought about becoming directly involved in the undercover aspects of a CIG investigation. She told Ms. Flanagan that the idea of working in the Department of Social Services under false pretenses made her feel a little uncomfortable, though she could see the importance of the investigation, given the reported problems in the department. Ruth said that she needed a day to think about the offer.

There is something in most of us which resists the idea of deliberately engaging in deceptive practices in order to achieve our purposes as social workers. Though our ends may be noble, there is something repugnant about using ignoble means such as lying or manipulation in order to reach them. The importance of being "honest" and "above board" in the practice of social work has long been revered. Many of us encounter circumstances during the course of our careers, however, which lead us to wonder if in some rare instances it might not be permissible to use some form of deception in order to bring about clearly desirable results. The practitioner whose seriously disturbed client is on a waiting list for hospitalization might wonder if it would be appropriate to exaggerate somewhat the client's symptoms in order to expedite admission. Or a director of a private agency might wonder if it is permissible to slightly overstate the accomplishments of his or her staff in order to secure funding necessary to keep the agency afloat.

The Legitimacy of Deceptive Practice

Arguments about the legitimacy of deception resemble arguments about the legitimacy of lying or other instances of reporting false information to others. Throughout history moral philosophers have argued that such practices are wrong. This is not surprising. Yet there has nonetheless been persistent debate between those moral philosophers who claim that under no circumstances is deception or lying permissible and those who claim that while these practices are generally unacceptable, there are rare instances when they are justifiable. According to the former, the deceptive practices engaged in by staff of the Committee for the Improvement of Government are never permissible, regardless of the desirability or appeal of the possible (or even likely) outcomes. According to the latter, deceptive practices carried out by staff of the CIG might be justifiable, depending on the amount and, perhaps, distribution of good that would result. What we have here, of course, is the standard conflict between deontologists, who believe it is necessary to abide by certain rules and values as a matter of principle, and teleologists, who claim that the rightness of any given action should be determined by the goodness of its consequences.

Immanuel Kant and the early Christian church father and philosopher Saint Augustine are well-known for their classic arguments in support of the view that deception is never permissible, regardless of the anticipated consequences. According to Augustine, the individual who engages in deceptive acts is defiled or tainted by the deception, regardless of the merits or demerits of the deception.[22] For Kant, deception or lying is wrong because "it is a perversion of one's uniquely human capacities irrespective of any consequences of the lie, and thus lying is not only intrinsically bad but wrong."[23]

This position contrasts sharply with that of strict utilitarians. According to Bentham, for example, deception is not necessarily wrong or even intrinsically bad: "Falsehood, take it by itself, consider it as not being accompanied by any other material circumstances, nor therefore productive of any material effects, can never, upon the principle of utility, constitute any offense at all."[24] For utilitarians deception and lying are wrong only to the extent that undesirable or bad consequences follow.

Deception in Social Work

The use of deception in social work has assumed a variety of forms. In general, though, deceptive practices have been primarily of two kinds. One has involved instances when it has seemed necessary, or at least advantageous, for a worker to deceive in order to advance the interests of a client, a colleague, the agency, or, more directly, him- or herself. Providing false information in order to gain or expedite the delivery of services, as I noted earlier, is not uncommon in practice. Providing false information in order to protect a colleague or to gain employment for oneself are also possible. In most instances we believe such tactics to be wrong on the grounds that individuals have a prima facie right to be told the truth. We know, however, that on occasion deception may be permissible, such as when it is necessary in order to prevent a client from seriously injuring or killing another person.

The second kind of deception which has been engaged in periodically in social work involves the gathering of information thought to be necessary for professional purposes. At one extreme are instances in which a researcher carrying out a formal study has believed it necessary to deceive research subjects in order to obtain valid and reliable data. For example, a practitioner who is interested in studying whether various leadership styles in group therapy affect patterns of interaction among members might resist telling the group about the study because of the likelihood that this would affect their behavior. Informing the group members of the hypothesis may represent a serious threat to the internal validity of the social worker's study.[25] As a result, the worker may believe that it is necessary to withhold information about her intentions from the group or provide them with a fabricated explanation of her treatment methods. Similarly, a researcher who is interested in comparing the effects of a voucher system and cash payments on the types of services and goods purchased by public aid recipients may not want to provide the subjects with a candid explanation of the purposes of the study in order to avoid biasing the results. It is not uncommon for practitioners and researchers who attempt to gather information or carry out a study to find themselves in a position where it seems that some degree of deception—either in the form of withholding information or deliberately providing false information—is necessary in order to ensure the validity of the results. This predicament is frequently encountered in the context of formal research studies. As the case involving Ruth Arnsparger and the Committee for the Improvement of Government illustrates, questions about the need for deception also arise in the context of somewhat less formal or scientific attempts to gather information.

Debate concerning the use of deception in research has a relatively short but eventful history. Some of the most intense controversy has arisen out of the famous study conducted by Stanley Milgram in 1963 concerning the limits of individuals' willingness to obey authority, a study of considerable importance to those interested in preventing an occurrence of holocaust-like experiences.[26] One of the experimental procedures designed by Milgram forced research subjects to administer what they believed to be increasingly severe electric shocks to another person. Each subject was told that he was playing the role of "teacher" in an experiment about learning. The subject was asked to administer an electric shock to another person (the "learner") whenever this person made an error. The "teacher" was instructed to increase the intensity of the shocks progressively from 15 volts to 450 volts. The "learner" was not actually shocked; he was a confederate in the experiment who was instructed to cry out in pain and to convulse as the level of the shock was increased. Thus, the research subjects were asked to further punish individuals who already appeared to be suffering. Milgram found that most of the research subjects complied with the experimenter's instructions despite the learner's apparent suffering. In Milgram's landmark study only 14 out of 40 subjects refused to complete the entire series of shocks; 26 of the subjects administered the maximum 450 volts.

As one would expect, Milgram's research generated considerable debate about the use of deception. A common concern has been that studies which rely on deception frequently place subjects under substantial psychological pressure.[27] Another argument against the use of deception has been that its use encourages the promotion of distrust and suspicion among people. According to Diener and Crandall, "deception may be adding to a cynical trend toward treating other people as objects to be used and manipulated. Deceptions that endanger traditional role relationships have very strong negative effects on society."[28] This statement appears to be a contemporary version of Kant's famous statement that "man and generally any rational being exists as an end in himself, not merely as a means to be arbitrarily used by this or that will, but in all his actions, whether they concern himself or other rational beings, must be always regarded at the same time as an end."[29] It has also been argued that engaging in deceptive practices in order to gather information can affect the well-being of the practitioner or researcher responsible for the effort. One claim is that the use of deception may lead one to view people as objects to be manipulated. A second is that the practitioner or researcher may later suffer guilt as a result of the deception.[30]

In response to such concerns, a number of authors has claimed that deception is justifiable on the grounds that it is frequently not possible to obtain important information in any other way. As Diener and Crandall observe: "The case for research deception can be summarized as follows: Because of practical, methodological, and moral considerations, much research would be difficult or impossible to carry out without deception. Important knowledge gained in the past would have been forfeited had the practice been totally abandoned. . . . As long as deception is practiced within the well-understood and circumscribed limits of research and no one is harmed, it is not unethical, and in fact it has been employed in some outstanding studies."[31] Proponents of the use of deception clearly take a teleological point of view when they argue that the results of studies based on deception can justify its use.

The Need for Disguised Observation

As I have already acknowledged, it may on rare occasions be necessary for social workers to use some degree of deception in order to gather needed information. It is important for us, however, to think carefully about the distinction between cases where deception is justifiable because of the circumstances involved and cases where it is both unnecessary and inappropriate.

It should be clear from the course of the discussion thus far that the critical variable to consider is the nature of the likely consequences of deception and those which are likely when we avoid its use. As always, consequences as they pertain to individuals' rights to freedom and well-being should be the focus of our attention. For example, there are good reasons to believe that it was permissible for the CIG to place staff in private abortion clinics to gather information about alleged abuses. Evidence presented to the CIG suggested that the health of a number of patients served by the clinics was being placed in serious jeopardy by a series of questionable medical practices. Detailed information about the quality of care being provided was not available from either public records or owners or employees of the clinics. The CIG's strategy seems permissible primarily because of the severity of the threat to the basic well-being of patients and because information needed to document abuses was not accessible by other means. It is unfortunate that deception needed to be used in order to gather relevant information, but such tactics, under such circumstances, seem justifiable because of the threat to patients' well-being. The duty to prevent harm to the health of these women must take precedence over the duty not to engage in deceptive practices, if it appears that the former duty can be fulfilled only by violating the latter (guideline 1).

This is in contrast to a case where, for example, a worker is planning to engage in deception in order to advance his own interests in obtaining a job promotion. The use of deception (such as falsifying employment records or credentials) would not be justified in this instance because the rights which would be violated as a result (that is, the right clients have to be served by practitioners who are qualified to fill a position and the right employers have to truthful information and to enforce personnel policies staff have voluntarily agreed to adhere to) take precedence over an individual's right to act deceptively in order to advance his or her own interests. Few would disagree with these conclusions. However, what do we believe is right and wrong when we consider a case which is less clear-cut, such as the dilemma faced by Ruth Arnsparger? What criteria should guide Ruth's decision about the rightness of accepting a position in the Department of Social Services under false pretenses in order to gather information about the quality of care and services provided by its staff?

Several criteria can be justified by the guidelines I have developed regarding individuals' rights to freedom and well-being and the duties which accompany these rights. First, Ruth must consider the extent to which the welfare of the clients served by the Department of Social Services depends upon the disclosure of information which might be obtained through the use of deception. According to staff of the CIG, staff of the department had been guilty of failing to respond to reported cases of abuse, placing children in unlicensed group and foster homes, not having records for a number of children who had been placed in foster care, and mismanaging departmental funds. To be sure, these charges suggest the possibility that there were very serious threats to the welfare of children and families served by the department. If the evidence were strong, there is reason to believe that deception may have been justifiable if it appeared likely that disclosure of agency practices would have helped remedy the department's problems. This brings us to a second condition which must be considered in order to justify the use of deception. It must not only appear that the severity of threats to individuals' welfare is such that deception is necessary in order to gather relevant information; there must also be a strong likelihood that the release of information obtained through deceptive means will in fact diminish the threat to the welfare of these individuals. Gathering information deceptively when there is little chance that release of it will substantially affect whatever threat exists would be wrong.

It may appear, for example, that the release of information Ruth might obtain would bring a great deal of pressure to bear on the Department of Social Services to clean its house and alter its inappropriate services. It is conceivable, however, that release of Ruth's information would not serve to goad the department to make necessary changes. It is also possible that adverse public reaction to publicity about the CIG's use of deception would dilute the impact of the organization's report and allegations.

Third, it would be important for Ruth to consider whether other, more legitimate means might be used to gather information about practices in the Department of Social Services. In many public social service agencies, for example, information about the expenditure of funds and the licensing of facilities is a matter of public record. It is quite possible that staff of the CIG could have gathered much of the desired information without resorting to deception. It may have been necessary to persevere in order to sidestep the variety of bureaucratic roadblocks which frequently frustrate attempts to obtain such information, but perseverance is to be preferred to deception whenever it is likely to reveal the information one needs. It is possible that in some instances certain relevant information is not available to the public and that to obtain it, one may feel compelled to use some degree of deception. Information about bribes paid to city building inspectors and about the mistreatment of patients in abortion clinics are examples. However, deception should be resorted to in only the most extreme of circumstances. The individuals with whom we have professional relationships also have rights not to be intentionally misled by contrived statements of intent. False information conveyed by an individual employed under false pretenses can interfere with the legitimate pursuits of colleagues. The rights our colleagues have not to be deceived, except under the most extreme circumstances, is very much akin to the rights individuals have not to be lied to. We ought ultimately to be guided by what Sissela Bok has referred to as the principle of veracity: "Such a principle need not indicate that all lies should be ruled out by the initial negative weight given to them, nor does it even suggest which lies should be prohibited. But it does make at least one immediate limitation on lying: in any situation where a lie is a possible choice, one must first seek truthful alternatives."[32]

WHISTLE-BLOWING

CASE 5.5 Jill Palmer was a caseworker at the state Department of Public Aid. She was one of eight caseworkers who staffed a branch office of the department. Her primary responsibility was to interview applicants for public aid, determine eligibility, and monitor clients who were receiving assistance. Jill had worked for the department for only four months; this was her first job after graduating from college. She had spent several months trying to find a job in an art museum, since she had majored in art history. Eventually, however, Jill gave up the idea of finding a job in her field and accepted the job at the Department of Public Aid.

Before long Jill began to feel frustrated in her position. She felt overwhelmed by the intricacy and detail of departmental regulations and found it difficult to tolerate the bureaucratic idiosyncrasies she frequently had to negotiate. She was also bothered by the insensitivity and cynicism of many of her coworkers. It seemed to Jill that her colleagues had very little patience for the difficulties many of the department's clients had.

What bothered Jill more than anything else was the inadequacy of the benefits available to many of the clients on her caseload. She knew that a few of her clients were not in dire need of public assistance and were taking advantage of loopholes in the welfare system. But Jill also knew that many of her clients lacked the skills, health, or ability to make ends meet and had a great deal of difficulty living off of the amount of aid current regulations permitted them to receive. Many of her clients were single mothers who complained that at the end of almost every month they were unable to feed their children adequately.

Jill shared her frustrations with one of her coworkers, Marilyn Robinson, during lunch one day. Marilyn had been a caseworker at the department for nearly three years and told Jill that she was well aware of the weaknesses and inequities embedded in the welfare regulations. Marilyn told Jill that during her first year in the department she performed her job "by the book," approving and denying benefits exactly as departmental policy required, but that when she realized how rigid and arbitrary many of the regulations were, she decided that she would begin to "bend" the regulations whenever they did not permit her to authorize a level of benefits which a client needed. She told Jill in detail about the various ways she had been able to work around the department's guidelines. Marilyn explained that she would occasionally overlook income she knew a client was receiving. For example, a number of Marilyn's clients worked as domestics and received wages in cash. Since there was no record of the income submitted to the Internal Revenue Service, Marilyn did not have to worry about a discrepancy ever appearing between records in the department and the IRS. Marilyn also explained to Jill that she would at times ignore the fact that a client was receiving support from her children's father, although according to regulations, caseworkers were required to adjust benefits in such cases. Marilyn told Jill that she regretted that the current welfare code forced her to violate certain guidelines, but that many of her clients simply would not have their needs met if she did not overlook some of the department's regulations.

The following week Marilyn excitedly told Jill that Marilyn had been recommended for promotion to casework supervisor. The promotion would mean a considerable increase in responsibility for Marilyn as well as an increase in salary. She would be responsible for supervising the office's caseworkers and would serve as a liaison between the office and central administration. Jill told Marilyn that she was very happy for her and asked when the decision would be made. Marilyn explained that she had to have an interview with the regional director first and would then have her file reviewed by the department's director of personnel.

Jill had the feeling that in most respects Marilyn would be an effective supervisor. But she was bothered by the fact that Marilyn might have responsibility for monitoring and enforcing department regulations she herself had been deliberately violating. Jill wondered if she should make the regional director or director of personnel aware of the fact that Marilyn had not been adhering to many of the department's guidelines and might not, in her capacity as casework supervisor, abide by them in the future.

According to the NASW Code of Ethics, "The social worker should not participate in, condone, or be associated with dishonesty, fraud, deceit, or misrepresentation" and "should take action through appropriate channels against unethical conduct by any other member of the profession." According to these prescriptions, it appears that Jill Palmer was obligated to report Marilyn's violations of departmental guidelines to a supervisor. However, the Code of Ethics also states that "The social worker should respect confidences shared by colleagues in the course of their professional relationships and transactions." Can this latter guideline be interpreted to mean that Jill was obliged to keep confidential the information Marilyn had shared with her? The Code of Ethics further asserts that "The social worker should act to prevent practices that are inhumane or discriminatory against any person or group of persons." Is it not possible to argue from Marilyn's point of view that welfare regulations failed to provide many clients with the level of assistance they needed and that, as a result, it was permissible for Marilyn to violate certain regulations of the Department of Public Aid in order to meet the needs of her clients? Once again we encounter an apparent conflict between the courses of action implied by several ethical guidelines.

The Need for Whistle-Blowing

It is not unusual for employees in both public and private organizations to encounter, accidentally or otherwise, information which indicates that colleagues have violated agency policy or a law or have engaged in some other indiscretion. Practitioners who become aware of wrongdoing by colleagues frequently, however, have difficulty deciding on a course of action. On the surface it may appear that a practitioner is obligated to report any violation of a policy or law to a supervisor or to some other responsible authority. As we have seen repeatedly, however, it is rarely possible to apply such a prescription uniformly to all cases without considering the merits of competing arguments. For example, it is not unheard of for an employee to become aware of violations of policy or law engaged in by a supervisor. Reporting such wrongdoing to a higher authority would almost certainly strain the worker's relationship with his or her supervisor and could very well jeopardize his or her own job. The dilemma becomes even more complicated when the suspected wrongdoer is a personal friend. No doubt these were thoughts that ran through Jill Palmer's mind as she pondered her obligation to share with a supervisor what Marilyn had told her about violating regulations of the Department of Public Aid.

There is little question that social workers have an obligation to report instances of wrongdoing when the violations of policy or law seriously threaten the welfare of others. For example, a practitioner who obtains evidence that a colleague is embezzling public funds which were to be used to provide emergency medical care to indigents would certainly have an obligation to report the offense. The severity of the threat to the basic well-being of the individuals whose medical care the funds were intended to purchase would require one to report the fraud. Similarly, a practitioner who discovers that several staff members in a group home for adolescents have abused several residents would have an obligation to make appropriate authorities aware of her evidence. The rights colleagues have to confidentiality must be overridden in such instances because of the seriousness of the threat to the well-being of the victims (guideline 1). A decision to report wrongdoing must rest, of course, on substantial evidence that seem incontrovertible.

Ambiguous Cases

In many instances it will not seem clear whether a practitioner has an obligation to report wrongdoing. The extent of injury others are exposed to because of the wrongdoings may be difficult to assess, the available evidence may not be conclusive, or the personal risk for the worker who obtains the evidence may seem too substantial. In such cases, where the obligation to report wrongdoing is not clear, social workers must make their decisions based on several considerations. First, as always, the severity of the threat to the well-being of the apparent victims must be a prime consideration. It would not be necessary, for example, for a social worker to report to a supervisor that a colleague has taken an extended lunch hour if this were an isolated incident and dire consequences for the colleague's clients did not result. The strain and ill will which would most likely follow such a report could very well have more damaging consequences for the agency's clients because of the disruption of working relationships among agency staff than would ignoring the incident. Clearly, the violation of certain agency rules does not warrant whistle-blowing.

A second consideration involves the nature of the evidence available concerning the alleged wrongdoing. A social worker may have only circumstantial evidence or evidence based on hearsay that a violation of a law or agency policy has occurred. A practitioner could make a very serious mistake if he or she alleged wrongdoing based on evidence that is ambiguous and disputable. Working relationships among staff in an agency can suffer irreparable damage if allegations are proved to be unfounded. Professional reputations can also suffer substantial harm.

It is also important for social workers who believe that they have discovered wrongdoing to attempt to distinguish between actions of colleagues which appear to have *broken* rules and those which appear to have *bent* them. It is not possible to construct rules and regulations which provide clear, unequivocal guides to the decisions social workers need to make in practice day to day. Social work is sufficiently complex that it is not possible to derive rules and regulations which take into account the unique characteristics of the many cases professionals encounter in practice. Discretion is to be expected and encouraged. The problem, however, is that what appears to one practitioner as an instance of rule breaking may appear to another as nothing more than rule bending of a sort many professionals believe is appropriate. It is quite possible, for example, that Marilyn Robinson viewed her actions as instances of rule bending. Her position as a social worker in a public agency obligated her to assist poor individuals in their attempts to obtain needed aid. For Marilyn, it may have seemed entirely justifiable, perhaps even obligatory, for her to overlook some of the details about her clients' lives in order to enable them to subsist. To Jill or to some other observer, however, Marilyn's actions may have constituted rule breaking.

Decisions to bend rules in order to accommodate client needs may at times be justifiable and within the boundaries of sound professional discretion. However, a blatant violation of regulations by an employee who, at the time he or she was hired, voluntarily agreed to abide by them is almost never permissible. If the consequences of the broken rule pose a serious threat to others, and if there is substantial evidence that the wrongdoing has in fact occurred, a social worker is ordinarily obligated to report the violation to a supervisor or some other appropriate authority.

Before a practitioner decides to report a colleague for violating a law or policy, he or she should consider carefully whether the wrongdoing might be remedied in a way that would not require disclosure to an agency official. As Fleishman and Payne observe, "There may be other ways to do right . . . than by blowing a whistle on a friend. A direct personal confrontation may serve both public interest and personal loyalty, if the corrupt practice can be ended and adequate restitution made."[33] For example, a social worker who discovers that a colleague has requested reimbursement for travel expenses that were not actually incurred might first approach the colleague and suggest that he or she withdraw the expense vouchers or make restitution. Whenever possible, a social worker should first approach the colleague who is suspected of wrongdoing in order to give the colleague an opportunity to defend or deny the alleged violation of law or policy. If the colleague denies any wrongdoing, the social worker will need to decide whether it is incumbent upon him or her to report the alleged wrongdoing by considering the severity of the apparent violation, the severity of harm it poses to others, and the reliability of the available evidence. If the colleague admits the wrongdoing, the worker will need to decide whether he or she is satisfied with the colleague's proposed solution. If the colleague agrees to report the wrongdoing him- or herself, the worker may be absolved of any further responsibility. If the colleague does not agree to report or remedy the wrongdoing, the worker will have to decide whether the circumstances are such that he or she should report the available evidence to an agency official.

For example, if Marilyn denied her past violations of department regulations, Jill may have been obligated to make a supervisor aware of the information Marilyn shared with her. It would have been entirely inappropriate for Marilyn to have assumed supervisory responsibilities when she herself had not acknowledged the importance of abiding by department regulations and had in fact condoned violating them. The public has a right to be served by administrators who adhere to regulations drafted by government agencies. It is possible, however, that Marilyn might have acknowledged her past violations and agreed to withdraw her name from consideration for the position of supervisor. Or she might have acknowledged her past violations and assured Jill that in the future she would abide by and enforce department regulations if she were offered the promotion to supervisor. Jill would then have to decide whether Marilyn should be given an opportunity to perform conscientiously as a supervisor or whether she should be denied the opportunity because of her questionable performance in the past. Jill would have to make this decision based on her judgment of Marilyn's sincerity and on her impressions about whether Marilyn deliberately broke department regulations or bent them believing that social workers are permitted such discretion. It would have been a serious mistake if Marilyn had become a casework supervisor firmly believing that it is appropriate for caseworkers to break department regulations. If this were Marilyn's professed point of view, Jill would have been obligated to share the information she had about Marilyn's past violations in an attempt to prevent her from being appointed as a supervisor.

Throughout her deliberations, it would have been important for Jill to be cognizant of her own motives for contemplating blowing the whistle on her colleague. It is imperative that any attempt to report a colleague for wrongdoing be based on a sincere concern for the welfare of those who stand to be harmed by the wrongdoing. Whistle blowing is sometimes an act of vengeance, growing out of resentment for past wrongs perpetrated on a worker by a colleague. We may personally resent misdeeds committed by colleagues in the past; however, reporting a colleague to a supervisor for wrongdoing should not be motivated by a desire for retribution. Rather, any attempt to expose a colleague who has apparently violated a law or policy should be pursued primarily because of the gravity of the wrongdoing and because of the threat it poses to the welfare of others.

Protecting Oneself

A social worker assumes considerable risk when he or she contemplates blowing the whistle on a colleague. On the one hand there is the strain and tension that is likely to pervade one's personal relationship with the colleague. Further, there is the risk that one will lose one's job or be disciplined in some other fashion. We can imagine how awkward it might be for Jill if she were to confront Marilyn with her concerns and if, despite Jill's allegations, Marilyn were to become Jill's supervisor.

Any social worker who considers blowing the whistle on a colleague or on an agency practice must make a difficult decision about the amount of personal and professional vulnerability he or she is willing to risk. It is one thing to preach that personal concerns should never stand in the way of professional or ethical obligations; it is of course another to always abide by such a principle. As Peters and Branch observe, "if an employee becomes a damaged good, tainted by a reputation as an organizational squealer, he may find so many doors locked that a drop in station or a change in profession will be required."[34]

Blowing the whistle on wrongdoing and wrongdoers is never easy. It is rarely approached without ambivalence. We know, however, that on occasion it may be required of us. The harms perpetrated by those who violate laws and policies are at times simply much too severe to ignore. Fleishman and Payne state it well: "The moral problems caused by other people's sins are an old story. When one discovers the corruption of a friend or political ally, personal or political loyalties may conflict with legal duty or devotion to the public interest. The high value of loyalty in politics may make the conflict a wrenching one, but on principled grounds the sacrifice of law or public interest to loyalty in such a case can hardly be justified."[35]

The ethical dilemmas that arise in social workers' relationships with colleagues are among the most difficult and dismaying. It is rarely easy to decide whether one has a right to violate an agency policy or use deception in order to obtain information. Ethical dilemmas involving colleagues are also frequently complicated by the loyalty we tend to feel for our professional associates. It is never pleasant to feel as if one must raise questions about the competence of a colleague or consider blowing the whistle on unprofessional practices. As the cases we have just examined illustrate, it is frequently difficult to settle on simple solutions to these dilemmas. These, like all of the cases we have considered, require careful thought informed by an appreciation of the rights people have to freedom and well-being and the conflicts which can arise among them.

6

Enduring Issues

It is a mark of the educated man and a proof of his culture that in every subject he looks for only so much precision as its nature permits—ARISTOTLE

In Thornton Wilder's *The Bridge of San Luis Rey,* Brother Juniper witnesses the sudden collapse of the finest bridge in all Peru and watches with horror as five travelers perish in the gulf below. Brother Juniper is taken by this wondrous event: "Why did this happen to *those* five?" As Wilder himself muses: "If there were any plan in the universe at all, if there were any pattern in a human life, surely it could be discovered mysteriously latent in those lives so suddenly cut off. Either we live by accident and die by accident, or we live by plan and die by plan. And on that instant Brother Juniper made the resolve to inquire into the secret lives of those five persons, that moment falling through the air, and to surprise the reason of their taking off."

There is much in Brother Juniper's mission that is reminiscent of our own as social workers. He faces a perplexing set of circumstances for which he is determined to find an explanation. His task is not unlike our own when we seek to understand why some people are beset with problems and how we might best help them. We persist in our efforts to uncover the mysteries of our various interventions into people's lives, just as Brother Juniper sought to reveal the secrets of the intervention which preceded the untimely deaths of those who wended their way across the bridge between Lima and Cuzco. The challenge is the same, to find rhyme and reason in our methods and our purposes.

In the profession of social work we have struggled for over a century to devise effective ways of assisting people in need. Our efforts have ranged from the friendly visitors of the nineteenth-century charity organization societies to contemporary techniques of casework and social planning. And of course the relatively modern methods of professional social work were foreshadowed by the social welfare apparatus which followed the enactment of the Elizabethan Poor Law. All along we have sought to understand how people can best be helped and to generate good reasons for intervening in people's lives as we do.

As I noted earlier, the theme of morality has persisted throughout the history of social work. During the early years of the profession there was considerable concern about the moral fiber and rectitude of the person in need. More recently there has been an abiding interest in the ethical aspects of the methods of social work and of the activities and decisions of its practitioners. We have seen how ethical issues can touch every facet of social work, including our decisions to intervene in individuals' lives in the first place, the methods we use when we do intervene, our obligation to abide by laws and formal policies, and our relationships with colleagues. The ethical dilemmas we encounter in practice are at times glaring and at times subtle.

It is clear that our ability to identify and think carefully about ethical dilemmas in social work practice can have profound consequences for clients' lives, for ourselves, and for the assumptions upon which the very foundation of the profession is built. What, however, can we hope to gain from a careful analysis of ethical dilemmas in social work, especially knowing that it is frequently difficult to devise clear-cut solutions to these dilemmas? What are reasonable goals to have when one embarks upon a systematic examination of ethical issues in social work?

THE GOALS OF ETHICAL ANALYSIS

It is apparent that many of the dilemmas we encounter in practice reduce to questions of right and wrong and are therefore by definition questions of ethics. Answers to questions about a worker's obligation to keep a promise of confidentiality or obey a law cannot, in the final analysis, be decided solely by reference to theories of social work practice or to the results of empirical research. Whether destitute people should be required to work in exchange for public aid, for example, or whether a community ought to be required to accept a group home cannot be determined entirely by principles of economics or theories of community development. Knowledge gained from research and the construction of theories can certainly help inform and guide our thinking but, as I observed in my discussion of the philosophical debate around the "is-ought" problem, normative conclusions about what is right and wrong cannot be deduced directly from descriptive statements of fact. In the end these decisions are ethical ones.

There are several reasons why it is important to pay attention to ethics.

Stimulating the Moral Imagination

It is important for practitioners to recognize that many of their decisions are, at their foundation, ethical ones. As we have seen, these decisions are frequently more than intellectual riddles; they involve difficult problems of human welfare and suffering and arouse our emotions as well as our intellect. We cannot afford to regard ethical dilemmas in social service merely as intriguing exercises to be run through for heuristic purposes. They frequently entail problems whose resolution will deeply affect the quality of people's lives. An important goal of attending to problems of ethics is to help practitioners become more sensitive to these profound dilemmas.[1] A report on the teaching of ethics has stated this goal well:

> Students should be encouraged to understand that there is a "moral point of view" (to use Kurt Baier's phrase), that human beings live their lives in a web of moral relationships, that a consequence of moral positions and rules can be actual suffering or happiness, and that moral conflicts are frequently inevitable and difficult. The ability to gain a feel for the lives of others, some sense of the emotions and the feelings that are provoked by difficult ethical choices,

and some insight into how moral viewpoints influence the way individuals live their lives would be important outcomes of attempts to stimulate the moral imagination.[2]

Distinguishing Ethical and Nonethical Issues

If practitioners are to become more sensitive to ethical dilemmas in social service, they must be able to distinguish ethical from nonethical issues, a goal closely related to the preceding one. Not every dilemma in practice is an ethical one. Whether a practitioner decides to design a group home for eight or fourteen youths may not be an ethical issue. However, whether the group home should be placed in a given community despite the protests of prospective neighbors is an ethical issue and should be treated as such. Issues of politics and economics might ultimately influence the resolution of such a dilemma, but it would be important for a practitioner to recognize the fundamentally ethical nature of the problem.

Earlier I drew distinctions among ethical, technical, and empirical aspects of social work. I argued that in many instances questions about social work technique and empirical evidence reduce to questions of ethics. Whether certain forms of casework should be used by practitioners may appear on the surface to depend on the empirical evidence available concerning the effectiveness of these methods. But if there are concerns that certain methods are manipulative or coercive, the debate becomes an ethical one. The effectiveness of the methods would become of secondary importance if we believed that social workers who used them were mistreating clients.

It is important to reiterate that social work methods are not right or justifiable simply because they appear to be effective. Our professional history is full of too many instances when appealing outcomes have been brought about through unconscionable means. The "is-ought" problem I referred to earlier is central to social work; we cannot afford to assume that descriptive statements of fact about the effectiveness of social work practice can lead us directly to normative conclusions about what methods should be used. Ethical considerations concerning what constitutes right and wrong behavior and justifiable and unjustifiable outcomes must intercede. It would be a mistake for us to become preoccupied with questions of technique and effectiveness. These are certainly important and at times critical issues; however, the foundation of our profession and many of the decisions we make are ethical in nature. It is incumbent upon us to pay close attention to questions of right and wrong. Max Siporin makes the point succinctly:

> The subject of philosophy, and particularly of . . . moral philosophy has not been very popular in social work in the past half-century. Rather, a value-free science, especially a value-free social science, has been an ideal model for social workers. This was associated with a belief that social workers could have a set of values so self-evidently true that they could be morally neutral and merely enable people to fulfill their needs and desires. There was an equation of morality with moralism, as if moral behavior meant being moralistic: being prejudiced, judgmental, and intolerant. In addition, social workers sought to be guided by a value system that could be quantified and measured, rather than contend with the ambiguities and large questions of a philosophy, even though it meant losing the larger dimensions of life meanings. Still further, there was a confusion as to a knowledge of fact and value, and therefore about the nature of knowledge itself. This has handicapped the development of both the moral philosophy and the scientific knowledge upon which an effective, viable theory and practice of social work need to be constructed.[3]

Developing Analytical Skills

As Siporin observes, philosophical problems in social work have not received adequate attention throughout the history of the profession. We are becoming increasingly aware, however, that some of the most persistent and critical questions for practitioners are ethical ones. It is therefore important for workers to cultivate skills which will enable them to critically assess and analyze ethical dilemmas in practice.

Earlier I concluded that social workers need to become acquainted with the various strategies which have been devised by philosophers for assessing ethical dilemmas and to understand the strengths and limitations of these approaches. Utilitarianism, for example, includes a set of guidelines which are frequently used by practitioners in their attempts to resolve difficult ethical dilemmas. As we have seen repeatedly, however, utilitarianism, despite its initial appeal, suffers from a variety of weaknesses, ranging from the difficulty we have in assigning quantitative values to qualitative phenomena to the abhorrent consequences strict utilitarianism can technically justify. Similarly, deontological principles—according to which certain actions or rules are inherently right and should therefore be obeyed—are frequently appealed to by social workers who want to justify ethical decisions. For example, practitioners who refuse to reveal to a colleague information which has been shared by a client often claim that it is inherently wrong to disclose confidential information. As we have also seen, it would be a mistake to adhere blindly to a given rule simply because one believes that this rule is inherently right and should therefore always be obeyed. Rules are important and useful, but exceptions to them are sometimes required.

Understanding the value and limitations of utilitarian approaches and of rules is an important skill to have if workers are to assess ethical dilemmas in a thoughtful, systematic fashion. Ethical dilemmas cannot be solved with simple formulae; social workers must therefore have an appreciation of the various ways in which ethical dilemmas can be thought about and the strengths and weaknesses of those various points of view.

The ability to understand principles of normative ethics and their relationship to dilemmas encountered in practice is thus an important skill for social workers to acquire. In addition, social workers must be sensitive to questions of metaethics—that is, questions about methods of justifying values and deriving ethical principles in the first place. Our profession has been guided for decades by values many of us hold dear—the client's right to self-determination, respect, confidentiality, and so on. But we must recognize that these values are not sacred simply because they have been asserted. Despite our fantasies, the values we have subscribed to throughout our professional history are not embraced universally. It is important for us to think carefully about the reasons why the values of freedom and well-being, and other values which can be derived from these basic ones, should guide our ethical decisions. There is a wide variety of opinion about ways of justifying values and ways of deriving ethical guidelines from them. Though we may not entirely resolve these debates, it is important to be aware that they exist.

THE USE OF ETHICS COMMITTEES

Although many ethical decisions are made privately or informally, in some instances it is appropriate and useful to refer ethical matters to a formal ethics committee. Many professional agencies have begun to develop ethics committees to provide colleagues with an opportunity to consult with one another about ethical issues in practice.[4] In hospitals, for example, institutional ethics committees (IECs) have existed for a number of years to provide opportunities for health care professionals to exchange ideas about ethical issues. In the 1920s special hospital committees were established to review decisions about the sterilization of patients, and in the 1950s and 1960s a number of hospitals formed committees to examine decisions related to abortion. In addition, institutional review boards (IRBs) to review ethical issues related to biomedical research and the use of human subjects have existed in hospitals for two decades now.[5] IRBs have since been established in a variety of public and private organizations, such as colleges and universities, state and federal agencies, and private rehabilitation programs.

The concept of IECs emerged most prominently in 1976, when the New Jersey Supreme Court ruled that Karen Anne Quinlan's family and physicians should consult an ethics committee in deciding whether to remove her from life-support systems. The court based its ruling in part on a seminal article that appeared in the *Baylor Law Review* in 1975, in which a pediatrician advocated the use of ethics committees in cases when health care professionals faced difficult ethical choices.[6]

A major endorsement of ethics committees was issued in March 1983 by the President's Commission for the Study of Ethical Problems in Medicine and Biomedical and Behavioral Research. The report of the commission suggested that health care institutions experiment with ethics committees in an effort to improve the quality of decision-making related to clinical care (especially decisions about whether to forgo life-sustaining treatment). It was subsequently applauded by many medical groups, such as the American Academy of Pediatrics and the American College of Hospital Administrators, which viewed this recommendation as an alternative to the type of regulations proposed by the U.S. Department of Health and Human Services following the notorious Baby Doe case.[7]

Ethics Committees in Social Work

The issues brought to the attention of ethics committees in health care settings are not unlike those that arise in social work generally. Social workers routinely face issues related to the treatment of clients, agency policy and administration, and relationships with third parties for which agency-based ethics committees can provide useful consultation. In principle, social work ethics committees can serve several functions:

Education. Among the most important functions is that of educating staff about ethical issues particularly relevant to the host agency. Sessions might be devoted specifically to issues that arise in the delivery of clinical services to individuals, families, and groups (for example, limits of the right to confidentiality and self-determination), truth-telling, informed consent, and the implications of privileged communication statutes. Other sessions might concentrate on ethical issues germane to agency policy and administration, such as the handling of personnel grievances; the use of coercion with clients; criteria for allocating scarce agency resources, such as program funds, workers' time, or shelter beds; compliance with a local law or agency policy; or whistle-blowing in response to unethical practices by agency staff.

Formulating Agency Policies. A related function concerns the formulation of agency policies and guidelines for use by staff who encounter ethical dilemmas. Thus, an ethics committee might develop detailed guidelines related to obtaining from clients in a drug rehabilitation program informed consent prior to treatment. An ethics committee in an agency that provides crisis intervention services, for example, might propose guidelines concerning the release of information to relatives or law enforcement officials. An ethics committee in an agency that provides services to the elderly might generate guidelines concerning the use of clients as research subjects.

Case Consultation. In some instances, staff may wish to call on the ethics committee for advice and consultation regarding a specific case. Social workers typically seek advice and consultation on ethical matters informally from colleagues and supervisors who may not have expertise or training in ethical issues in the profession. An ethics committee can offer an opportunity for staff to think through case-specific issues with colleagues who in principle have more thorough knowledge of ethical issues in social work as a result of their experiences, familiarity with literature on professional ethics, and specialized training in the area.

Few agencies require that their staff consult with an ethics committee or follow its recommendations. Rather, most ethics committees offer consultation to staff who wish it, with the understanding that the committee's aim is to provide information and opinions, not a mandatory prescription or binding solution. In this respect, most ethics committees are advisory.[8]

Case Review. In addition to providing consultation to staff in advance of a decision, ethics committees can also provide a valuable service to staff who wish to examine cases retrospectively. One of the distressing features of social work practice is that ethically complex situations cannot always be anticipated in advance. Occasionally, crises arise that demand immediate decisions. Ethics committees can thus provide a forum for staff to review after the fact the ways in which ethical dilemmas were handled when the press of time did not permit thoughtful deliberation.

Composition of Committees

The membership of an ethics committee will depend in large part on the nature of the host agency. An agency comprised primarily of social work staff may not be in a position to form an interdisciplinary committee unless it draws on individuals from outside the agency. Agencies that employ interdisciplinary staff, such as hospitals and many residential treatment centers, ordinarily seek to represent the respective professions. Institutional ethics committees in hospitals, for example, frequently include physicians, social workers, nurses, clergy, administrators, attorneys, and psychologists. Many committees also include a lay person not on the agency's staff, such as a client or community representative.

Many ethics committees have also found it valuable to include someone who is trained in the subject of ethics. Often this is a philosopher who has a special interest in professional ethics and who has formal training in the methods of ethical analysis. Benjamin Freedman, a philosopher who is a member of an ethics committee, notes in his reflections:

> An ethics group needs somebody who is used to analyzing issues, someone who can identify relevant points and recognize red herrings. And they need someone sufficiently well read in the literature to be able to confront the group with the best arguments for and against proposed ethical positions.[9]

Because ethics committees frequently are interdisciplinary and include representatives from a variety of administrative and line-staff positions, it is important for members to acknowledge the possibility of conflicts among their vested interests. For example, whereas an agency social worker may be inclined to advocate primarily on behalf of clients, an administrator may feel obliged to protect the interests of the agency. Attorneys employed by an agency also pose a special problem because of their traditional duty to uphold the interests of their client first and foremost.[10] An option some ethics committees have used to avoid such conflicts is to invite legal staff to participate as advisors rather than as full members.[11]

It is especially important for committee members to acknowledge that often they will not reach consensus. This is not, as it might appear, a defect in the functioning of ethics committees. It is unrealistic to expect that a group of professionals, especially when they represent different disciplines, will always agree on matters that are as complex as ethical issues tend to be. One can argue, in fact, that if consensus is consistently achieved, such consensus is either artificial and deceptive or the committee is not examining critically the issues that come before it. These issues are often complex and controversial. That they could not be resolved prior to being presented to an ethics committee indicates that they do not lend themselves to simple or obvious solutions. Thus, it is reasonable to expect that these issues would typically generate significant differences of opinion and disagreement among committee members. To push for consensus might camouflage important differences of opinion and might also promote the mistaken impression that the mission of the ethics committee is to make decisions for staff, clients, and other concerned parties, when such may not be its purpose.[12]

Limitations

It is important for social workers to keep in mind that there are risks accompanying the substantial contributions ethics committees make to the quality of care provided in human service agencies. These risks primarily concern issues of influence, neutrality, and efficacy.

Influence. The vast majority of agency ethics committees is advisory. These committees are neither designed nor do they seek to impose their members' beliefs on staff, clients and their families, or other parties. Nonetheless, the very existence of an ethics committee, especially a visible and active one, may lead staff, clients, and others to assume that its role is more than advisory and that the product of its deliberations is binding. Members of ethics committees may also have a mistaken view of a committee's function, and untoward pressure may be brought to bear on staff and clients as a result. Social workers ordinarily believe that clients ought to assume the principal responsibility for decisions that affect their lives. It is thus important that the formation of ethics committees not lead to an abrogation of this responsibility or to interference with clients' autonomy. Similarly, ethics committee members must ensure that their activities do not lead to gratuitous meddling in clients' lives. Committees sometimes need to gather information from clients and probe into sensitive areas of their lives in order to render sound, informed opinions. Yet, there is a fine line between collecting pertinent data and unwarranted intrusion.

Of course, there is also the possibility that the advisory, rather than binding, nature of an ethics committee's function may dilute its influence with staff and clients. If its goal is merely to provide consultation and if its members are not expected to reach consensus, there is a danger that the committee's recommendations will lose their forcefulness. Committee members themselves may lose some incentive to debate the issues with vigor and conviction. To avoid this pitfall, prospective committee members must be selected in part because of their clear understanding of the committee's advisory function and of the value of sustained discussion about ethical matters that does not always lead to consensus. Freedman's comments on this point, based on his participation in the Ethics Consultation Service at the Foothills General Hospital in Calgary, Canada, are cogent:

> The . . . danger confronting this group is a degeneration into indecisiveness or bland compromise. Imagine for a moment that you are a member of the group, and you will begin to sense the temptation to temporize and to commit intellectual ambidexterity ("On the one hand . . . on the other hand . . ."). Anyone who advises a person who must make a decision of great moment is prey to the same temptation. (Harry Truman used to complain that he needed a one-handed lawyer.) The only way to avoid indecisiveness is to choose members who have done some thinking about a particular area and have arrived at some settled convictions. But the delicate tension between being opinionated and being an ethical *tabula rasa* must be preserved. A member must be knowledgeable and principled, but at the same time openminded.[13]

Neutrality. In principle ethics committees aim to provide consultation that is free of influence from the vested interests of their members. Cases are to be reviewed in terms of their merits. In practice, however, it is sometimes difficult for committee members to abandon their loyalties and commitments to the parties and interests they represent as part of their day-to-day responsibilities. Thus, a social worker on the committee may have some difficulty balancing his or her ordinary obligations to clients with the neutrality that may be expected of committee members. As I noted earlier, a particular risk is that an ethics committee may ultimately be used to protect the interests of its host agency. Annas has argued, for example, that a number of hospital ethics committees were established essentially to protect their respective institutions and that it is naive to expect that committees will be altruistic consistently and concerned only with client welfare.[14]

A related problem concerns the possibility that over time an ethics committee may become dominated by an ideological faction or a particular professional group. Diversity on a committee is not always a virtue; however, in the case of ethics committees it is essential to ensure that the committee does not serve merely to endorse the views of like-minded colleagues.[15]

Efficacy. Although ethics committees generally have encouraged agency staff to increase their awareness of ethical issues in professional practice, there is a danger that the availability of an ethics committee may lead some staff to set aside their responsibility to reflect carefully on these issues. This is especially likely if a committee assumes too much authority and isolates itself from agency staff and clients. In time staff and clients may begin to assume erroneously that ethical deliberations should be carried out only by the ethics committee. At the other extreme, ethics committees must avoid diffusing responsibility for ethical consultation so widely that staff and clients are left to feel as if no one is assuming primary responsibility for it.

The formation of an ethics committee does not necessarily lead to expansion of an agency's bureaucracy or organizational chart. In a number of agencies these functions have been assumed by an existing committee, such as a director's advisory committee. What is important is that some committee within an agency be charged with providing consultation on ethical matters and that its members be knowledgeable about these issues. Whether this is best done under the auspices of an existing committee or a newly created one depends on the nature and efficacy of committees extant in the host agency.

Although it is tempting to applaud the accomplishments of existing ethics committees and to encourage the introduction of such committees throughout the profession, it is important for social workers to appreciate that ethics committees cannot replace individual practitioners in their responsibility to reflect on ethical aspects of their work. Ethics committees can help to raise issues and examine them critically. They can provide informed judgments and advice. Ultimately, however, individual social workers have the responsibility to recognize the relevance of ethical considerations to their professional duties. As Albert Jonsen observes, guidelines provided by ethics committees

> are not the modern substitute for the Decalogue. They are, rather, shorthand moral education. They set out the concise definitions and the relevant distinctions that prepare the already well-disposed person to make the shrewd judgment that this or that instance is a typical case of this or that sort, and, then, decide how to act. Good guidelines will reflect the body of critical opinion that thoughtful persons have produced about a problem.[16]

PROFESSIONAL PRIORITIES

As social workers, we ordinarily view our mission as the promotion of human happiness. In short, we seek to bring about the greatest good for the greatest number. This is certainly a noble goal. Yet there is debate about its merit, debate which has important implications for our profession.

Social workers engage in a wide variety of activities. Some spend the greatest portion of their time working with individuals, families, and groups. Their duties may involve traditional casework, advocacy, psychotherapy, or case management. They may work with the emotionally disturbed, the elderly, the poor, the infirm, or the delinquent. Some are self-employed, some work in private agencies, and some work in public agencies. Other workers spend most of their professional time in administrative or planning positions. They may, for example, direct a family service agency, work in a public social service agency, or own and operate a private consulting firm. The range of activities social workers engage in today is much wider than it was during the first half-century of the profession's life. We have branched out in a staggering number of directions using a variety of skills with a variety of populations, in sharp contrast to the early years of the profession, when a concern with the poor occupied a much greater portion of our attention.

Our professional boundaries now include work with relatively affluent populations. Significant numbers of practitioners are being trained to become psychotherapists who will serve individuals who have problems in both living and the means to purchase private weekly sessions. In addition, social workers have been moving out of public service in unusually large numbers. Between 1972 and 1982 there was an 18 percent decline in the number of National Association of Social Workers members employed in public sector agencies, such as those responsible for public assistance and child welfare programs. On the other side of the coin, employment in private sectarian agencies and proprietary (for-profit) agencies—the vast majority of which provide casework and psychotherapy services—increased 132 percent and 264 percent, respectively. As the *New York Times* reported recently, between 1975 and 1985 the number of clinical social workers in the United States increased from 25,000 to 60,000 (an increase of 140 percent), placing social workers first in the list of professional groups providing mental health services (followed by psychiatrists, clinical psychologists, and marriage and family counselors).[17]

This trend has not gone unnoticed and without controversy. On the one hand are arguments that the profession of social work has been enriched and its status enhanced by the breadth of activities its practitioners now engage in. On the other hand some protest vigorously that the original purposes and goals of the profession have been substantially distorted or abandoned as a result of the aggressive pursuit by practitioners of professional positions which have little to do with problems of poverty and destitution. Complaints that social workers have become more concerned with self-aggrandizement and status than with the perennial problems of the needy are now common. Of course, such critical comments are sometimes tempered by an acknowledgement of the decline since the 1970s in government funding of and commitment to social service programs, and, hence, a decline in the number of jobs in the public sector. It is difficult for social workers to pursue a mission that is not embraced by the broader culture.[18]

This debate is closely tied to one that has persisted for decades in moral philosophy, at least since the advent of utilitarianism. The conventional view of utilitarianism entails that it is each individual's responsibility to do what he or she can to bring about the greatest good for the greatest number—positive utilitarianism. However, a close look at this prescription suggests that it is important to ask whether this implies that our primary goal should be the promotion of as much happiness as possible or, in contrast, what Sir Karl Popper refers to as the minimization of suffering[19] (and what J. J. C. Smart labels *negative* utilitarianism[20]). This is an important distinction. It may in fact be that both the greatest happiness and the least suffering can be pursued through the same means, that these phrases merely represent two ways of saying the same thing. But is this necessarily the case? It appears not.

We have seen repeatedly that instances arise in social work which require us to make decisions about which values should take precedence over which others. I concluded that there must be a lexical ordering among values, such that in cases of conflict, threats to basic goods such as life and health must take precedence over threats to goods such as excessive wealth, products for entertainment and recreation, sensual pleasure, and other goods which tend to help make life enjoyable but upon which basic subsistence does not depend. This reasoning can be extended to the debate concerning the mission of social work and the professional priorities of its practitioners. On the face of it this conclusion suggests that social workers should devote themselves to the poor and helpless because of the severity of their needs and the threats to their well-being, in contrast to the needs of those who are more affluent or who have greater wherewithal for helping themselves. However, such exhortations must be tempered by an appreciation of the frustrations and obstacles which often stand in the way of well-intentioned practitioners who feel very committed to assisting people in dire need. The reality of work in public bureaucracies and social service agencies is such that the most devoted and skilled among us can be battered and worn by the vagaries of contemporary welfare policies, regulations, and working conditions. The problems can be monumental and the satisfactions few. A wide gulf frequently stands between our hopes for helping those who suffer and our ability to intervene effectively. Yet we must each make a personal decision about the activities we will engage in as practitioners. I would argue that in general we should be more concerned with the alleviation of suffering than with the maximization of aggregate happiness whenever the two conflict. This is not to say that social workers who have lucrative private practices address problems that are less compelling than those addressed by caseworkers in our inner cities. Psychic pain and deep emotional trauma are not trivial forms of suffering. However, it is not unfair to conclude that some of our activities as social workers are more important than others and have a greater likelihood of helping to relieve some of the profound pain under which many people labor.

We must constantly reflect on the various needs of various populations of clients. The relative need of different client groups will no doubt change over time. At a particular time in a particular community it may be important to devote considerable attention to establishing noninstitutional programs for mentally retarded youths. Or there may be a particular need to advocate for changes in eligibility requirements for public assistance. Certain needs will undoubtedly remain constant. It will always be important to pay close attention to the needs of the poor, physically disabled, mentally disturbed, and other individuals whose disabilities threaten their basic welfare or access to basic goods. However, social workers must think carefully about which other client groups—that is, beyond those which have dire needs—should be served. One can only hope that the decisions social workers make about their professional activities will be guided by a primary concern for those whose welfare is most threatened. It has been our tradition as a profession to serve those individuals who are least capable of helping themselves. There are sound ethical reasons for us to uphold this tradition. As J. J. C. Smart remarks, "Even though we may not be attracted to negative utilitarianism as an ultimate principle, we may concede that the injunction 'worry about removing misery rather than about promoting happiness' has a good deal to recommend it as a subordinate rule of thumb. For in most cases we can do most for our fellow men by trying to remove their miseries."[21]

THE LIMITS OF OBLIGATION

How do we know where to draw the line between activities which we should feel obligated to engage in as social workers and activities which, while perhaps commendable and meritorious, extend beyond what is required of us? It was certainly commendable for Michael Bunker to be concerned about the elderly woman, Helen, who lived in a dilapidated, abandoned garage, but was he obligated to be concerned about her welfare? It is certainly commendable for social workers to promote the development of community-based group homes for the mentally retarded, but is there an obligation to provide the mentally retarded with such care? In short, where does obligation end and altruism begin?

Philosophers make a useful distinction between actions which are considered obligatory and those which, while perhaps worthy of praise and to be encouraged, are not obligatory in the strict moral sense of the term. John Rawls, for example, refers to obligatory actions as *natural duties:* the duty of helping another when he or she is in need or jeopardy, provided that one can do so without excessive risk or loss to oneself; the duty not to harm or injure another; and the duty not to cause unnecessary suffering.[22] Other actions are considered commendable and praiseworthy, but not obligatory; these actions are called *supererogatory:*

> These are acts of benevolence and mercy, of heroism and self-sacrifice. It is good to do these actions but it is not one's duty or obligation. Supererogatory acts are not required, though normally they would be were it not for the loss or risk involved for the agent himself. A person who does a supererogatory act does not invoke the exemption which the natural duties allow. For while we have a natural duty to bring about a great good, say, if we can do so relatively easily, we are released from this duty when the cost to ourselves is considerable.[23]

The distinction between natural and supererogatory acts has important implications for the conclusions we reach about the extent of our duty to aid other people.[24] For example, a strict utilitarian might argue that social workers are obliged to do whatever they can to promote the greatest good for the greatest number; however, this point of view does not clarify whether boundaries exist between what is required and what is supererogatory. One can't help but wonder whether a utilitarian would have us working endlessly, without respite, promoting good and engaging in altruistic activities. Though it is perhaps unfair to attribute this point of view to utilitarianism, it is fair to say that utilitarianism does not help us to decide where obligation ends and generosity begins.

Most of us have a limited capacity for assisting others. We are constrained by both our physical and emotional resources. All of us occasionally reach a point where we feel unable to muster the wherewithal to counsel another client, make another home visit, or write another annual report. It is important for us to keep in mind, however, that certain actions are important for us to engage in, though at times we may not feel up to them. Decisions about which actions can be postponed and which cannot should be guided by more than casual reflection about what we feel like doing at any given moment. The distinction between natural duties and supererogatory acts can help us think carefully about the limits of our duty to aid.

There is much we can do to help relieve the suffering of others; it is important to acknowledge, however, that despite our good intentions and sentiments, we cannot be expected to do everything. Charles Fried makes this point nicely in his *Right and Wrong:*

> The . . . difficult problem, to which I have no satisfactory solution, is our duty to concrete persons who are the victims of unjust institutions. It seems insufficient to say that our duty is wholly discharged by working to change

> these institutions. And yet the duty we have to our fellow men is to contribute a *fair* share; it is not a duty to give over our whole lives. Can it be that we do wrong, violate our duty to contribute, when we refrain from a total sacrifice which is necessitated only by the plain violation of duty on the part of others? I cannot give an answer. I suggest that compassion and solidarity demand a great deal of us—and particularly if we are the (unwilling) beneficiaries of the unjust situation. But they do not demand everything.[25]

Where does this sober conclusion leave us? It is clear that we are still saddled with the responsibility for making difficult, often excruciating, ethical decisions about our obligation to intervene in people's lives and about ways of doing so. I have devoted considerable space to a review of various theories of ethics and have speculated about their application to the sorts of ethical dilemmas social workers encounter in practice. In the end we must still entertain the most basic of all our questions: Can ethics provide answers?

ETHICS AND ANSWERS

I have attempted to show that many of the decisions social workers make involve ethical judgments. It is clear by now that many of the ethical dilemmas practitioners face do not lend themselves to quick or simple answers. It frequently seems that as many arguments can be provided against a particular point of view as for it, though such is not always the case. As I noted earlier, there has been a tendency in our profession to regard ethical dilemmas as problems which should be resolved on a case by case basis without any systematic appeal to ethical rules or principles. Our intuition regarding the circumstances of individual cases has been the primary determinant of the judgments we have made about right and wrong. We have been largely without ethical principles or guidelines for helping us assess the dilemmas we encounter in our work. What we have tended to practice is *situational* ethics.

We know, however, that decisions about how to intervene in clients' lives require a careful consideration of principles. When we develop a treatment plan for a depressed child, for example, we know that it is important to rely on more than intuition about what methods will be most effective. We know that there is a considerable fund of knowledge and practice principles concerning ways of treating depressed children. We know that as a matter of routine we should take into account factors such as a child's age, developmental history, family circumstances, school experiences, and so on, when we devise a treatment approach. We know in addition that certain treatment techniques have been shown to be more or less effective with depressed children.

Similarly, when we are faced with the task of developing a plan for reviving a deteriorating community, we know that it is important to rely on more than intuition about what strategies are likely to work best. We know that it is important to consider such factors as a community's tax base, unemployment rate, median income, housing patterns, political climate, and so on, before devising a plan. Whenever we develop intervention plans—whether for an individual, a family, a neighborhood, a region, or a nation—we know that it is important to consult principles of practice developed from theory and research to help guide our thinking.

Our approach to ethical dilemmas should be no different. A purely intuitionistic approach to ethics is no more satisfactory than a purely intuitionistic approach to treatment plans. We have a right to expect good reasons for proposed solutions to ethical dilemmas, just as we have a right to good reasons for proposed treatment plans that do not involve ethical issues. For thousands of years philosophers have given careful thought to problems of ethics and to ways of approaching them. It is important to engage in rational discourse about the merits and demerits of various approaches. We know by now that people will frequently disagree about what is right and wrong, but this fact of life should not discourage us from engaging in the debate. It is important for us to present reasons for the opinions we have about what is right and wrong, and it is important for us to challenge both ourselves and one another on the cogency and validity of our reasons. Such reflection and dialogue will sometimes lead us to change our minds about what is right and wrong. Sometimes we will change the minds of others as a result. Whatever we decide in the end, however, should be based on careful thought about the nature of the rights individuals have to freedom and well-being and about the most appropriate ways of promoting and protecting these rights. Careful thought, combined with a deep sense of caring about the welfare of others, can substantially affect the quality of individuals' lives. James Rachels makes the point eloquently:

> Aristotle even suggested that there are two distinct pieces of knowledge: first, the sort of knowledge possessed by one who is able to recite facts, "like the drunkard reciting the verses of Empedocles," but without understanding

their meaning; and second, the sort of knowledge possessed when one has thought carefully through what one knows. An example might make this clearer. We all know, in an abstract sort of way, that many children in the world are starving; yet for most of us this makes little difference to our conduct. We will spend money on trivial things for ourselves, rather than spending it on food for them. How are we to explain this? The Artistotelian explanation is that we "know" the children are starving only in the sense in which the drunkard knows Empedocles' verses—we simply recite the fact. Suppose, though, that we thought carefully about what it must be *like* to be a starving orphan. Our attitudes, our conduct, and the moral judgments we are willing to make, might be substantially altered. . . .

The fact that rationality has limits does not subvert the objectivity of ethics, but it does suggest a certain modesty in what can be claimed for it. Ethics provides answers about what we ought to do, given that we are the kinds of creatures we are, caring about the things we will care about when we are as reasonable as we can be, living in the sort of circumstances in which we live. This is not as much as we might want, but it is a lot. It is as much as we can hope for in a subject that must incorporate not only our beliefs but our ideals as well.[26]

OF CLOUDS AND CLOCKS

In a lecture concerning the use of reason to pursue freedom and well-being, Sir Karl Popper speculated about our yearning for certainty, our collective wish for determinate answers to the perplexing problems people face. Popper used the image of clouds and clocks to convey, on the one hand, the uncertainty which characterizes much of life and the methods we devise for coping with it and, on the other, the precision and order which we would like to be able to impose upon our world: "My clouds are intended to represent physical systems which, like gases, are highly irregular, disorderly and more or less unpredictable. I shall assume that we have before us a schema or arrangement in which a very disturbed or disorderly cloud is placed on the left. On the other extreme of our arrangement, on its right, we may place a very reliable pendulum clock, a precision clock, intended to represent physical systems which are regular, orderly, and highly predictable in their behavior."[27]

I too have been speaking of clouds and clocks. The professional journey of every social worker includes encounters with complex and troubling ethical dilemmas which cannot be skirted. On occasion we face ethical decisions which are relatively easy, such as when a worker decides to report confidential information to law enforcement officials in order to save a life. Very often, however, we are required to choose, not between something bad and something good, but between two or more goods (or "bads"). Even after considerable thought and reflection a clear resolution, one with which we can live comfortably, may not be apparent. Despite our best efforts to impose rationality and systematic analysis upon ethical dilemmas, unambiguous resolutions frequently elude us. The clouds of ethical dilemmas often seem to overshadow the best analytical tools available to us—our clocks.

But this is not always the case. Good reasons can be provided for believing in certain values and for ways of reconciling conflicts among them. The application of principles of moral philosophy to nagging ethical dilemmas has matured considerably since the days of the early Greek sophists. The utilitarian principles generated by Bentham and Mill, for example, have done much to help us organize our thinking concerning problems of ethics. In recent years, however, we have come to appreciate some of the limitations and hazards of a strict utilitarian point of view. We have learned that a blind embrace of utilitarianism can engender some rather disquieting and distasteful outcomes. In short, we have learned that our concern about the consequences of our decisions and actions must be tempered with a concern about the means used to pursue them and their effect upon individual freedom and well-being.

A challenge which will require continuing attention concerns the ever-present need to reconcile conflicts of professional duty. It is clear from our review of ethical dilemmas that social work practice will always contain instances when difficult choices must be made from among values and duties which, though justifiable when considered independently of one another, cannot be satisfied simultaneously. These choices are the most troubling and require the greatest care. The consequences of such decisions are often profound. We know that simplistic formulae cannot be derived for resolving these dilemmas. We also know, however, that it is important for us to be skilled at identifying the questions which need to be raised about ethical dilemmas in practice. Easy solutions may not be available; however, asking the right question is necessary if we are to do our best to protect and enhance the rights individuals have to freedom and well-being. As John Tukey asserts: "Far better an approximate answer to the right question, which is often vague, than an exact answer to the wrong questions, which can always be made precise."[28]

Popper was right when he concluded that to some degree all clocks are clouds. But he also knew that we are capable of rendering considerable order among our clouds. Our abiding obligation as social workers is to use our abilities to respond sensitively and compassionately to the needs of those who suffer, and to use our capacity to reason to make sound judgments about what is right and wrong. Our attempts to think carefully about ethics will not always make a difference. There will always be individuals who will not be persuaded by the most compelling of ethical arguments and circumstances which resist the introduction of ethical content. All of us, however, must at times make personal decisions about our professional commitments and the ethical aspects of our relationships with clients and colleagues. It is our private thoughts and conclusions with which we must eventually live, and in these, as we all know, there is always room for speculation about what is right and wrong.

Notes

1. THE NATURE OF ETHICS

1. Walter I. Trattner, *From Poor Law to Welfare State* (2d ed.; New York: Free Press, 1979), pp. 42–47.
2. Trattner, p. 47.
3. Trattner, p. 50.
4. Allen F. Davis, *Spearheads for Reform* (New York: Oxford University Press, 1967), pp. 18–20.
5. NASW, *Code of Ethics* (rev. ed.; New York: National Association of Social Workers, 1980).
6. Felix P. Biestek, "Client Self-Determination," in F. E. McDermott, ed., *Self-Determination in Social Work* (London: Routledge and Kegan Paul, 1975), p. 19.
7. Florence Hollis, "Principles and Assumptions Underlying Casework Practice," in Eileen Younghusband, ed., *Social Work and Social Values* (London: Allen and Unwin, 1967), p. 26.
8. See *Encyclopedia Britannica,* 15th ed. (1978), s.v. "Ethics"; William K. Frankena, *Ethics* (2d ed.; Englewood Cliffs, N.J.: Prentice-Hall, 1973), pp. 95–116; and Roger N. Hancock, *Twentieth-Century Ethics* (New York: Columbia University Press, 1974), pp. 3–17.
9. See Dorothy Emmet, "Ethics and the Social Worker," *British Journal of Psychiatric Social Work* (1962), 6:165–172; Charles Frankel, "Social Philosophy and the Professional Education of Social Workers," *Social Service Review* (1959),

33:345–359; Frederic G. Reamer, "Values and Ethics," *Encyclopedia of Social Work* (18th ed.; Washington, D.C.: National Association of Social Workers, 1987), pp. 801–809; Frederic G. Reamer, "Ethical Dilemmas in Social Work Practice," *Social Work* (1983), 28:31–35.

10. Joseph L. Vigilante, "Between Values and Science: Education for the Profession During A Moral Crisis or Is Proof Truth?" *Journal of Education for Social Work* (1974), 10:114.
11. See Frankena, *Ethics,* pp. 16–17, 23–28.
12. Frankena, pp. 14–23.
13. For a review of utilitarianism, see Jeremy Bentham, *An Introduction to the Principles of Morals and Legislation* (New York: Hafner, 1948; originally published 1789); Frankena, *Ethics,* pp. 34–43; Samuel Gorovitz, ed., *Mill: Utilitarianism* (Indianapolis: Bobbs-Merrill, 1971); John Stuart Mill, *Utilitarianism* (Indianapolis: Bobbs-Merrill, 1957; originally published 1863); J. J. C. Smart and Bernard Williams, *Utilitarianism: For and Against* (Cambridge: Cambridge University Press, 1973).
14. For a review of labeling theory, see Charles H. Shireman and Frederic G. Reamer, *Rehabilitating Juvenile Justice* (New York: Columbia University Press, 1986), pp. 47–53; Edwin M. Lemert, "The Juvenile Court: Quest and Realities," in U.S. President's Commission on Law Enforcement and Administration of Justice, *Task Force Report: Juvenile Justice and Youth Crime* (Washington, D.C.: GPO, 1967), pp. 92–94; Ann Rankin Mahoney, "The Effect of Labeling Upon Youths in the Juvenile Justice System: A Review of the Evidence." *Law and Society Review* (1974), 8:583–614; Raymond Paternoster, Gordon P. Waldo, Theodore G. Chiricos, and Linda S. Anderson, "The Stigma of Diversion: Labeling in the Juvenile Justice System," in Patricia Brantingham and Thomas G. Blomberg, eds., *Courts and Diversion* (New York: Sage, 1979), pp. 127–142.
15. See Frankena, *Ethics,* pp. 34–43; Smart and Williams, *Utilitarianism: For and Against.*
16. See Smart and Williams, pp. 12–27.
17. Fyodor Dostoevsky, *Crime and Punishment* (London: William Heinemann, 1914), pp. 60–61.
18. Emmet, "Ethics and the Social Worker," pp. 170, 171.
19. See Alan Gewirth, *Reason and Morality* (Chicago: University of Chicago Press, 1978), pp. 1–26; Joel Feinberg, *Social Philosophy* (Englewood Cliffs, N.J.: Prentice-Hall, 1973), pp. 4–35, 84–119; Frankena, *Ethics;* Hancock, *Twentieth-Century Ethics;* pp. 1–17.
20. See, for example, Vigilante, "Between Values and Science," pp. 107–115.
21. See Malcolm W. Klein, "Deinstitutionalization and Diversion of Juvenile Offenders: A Litany of Impediments," in Norval Morris and Michael Tonry, eds., *Crime and Justice: An Annual Review of Research* (Chicago: University of Chicago Press, 1979), 1:145–201; Solomon Kobrin and Malcolm W. Klein, *Final Report: National Evaluation of the Program for the Deinstitutionalization of Status Offenders* (Los Angeles: University of Southern California, 1979).

22. John R. Searle, "How to Derive 'Ought' from 'Is,' " in W. D. Hudson, ed., *The Is/Ought Question* (New York: St. Martin's Press, 1969), p. 120.
23. See for example, Frederic G. Reamer, "Protecting Research Subjects and Unintended Consequences: The Effects of Guarantees of Confidentiality," *Public Opinion Quarterly* (1979), 43:497–506; H. W. Riecken, "A Program for Research on Experiments in Social Psychology," in N. F. Washburne, ed., *Decisions, Values, and Groups* (New York: Pergamon Press, 1962) 2:25–41; Milton J. Rosenberg, "Conditions and Consequences of Evaluation Apprehension," in Robert Rosenthal and Ralph L. Rosnow, eds., *Artifact in Behavioral Research* (New York: Academic Press, 1969), pp. 279–349; Seymour Sudman and Norman M. Bradburn, *Response Effects in Surveys* (Chicago: Aldine, 1974); J. Allen Williams, Jr., "Interview-Respondent Interaction: A Study of Bias in the Information Interview," *Sociometry* (1964), 27:338–352.
24. See Richard M. Grinnell, Jr., ed., *Social Work Research and Evaluation* (3d ed.; Itasca, Ill.: F. E. Peacock, 1988).
25. For discussion of the limitations of research methodology in social work, see Colin Peile, "Research Paradigms in Social Work: From Stalemate to Creative Synthesis," *Social Service Review* (1988), 62:1–19; Martha B. Heineman, "The Obsolete Scientific Imperative in Social Work Research and Practice," *Social Service Review* (1981), 55:371–397; Walter H. Hudson, "Scientific Imperatives in Social Work Research and Practice," *Social Service Review* (1982), 56:242–258; Edward J. Mullen, "Methodological Dilemmas in Social Work Research," *Social Work Research and Abstracts* (1985), 21:12–20.
26. W. D. Ross, *The Right and the Good* (Oxford: Clarendon Press, 1930).
27. Alan Donagan, *The Theory of Morality* (Chicago: University of Chicago Press, 1977), p. 152.
28. Quoted in *Encyclopedia Britannica,* s.v. "Ethics," pp. 982–983.
29. Donagan, *The Theory of Morality,* p. 152.

2. FUNDAMENTAL ETHICAL ISSUES IN SOCIAL WORK

1. Charles Frankel, "Social Philosophy and the Professional Education of Social Workers," *Social Service Review* (1959), 33:348.
2. Robert Nozick, *Anarchy, State, and Utopia* (New York: Basic, 1974), p. ix.
3. Sir Isaiah Berlin, *Four Essays on Liberty* (Oxford: Oxford University Press, 1969), pp. 121–134.
4. Sir Isaiah Berlin, "Two Concepts of Liberty," in F. E. McDermott, ed., *Self-Determination in Social Work* (London: Routledge and Kegan Paul, 1975), p. 149.
5. See Gaston V. Rimlinger, *Welfare Policy and Industrialization in Europe, America, and Russia* (New York: Wiley, 1971), p. 2.
6. Quoted in Rimlinger, p. 94. Rimlinger included only certain stipulations from the original document but kept the original numbering.

7. Concerning the visibility of government in social welfare programs, see Maurice Bruce, *The Coming of the Welfare State* (London: B. T. Botsford, 1965); Norman Furniss and Timothy Tilton, *The Case for the Welfare State* (Bloomington: Indiana University Press, 1977); Fred Krinsky and Joseph Boskin, eds., *The Welfare State: Who Is My Brother's Keeper?* (Beverly Hills: Glencoe Press, 1968); Robert Pinker, *The Idea of Welfare* (London: Heinemann, 1979); Harold Wilensky, *The Welfare State and Equality* (Berkeley: University of California Press, 1975).
8. "Chrysler Aid Bill is Facing Tough Battle in Senate Panel Due to Bankers' Doubts," *Wall Street Journal*, November 23, 1979.
9. Lee Iacocca, "Chrysler Deserves Federal Help," *Wall Street Journal*, December 3, 1979.
10. See Joseph A. Schumpeter, *History of Economic Analysis* (London: Allen and Unwin, 1963), pp. 251–252.
11. Pinker, *The Idea of Welfare*, pp. 75–80.
12. Pinker, p. 78.
13. Pinker, p. 80.
14. Pinker, pp. 85–94.
15. See Oliver MacDonagh, *A Pattern of Government Growth, 1800–1860* (London: MacGibbon and Kee, 1961).
16. Quoted in Pinker, *The Idea of Welfare*, p. 113.
17. John Maynard Keynes, *The General Theory of Employment, Interest, and Money* (London: Macmillan, 1960), p. 372.
18. Keynes, p. 378.
19. Pinker, *The Idea of Welfare*, p. 115.
20. Sir William Beveridge, *Social Insurance and Allied Services* (New York: Macmillan, 1942), p. 6.
21. Rimlinger, *Welfare Policy and Industrialization in Europe, America, and Russia*, p. 150.
22. Beveridge, *Social Insurance and Allied Services*, pp. 6–7.
23. See Joel Feinberg, *Social Philosophy* (Englewood Cliffs, N.J.: Prentice-Hall, 1973), pp. 109–111.
24. John Rawls, *A Theory of Justice* (Cambridge: Harvard University Press, 1971).
25. Alan Donagan, *The Theory of Morality* (Chicago: University of Chicago Press, 1977).
26. Donagan, p. 85.
27. Donagan, p. 86.
28. Donagan, p. 209.
29. See Walter Stace, "Ethical Absolutism and Ethical Relativism," in Karsten J. Struhl and Paula Rothenberg Struhl, eds., *Ethics in Perspective* (New York: Random House, 1975), pp. 51–60.
30. Alan Gewirth, *Reason and Morality* (Chicago: University of Chicago Press, 1978), p. ix.
31. See, for example, Kathleen Woodroofe, *From Charity to Social Work in England and the United States* (Toronto: University of Toronto Press, 1971).

32. See, for example, Dale G. Hardman, "Not With My Daughter You Don't!" *Social Work* (1975), 20:278–285; Max Siporin, "Moral Philosophy in Social Work Today," *Social Service Review* (1982), 56:527–528.
33. Dorothy Emmet, "Ethics and the Social Worker," *British Journal of Psychiatric Social Work* (1962), 6:169.
34. Gewirth, *Reason and Morality*, p. 5.
35. See G. E. Moore, *Principia Ethica* (Cambridge: Cambridge University Press, 1903).
36. See Kurt Baier, *The Moral Point of View* (New York: Random House, 1965); Donagan, *The Theory of Morality*, pp. 218–221; William K. Frankena, *Ethics* (2d ed.; Englewood Cliffs, N.J.: Prentice-Hall, 1973), pp. 113–114.
37. Donagan, *The Theory of Morality*, pp. 218–221.
38. See Gewirth, *Reason and Morality*, p. 21.
39. Ludwig Wittgenstein, "Lecture on Ethics," *Philosophical Review* (1965), 74:12.
40. Gewirth, *Reason and Morality*.
41. Gewirth, pp. 342–345.

3. ETHICAL DILEMMAS IN SERVICE TO INDIVIDUALS AND FAMILIES

1. President's Committee on Mental Retardation, *Mental Retardation: The Known and the Unknown* (Washington, D.C.: Department of Health, Education, and Welfare, 1975), p. 78.
2. Immanuel Kant, "On the Supposed Right to Tell Lies from Benevolent Motives," in Thomas Kingsmill Abbott, trans., *Kant's Critique of Practical Reason and Other Works on the Theory of Ethics* (London: Longmans, 1909), pp. 361–365. For a thorough discussion of truth-telling, see Sissela Bok, *Lying: Moral Choice in Public and Private Life* (New York: Pantheon, 1978).
3. J. J. C. Smart, "Extreme and Restricted Utilitarianism," in Samuel Gorovitz, ed., *Mill: Utilitarianism* (Indianapolis: Bobbs-Merrill, 1971), p. 199.
4. See *Diagnostic and Statistical Manual of Mental Disorders* (3d ed., revised; Washington, D.C.: American Psychiatric Association, 1987), pp. 28–33.
5. See, for example, Benjamin B. Wolman and Herbert H. Krauss, eds., *Between Survival and Suicide* (New York: Gardner Press, 1976); and Edwin S. Shneidman, ed., *On the Nature of Suicide* (San Francisco: Jossey-Bass, 1969).
6. Felix P. Biestek, "Client Self-Determination." in F. E. McDermott, ed., *Self-Determination in Social Work* (London: Routledge and Kegan Paul, 1975), p. 19.
7. David Soyer, "The Right to Fail," *Social Work* (1963), 8:72–78. Also see Gerald Dworkin, "Paternalism," in Richard A. Wasserstrom, ed., *Morality and the Law* (Belmont, Calif.: Wadsworth, 1971), pp. 107–126.
8. John Stuart Mill, "On Liberty," in *The Utilitarians* (New York: Anchor, 1973), p. 484.
9. Dworkin, "Paternalism," p. 108. Dworkin's original version of this essay was written in 1968 and presented at a conference on legal philosophy and the law of torts.

10. Rosemary Carter, "Justifying Paternalism," *Canadian Journal of Philosophy* (1977), 7:133–145, especially p. 133 (emphasis added).
11. Allen Buchanan, "Medical Paternalism," *Philosophy and Public Affairs* (1978), 7:370–390, especially p. 372.
12. Alan Gewirth, *Reason and Morality* (Chicago: University of Chicago Press, 1978), p. 264.
13. Charles S. Levy, *Social Work Ethics* (New York: Human Sciences Press, 1976), pp. 168–169.
14. This case raises important, complicated, and controversial questions about the right to life and the use of extraordinary medical measures to sustain it. These questions have been debated extensively in the literature on medical ethics and should be considered thoroughly by those who are inclined to consider these issues in depth. See, for example, Daniel Callahan, *Setting Limits: Medical Goals in an Aging Society* (New York: Simon and Schuster, 1987); Gary R. Anderson and Valerie A. Glesnes-Anderson, eds., *Health Care Ethics: A Guide for Decision Makers* (Rockville, Md.: Aspen, 1987); Ruth Macklin, *Mortal Choices: Bioethics in Today's World* (New York: Pantheon, 1987); Rem B. Edwards and Glenn C. Graber, eds., *Bio-ethics* (San Diego: Harcourt Brace Jovanovich, 1988); John Freeman and Kevin McDonnell, *Tough Decisions: A Casebook in Medical Ethics* (New York: Oxford University Press, 1987); Tom Beauchamp and James Childress, *Principles of Biomedical Ethics* (New York: Oxford University Press, 1979); Howard Brody, *Ethical Decisions in Medicine* (Boston: Little, Brown, 1976).
15. See, for example, Anthony N. Maluccio, Edith Fein, and Kathleen A. Olmstead, *Permanency Planning for Children* (New York: Tavistock, 1986); Alfred Kadushin and Judith A. Martin, *Child Welfare Services* (4th ed.; New York: Macmillan, 1988); Joan Laird and Ann Hartman, eds., *A Handbook of Child Welfare* (New York: Free Press, 1985); and Brenda G. McGowan and William Meezan, eds., *Child Welfare* (Itasca, Ill.: F. E. Peacock, 1983).
16. See Theodore J. Stein, Eileen D. Gambrill, and Kermit T. Wiltse, *Children in Foster Homes: Achieving Continuity of Care* (New York: Praeger, 1978), pp. 17–22.
17. See Stein, Gambrill, and Wiltse, p. 19; David Fanshel and Eugene B. Shinn, *Dollars and Sense in the Foster Care of Children: A Look at Cost Factors* (New York: Child Welfare League of America, 1972).
18. California State Department of Health, *Adoption and Foster Care Study* (Sacramento: California State Department of Health, 1973), p. 17.
19. For discussion of this dilemma see Scott Briar and Henry Miller, *Problems and Issues in Social Casework* (New York: Columbia University Press, 1971), pp. 37–45; and Raymond Plant, *Social and Moral Theory in Casework* (London: Routledge and Kegan Paul, 1970).
20. See Biestek, "Client Self-Determination"; Saul Bernstein, "Self-Determination: King or Citizen in the Realm of Values," *Social Work* (1960), 5:3–8; Alan Keith-Lucas, "A Critique of the Principle of Client Self-Determination," *Social Work* (1963), 8:66–71; Helen Harris Perlman, "Self-Determination: Reality or

Illusion?" *Social Service Review* (1965), 39:410–421; R. F. Stalley, "Determinism and the Principle of Client Self-Determination," in F. E. McDermott, ed., *Self-Determination in Social Work* (London: Routledge and Kegan Paul, 1975), pp. 93–117.

21. Levy, *Social Work Ethics*, pp. 50–51, 141–142. See also Suanna J. Wilson, *Confidentiality in Socal Work* (New York: Free Press, 1978).
22. See W. D. Ross, *The Right and the Good* (Oxford: Clarendon Press, 1930) for further discussion of prima facie duties and their relationship to actual duties.
23. *Tarasoff v. Board of Regents of the University of California*, 17 Cal.3d 425, 551 P.2d 334, 131 Cal. Rptr. 14 (1976).
24. Charles H. Huber and Leroy G. Baruth, *Ethical, Legal, and Professional Issues in the Practice of Marriage and Family Therapy* (Columbus, Ohio: Merrill, 1987), pp. 92–97.
25. "Acquired Immune Deficiency Syndrome," a policy statement of the National Association of Social Workers approved by the 1984 Delegate Assembly, *Compilation of Public Social Policy Statements* (Washington, D.C.: National Association of Social Workers, June 1985); Carl G. Leukefeld and Manuel Fimbres, eds., *Responding to AIDS: Psychosocial Initiatives.* (Silver Spring, Md.: National Association of Social Workers, 1987); Joseph J. O'Hara and Gary J. Stangler, "AIDS and the Human Services," *Public Welfare* (1986), 44:12–13; Ruth Macklin, "Predicting Dangerousness and the Public Health Response to AIDS," *Hastings Center Report Supplement* (1986), 16:22; Deborah Jones Merritt, "The Constitutional Balance Between Health and Liberty," *Hastings Center Report Supplement* (1986), 16:6–7; James Barron, "A Debate Over Disclosure to Partners of AIDS Patients," *New York Times*, May 8, 1988, p. E8; Sheldon H. Landesman, "AIDS and the Duty to Protect," *Hastings Center Report* (1987), 17:22–23.
26. See Leukefeld and Fimbres, eds., *Responding to AIDS.*
27. Douglas S. Besharov, *The Vulnerable Social Worker* (Silver Spring, Md.: National Association of Social Workers, 1985); Steven R. Smith and Robert G. Meyer, *Law, Behavior, and Mental Health* (New York: New York University Press, 1987), pp. 7–33.
28. Saul Bernstein, "Self-Determination: King or Citizen in the Realm of Values?" *Social Work* (1960), 5:3–8; Alan Keith-Lucas, "A Critique of the Principle of Client Self-Determination," *Social Work* (1963), 8:66–71; Helen Harris Perlman, "Self-Determination: Reality or Illusion?" *Social Service Review* (1965), 39:410–421; F. E. McDermott, ed., *Self-Determination in Social Work.*
29. Quoted in President's Commission for the Study of Ethical Problems in Medicine and Biomedical and Behavioral Research, *Making Health Care Decisions: The Ethical and Legal Implications of Informed Consent in the Patient-Practitioner Relationship,* vol. 3 (Washington, D.C.: GPO, 1982) p. 5; Mark Siegler, "Searching for Moral Certainty in Medicine: A Proposal for a New Model of the Doctor-Patient Encounter," *Bulletin of the New York Academy of Medicine*, (1981), 57:68; Fay A. Rozovsky, *Consent to Treatment: A Practical Guide* (Boston: Little, Brown, 1984), pp. xxxi–xxxii.

30. President's Commission for the Study of Ethical Problems in Medicine and Biomedical and Behavioral Research, *Making Health Care Decisions,* vol. 3.
31. *Ibid.*
32. Quoted in *ibid.*, pp. 28–29. See Schloendorff v. Society of New York Hospital, 105 N.E. 92 (N.Y. 1914).
33. *Ibid.*, vol. 1.
34. *Ibid.* See Salgo v. Leland Stanford Jr. Univ. Bd. of Trustees, 317 P.2d 170 (Cal. Ct. App. 1957).
35. Rozovsky, *Consent to Treatment,* pp. 235–236; Jane Cowles, *Informed Consent* (New York: Coward, McCann and Geoghegan, 1976).
36. Rozovsky, *Consent to Treatment,* p. 240.
37. Rozovsky, pp. 242–243.
38. See, for example, Conn. Gen. Stat., sec. 19-89A (1977); Neb. Rev. Stat., sec. 71–1121 (1972); Okla. Stat. Ann. tit. 63, sec. 2602 (West 1976); Ga. Code, sec. 74–104.3 (1971); Ill. Ann. Stat. ch. 111, sec. 4505 (Smith-Hurd 1980); La. Rev. Stat. Ann., sec. 1065.1 (West 1970); Me. Rev. Stat. Ann. tit. 32, sec. 2595 (1979); Or. Rev. Stat., sec. 109.650 (1977); Vt. Stat. Ann. tit. 18, sec. 4226 (1975).
39. See Mo. Ann. Stat., sec. 632.110 (Vernon 1980); Or. Rev. Stat., sec. 426.220 (1975); Cal. Civ. Code, sec. 25.9 (West 1979); Mont. Code Ann., sec. 41–1–406 (1977).
40. See *Matter of Quinlan,* 70 N.J. 10, 355 A.2d 647 (1976); *Superintendent of Belchertown State School v. Saikewicz,* 373 Mass. 728, 370 N.E. 2d 417 (1977).
41. Rozovsky, *Consent to Treatment,* pp. 195–234.
42. Rozovsky, pp. 8–41.
43. Frederic G. Reamer, "Protecting Research Subjects and Unintended Consequences: The Effect of Guarantees of Confidentiality," *Public Opinion Quarterly,* (1979), 43:497–506; Peggy C. Giordano, "The Client's Perspective in Agency Evaluation," *Social Work* (1977), 22:34–39.
44. *Reif v. Weinberger,* 372 F. Supp. 1196 (D.D.C. 1974).
45. President's Commission for the Study of Ethical Problems in Medicine and Biomedical and Behavioral Research, *Making Health Care Decisions,* vol. 1.
46. *Ibid.*
47. *Ibid.*
48. *Ibid.*
49. *Ibid.*
50. Rozovsky, *Consent to Treatment,* p. 18.
51. In *Winfrey v. Citizens Southern Natl. Bank,* 149 Ga. App. 488, 254 S.E.2d 725 (1979), a female patient challenged her physician's authority to perform a complete hysterectomy, based on her consent to an exploratory operation. In *Darrah v. Kite,* 32 A.D. 2d 208, 301 N.Y.S.2d 286 (1969), the father of a young child challenged a neurosurgeon's authority to conduct a ventriculogram on the child when the consent form referred only to "routine brain tests" and a "workup."
52. Rozovsky, *Consent to Treatment,* p. 26.

53. President's Commission for the Study of Ethical Problems in Medicine and Biomedical and Behavioral Research, *Making Health Care Decisions,* vol. 1, p. 195, and Rozovsky, pp. 41–51.
54. Rozovsky, *Consent to Treatment,* p. 89.
55. *Ibid.*, pp. 103–106.
56. *Holt v. Nelson,* 11 Wash. App. 230, 523 P.2d 211 (1974); Alaska Stat., sec. 09.55.556 (1976); Del. Code Ann. tit. 18, sec. 6852 (1976); N.Y. Pub. Health Law sec. 2805-d (McKinney 1975); Utah Code Ann., sec. 78-14-5 (1976); Vt. Stat. Ann. tit. 12, sec. 1909 (1976). See also *Ferrara v. Galluchio,* 5 N.Y.2d 16, 176 N.Y.S.2d 996, 152 N.E.2d 249 (1958).
57. Alaska Stat., sec. 09.55.556 (1976); N.Y. Public Health Law, sec. 2805-d (McKinney 1975); Pa. Stat. Ann. tit. 40, sec. 1301.103 (Purdon 1976); Utah Code Ann., sec 78-14-5 (1976). See also Frederic G. Reamer, "The Concept of Paternalism in Social Work," *Social Service Review* (1983), 57:254–271.
58. For additional discussion of exceptions to informed consent, see Rozovsky, *Consent to Treatment,* pp. 114–123.
59. David J. Rothman, "Were Tuskegee and Willowbrook 'Studies in Nature'?" *Hastings Center Report* (1982), 12:5–7.
60. President's Commission for the Study of Ethical Problems in Medicine and Biomedical and Behavioral Research, *Making Health Care Decisions,* vol. 1, p. 100.
61. *Ibid.*
62. Cited in *ibid.*, vol. 3, pp. 55–56.
63. *Ibid.*, p. 56.

4. ETHICAL DILEMMAS IN SOCIAL PLANNING AND POLICY

1. Anthony M. Platt, *The Child Savers* (Chicago: University of Chicago Press, 1969), p. 50.
2. Platt, p. 106.
3. Francis A. Allen, *The Borderland of Criminal Justice* (Chicago: University of Chicago Press, 1964), p. 18.
4. See Charles H. Shireman and Frederic G. Reamer, *Rehabilitating Juvenile Justice.* (New York: Columbia University Press, 1986); Frederic G. Reamer and Charles H. Shireman, "Alternatives to the Juvenile Justice System: Their Development and the Current State of the Art," *Juvenile and Family Court Journal* (1981), 32:17–32; Robert M. Carter and Malcolm W. Klein, eds., *Back on the Street: The Diversion of Juvenile Offenders* (Englewood Cliffs, N.J.: Prentice-Hall, 1976).
5. Edwin M. Lemert, "The Juvenile Court: Quest and Realities," in President's Commission on Law Enforcement and Administration of Justice, *Task Force Report: Juvenile Justice and Youth Crime* (Washington, D.C.: GPO, 1967).
6. See Malcolm W. Klein, "Deinstitutionalization and Diversion of Juvenile Offenders: A Litany of Impediments," in Norval Morris and Michael Tonry, eds.,

Crime and Justice: An Annual Review of Research (Chicago: University of Chicago Press, 1979), 1:145–201.

7. Ted Palmer, "The Youth Authority's Community Treatment Project," *Federal Probation* (1974), 38:3–14.
8. LaMar T. Empey and Maynard L. Erickson, *The Provo Experiment* (Lexington, Mass.: Lexington/D. C. Heath, 1972).
9. Robert B. Coates, Alden D. Miller, and Lloyd E. Ohlin, *Diversity in a Youth Correctional System: Handling Delinquents in Massachusetts* (Cambridge, Mass.: Ballinger, 1978). The authors do state, however, that greater success was achieved in areas where alternative programs that emphasized youths' relationships with family, friends, and community organizations had been developed.
10. See LaMar T. Empey and Steven G. Lubeck, *The Silverlake Experiment: Testing Delinquency Theory and Community Intervention* (Chicago: Aldine, 1971); Charles A. Murray and Louis A. Cox, Jr., *Beyond Probation* (Beverly Hills: Sage, 1979); LaMar T. Empey, "Juvenile Justice Reform: Diversion, Due Process, and Deinstitutionalization," in Lloyd E. Ohlin, ed., *Prisoners in America* (Englewood Cliffs, N.J.: Prentice-Hall, 1973).
11. Marvin Wolfgang, Robert M. Figlio, and Thorsten Sellin, *Delinquency in a Birth Cohort* (Chicago: University of Chicago Press, 1972).
12. Paul A. Strasberg, *Violent Delinquents: A Report to the Ford Foundation from the Vera Institute of Justice* (New York: Monarch Press, 1978).
13. Donna Martin Hamparian, Richard Schuster, Simon Dinitz, and John P. Conrad, *The Violent Few: A Study of Dangerous Juvenile Offenders* (Lexington, Mass.: Lexington, 1978).
14. Ernest A. Wenk, James O. Robison, and Gerald W. Smith, "Can Violence Be Predicted?" *Crime and Delinquency* (1972), 18:393–402.
15. Martin Rein, *Social Policy: Issues of Choice and Change* (New York: Random House, 1970), p. 214.
16. See Coates, Miller, and Ohlin, *Diversity in a Youth Correctional System*, and Murray and Cox, *Beyond Probation*.
17. See Coates, Miller, and Ohlin, *Diversity in a Youth Correctional System*.
18. Sar A. Levitan, *Programs in Aid of the Poor* (3d ed.; Baltimore: Johns Hopkins University Press, 1976), pp. 1–12; Ralph Dolgoff and Donald Feldstein, *Understanding Social Welfare* (New York: Harper and Row, 1980), pp. 134–149.
19. U.S. Bureau of the Census, Current Population Reports, Series P-60, No. 157, *Money Income and Poverty Status of Families and Persons in the United States: 1986* (Washington, D.C.: GPO, 1987).
20. *Ibid.*
21. Joseph A. Califano, Jr., "Putting the Public Into Public Policy Development," *Journal of the Institute for Socioeconomic Studies* (1978), 3(2):3.
22. James N. Morgan et al, *Five Thousand American Families—Patterns of Economic Progress: Analysis of the Panel Study of Income Dynamics* (Ann Arbor, Mich.: Institute for Social Research, University of Michigan Press, 1974–1977).
23. W. Joseph Heffernan, *Introduction to Social Welfare Policy: Power, Scarcity, and Common Human Needs* (Itasca, Ill.: F. E. Peacock, 1979), p. 116.

24. Alan Gewirth, *Reason and Morality* (Chicago: University of Chicago Press, 1978), p. 330.
25. To avoid instances where recipients with some degree of disability are inappropriately required to work in exchange for benefits, an appeal procedure ought to be made available to provide such recipients an opportunity to object to a job assignment and to have the benefit of an administrative review.
26. See Dexter D. MacBride, *Power and Process: A Commentary on Eminent Domain* (Washington, D.C.: American Society of Appraisers, 1969).
27. *Ibid.*
28. *Encyclopedia Americana* (1968), s.v. "Eminent Domain," p. 295.
29. Gewirth, *Reason and Morality,* pp. 53–58.
30. Gewirth, pp. 62–63 (emphasis added).
31. See chapter 2.
32. See Lynn M. Irvine, Jr, and Jerry B. Brelje, *Law, Psychiatry, and the Mentally Disordered Offender,* vol. 2 (Springfield, Ill.: Charles C. Thomas, 1973).
33. Governor's Task Force on the Mental Health of Juvenile Offenders, *Report and Recommendations of the Governor's Task Force on the Mental Health of Juvenile Offenders* (Harrisburg, Pa.: Pennsylvania Department of Public Welfare, 1978), p. 45.
34. Evan McKenzie and Robert A. Roos, "The Mentally-Disordered Juvenile Offender: An Inquiry into the Treatment of the Kids Nobody Wants," *Juvenile and Family Court Journal* (1979), 30:47.
35. See, for example, *The Children at Bridgewater.* Report prepared by the Commonwealth of Massachusetts, Office for Children, 1974.
36. Alan Donagan, *The Theory of Morality* (Chicago: University of Chicago Press, 1977), p. 85.
37. *Ibid.*
38. See Irvine and Brelje, *Law Psychiatry, and the Mentally Disordered Offender.*
39. This information was obtained from a review of programs surveyed in 1980 by the National Center for the Assessment of Alternatives to Juvenile Justice Processing, University of Chicago.
40. See, for example, Dorothy O. Lewis and Shelley S. Shanok, *Delinquency and Psychopathology* (New York: Grune and Stratton, 1976).
41. *Mental Health Needs of Juvenile Delinquents.* Report prepared by the District of Columbia Department of Public Health, 1964.
42. Arthur Bolton and Associates, *A Study of the Need and Availability of Mental Health Services for Mentally Disordered Jail Inmates and Juveniles in Detention Facilities.* Report prepared for California Department of Health, 1976.
43. Task Force on Secure Facilities, *The Issue of Security in a Community-Based System of Juvenile Corrections.* Report prepared for the Massachusetts Department of Youth Services, 1977.
44. Gary E. Bodner, Curtis D. Booraem, and Bruce J. Tapper, "A Cognitive-Behavioral Program for Psychotic Youthful Offenders" (Norwalk: California Department of the Youth Authority, 1976), manuscript.
45. For further discussion see Kathleen V. Turney, "The Provision of Intensive

Mental Health Services to Adjudicated Delinquents: A Survey of State Practices" (Harvard Law School, 1980), manuscript.

46. *Ibid.*
47. *Ibid.*
48. See Dwight Frankfather, "Provider Discretion and Consumer Preference in Long-Term Care for Seriously Disabled Elderly" (University of Chicago, School of Social Service Administration, 1980), manuscript.
49. *Ibid.*
50. See William Pollak, "Organizational Issues in the Provision of Community Care to the Impaired Elderly," in Joel Bergsman and Howard Weiner, eds., *Urban Problems and Public Policy* (New York: Praeger, 1975), pp. 23–43.
51. See Frankfather, "Provider Discertion and Consumer Preference."
52. See Joel F. Handler, *The Coercive Social Worker: British Lessons for American Social Services* (Chicago: Markham, 1973); and Jeffrey Manditch Prottas, *People-Processing* (Lexington, Mass.: Lexington Books, 1979).
53. See Peter Blau, *The Dynamics of Bureaucracy* (Chicago: University of Chicago Press, 1963).
54. See Frankfather, "Provider Discretion and Consumer Preference," p. 6.
55. Sidney Katz, Thomas Downs, Helen Cash, and Robert Grotz, "Progress in Development of the Index of ADL." *The Gerontologist* (1970), 10:20–30.
56. Details of this approach to the design of services for the disabled elderly were provided in part by Dwight L. Frankfather.

5. ETHICAL DILEMMAS IN RELATIONSHIPS AMONG PRACTITIONERS

1. See J. J. C. Smart and Bernard Williams, *Utilitarianism: For and Against* (Cambridge: Cambridge University Press, 1973), pp. 98–99.
2. Smart and Williams, p. 95.
3. Charles Fried, *Right and Wrong* (Cambridge: Harvard University Press, 1978), pp. 13–14.
4. Alan Gewirth, *Reason and Morality* (Chicago: University of Chicago Press, 1978), p. 218.
5. Fried, *Right and Wrong,* pp. 34–35.
6. John Rawls, "The Justification of Civil Disobedience," in Richard Wasserstrom, ed., *Today's Moral Problems* (New York: Macmillan, 1975), p. 352.
7. Richard Wasserstrom, "The Obligation to Obey the Law," in Richard Wasserstrom, ed., *Today's Moral Problems* (New York: Macmillan, 1975), p. 383.
8. Gewirth, *Reason and Morality,* p. 284.
9. Gewirth, p. 286.
10. For a comprehensive discussion of problems of confidentiality in social work, see Suanna J. Wilson, *Confidentiality in Social Work* (New York: Free Press, 1978). Also see Selma Arnold, "Confidential Communication and the Social Worker," *Social Work* (1970), 15:61–67; Mildred M. Reynolds, "Threats to

Confidentiality," *Social Work* (1976), 21:108–113; and Estelle Promislo. "Confidentiality and Privileged Communication." *Social Work* (1979), 24:10–13.

11. For further discussion of lying see Sissela Bok, *Lying: Moral Choice in Public and Private Life* (New York: Pantheon, 1978); and Fried, *Right and Wrong*, pp. 54–78.
12. Wilson, *Confidentiality in Social Work*, pp. 97–110.
13. See John H. Wigmore, *Evidence in Trials at Common Law* (revised by J. T. McNaughton) (Boston: Little, Brown, 1961), 8:52.
14. See Gordon Hamilton, *Theory and Practice of Social Case Work* (2d ed.; New York: Columbia University Press, 1951), p. 39.
15. Wilson, *Confidentiality in Social Work;* Leon VandeCreek, Samuel Knapp, and Cindy Herzog, "Privileged Communication for Social Workers," *Social Casework* (1988), 69:28–34; Martin Lakin, *Ethical Issues in the Psychotherapies* (New York: Oxford University Press, 1988), pp. 131–134.
16. "Note: Social-Worker Client Relationship and Privileged Communication," *Washington University Law Quarterly* (1965), pp. 386–387; cited in Wilson, *Confidentiality in Social Work*, pp. 114–115.
17. See Wilson, *Confidentiality in Social Work*, pp. 143–146.
18. Maurice Grossman, "The Psychiatrist and the Subpoena," *Bulletin of the American Academy of Psychiatry and the Law* (1973), 1:245; cited in Wilson, *Confidentiality in Social Work*, pp. 145–146.
19. See *Humphrey v. Norden*, 359 N.Y.S. 2d 733 (S. Court 1974); Wilson, *Confidentiality in Social Work*, p. 100; Barton E. Bernstein, "The Social Worker as a Courtroom Witness," *Social Casework* (1975), 56:521–525; Robert M. Fisher, "The Psychotherapeutic Professions and the Law of Privileged Communication," *Wayne Law Review* (1963–1964), 10:609–654.
20. For a case in which a counselor was *not* in the end required to testify in a custody dispute, see *Simrim v. Simrim*, 43 Cal. Rptr., 376 (Dist. Ct. App. 1965).
21. Wilson, *Confidentiality in Social Work*, p. 138.
22. See Fried, *Right and Wrong*, p. 60.
23. *Ibid.*
24. Jeremy Bentham, "An Introduction to the Principles of Morals and Legislation" (originally published 1789), in *The Utilitarians* (New York: Anchor, 1973), p. 205.
25. See Donald T. Campbell and Julian C. Stanley, *Experimental and Quasi-Experimental Designs for Research* (Chicago: Rand McNally, 1963); Robert Rosenthal, "Interpersonal Expectations: Effects of the Experimenter's Hypothesis," in Robert Rosenthal and Ralph L. Rosnow, eds., *Artifact in Behavioral Research* (New York: Academic Press, 1969).
26. Stanley Milgram, "Behavioral Study of Obedience," *Journal of Abnormal and Social Psychology* (1963), 67:371–378; Stanley Milgram, "Liberating Effects of Group Pressure," *Journal of Personality and Social Psychology* (1965), 1:127–134.
27. For a comprehensive review of these issues, see Edward Diener and Rick

Crandall, *Ethics in Social and Behavioral Research* (Chicago: University of Chicago Press, 1978).

28. Diener and Crandall, p. 86.
29. Immanuel Kant, "The Categorical Imperative," in Maurice Mandelbaum, Francis W. Gramlich, Alan Ross Anderson, and Jerome B. Schneewind, eds., *Philosophic Problems: An Introductory Book of Readings* (New York: Macmillan, 1967), p. 579.
30. Diener and Crandall, *Ethics in Social and Behavioral Research,* p. 87; see also Margaret Mead, "The Human Study of Human Beings," *Science* (1961), 133:163.
31. Diener and Crandall, *Ethics in Social and Behavioral Research,* p. 79.
32. Bok, *Lying: Moral Choice in Public and Private Life,* p. 31.
33. Joel L. Fleishman and Bruce L. Payne, *Ethical Dilemmas and the Education of Policymakers* (New York: Institute of Society, Ethics, and the Life Sciences, 1980), p. 43. Also see Vincent Barry, *Moral Issues in Business,* (3d ed.; Belmont, Calif.: Wadsworth, 1986), pp. 238–267.
34. Charles Peters and Taylor Branch, *Blowing the Whistle: Dissent in the Public Interest* (New York: Praeger, 1972), p. 280. For additional discussion of personal and professional risks, see Ralph Nader, Peter J. Petkas, and Kate Blackwood, eds., *Whistle Blowing* (New York: Grossman, 1972); and Sissela Bok, "Whistleblowing and Professional Responsibility," *New York University Education Quarterly* (1980), 11:2–10.
35. Joel L. Fleishman and Bruce L. Payne, *Ethical Dilemmas and the Education of Policymakers* (Hastings-on-Hudson, N.Y.: Hastings Center, Institute of Society, Ethics, and Life Sciences, 1980), p. 43.

6. ENDURING ISSUES

1. For additional discussion of this goal of ethical analysis, see The Hastings Center, *The Teaching of Ethics in Higher Education* (New York: Institute of Society, Ethics, and the Life Sciences, 1980), p. 48.
2. *Ibid.*
3. Max Siporin, *Introduction to Social Work Practice* (New York: Macmillan, 1975), p. 63.
4. Cynthia B. Cohen, "Ethics Committees," *Hastings Center Report* (1988), 18:11; Thomas H. Murray, "Where are the Ethics in Ethics Committees?" *Hastings Center Report* (1988), 18:12–13; Andrew L. Merritt, "Assessing the Risk of Legal Liability," *Hastings Center Report* (1988), 18:13–14; Ruth Macklin, "The Inner Workings of an Ethics Committee: Latest Battle Over Jehovah's Witness," *Hastings Center Report* (1988), 18:15–20; Carole Levine, "Questions and (Some Very Tentative) Answers About Hospital Ethics Committees," *Hastings Center Report* (1984), 14:9–12.
5. Frederic G. Reamer, "Ethics Committees in Social Work," *Social Work* (1987), 32:425–429; Frederic G. Reamer, "The Emergence of Bioethics in Social Work," *Health and Social Work* (1985), 10:271–281.

6. *In re Quinlan,* NJ 835 A 2d 647. See Karen Teel, "The Physician's Dilemma: A Doctor's View: What the Law Should Be," *Baylor Law Review,* (1975), 27:6–9.
7. Levine, "Questions and (Some Very Tentative) Answers About Hospital Ethics Committees," p. 9, citing President's Commission for the Study of Ethical Problems in Medicine and Biomedical and Behavioral Research, *Deciding to Forgo Life-Sustaining Treatment* (Washington, D.C.: GPO, 1983). The Baby Doe case (*Am. Academy of Pediatrics v. Heckler,* No. 83-0774, U.S. District Court, D.C., April 14, 1983) involved an infant in Indiana born in 1982 with Downs syndrome and tracheo-esophageal fistula, a condition in which the esophagus is not connected to the stomach, preventing normal feeding. His parents, with the approval of the courts, denied him food, water, and surgical aid. See George J. Annas, "Disconnecting the Baby Doe Hotline," *Hastings Center Report* (1983), 13:14–16.
8. Levine, "Questions and (Some Very Tentative) Answers About Hospital Ethics Committees."
9. Benjamin Freedman, "One Philosopher's Experience on an Ethics Committee," *Hastings Center Report* (1981), 11:22.
10. Levine, "Questions and (Some Very Tentative) Answers About Hospital Ethics Committees," p. 12.
11. *Ibid.* See, for example, American Hospital Association, "Guidelines: Hospital Ethics Committees on Biomedical Ethics" (Chicago, Ill.: American Hospital Association, 1984).
12. Freedman, "One Philosopher's Experience on an Ethics Committee," p. 21.
13. Freedman, pp. 21–22.
14. George J. Annas, as cited in a paper presented at a conference of the American Society of Law and Medicine, "Institutional Ethics Committees: Their Role in Medical Decision Making," Washington, D.C., April 21–23, 1983; cited by Judith Randal, "Are Ethics Committees Alive and Well?" *Hastings Center Report* (1983), 13:10–12.
15. Alan R. Fleischman and Thomas H. Murray, "Ethics Committees for Infants Doe?" *Hastings Center Report* (1983), 13:9.
16. Albert R. Jonsen, "A Guide to Guidelines," *American Society of Law and Medicine: Ethics Committee Newsletter* (1984), 2:4. Social workers also must not lose sight of the fact that the availability of ethical guidelines does not guarantee their use. Jonsen noted, for example, the recent discovery of guidelines prepared by the German Ministry of Health for experimentation with human subjects. These guidelines, issued in 1928 and in force until 1945, are an impressive statement of the rights of human subjects. Sadly, they lacked efficacy. See also Ronald E. Cranford and Edward Doudera, eds., *Institutional Ethics Committees and Health Care Decision Making* (Ann Arbor, Mich.: Health Administration Press, 1984).
17. Daniel Goleman, "Social Workers Vault into a Leading Role in Psychotherapy," *New York Times,* April 30, 1985, pp. C1 and C9; "Membership Survey Shows Practice Shifts," *NASW News* (1983), 28:6.

18. Frederic G. Reamer, "Social Work: Calling or Career?" *Hastings Center Report Supplement* (1987), 17:14–15. Also see James F. Gustafson, "Professions as 'Callings,'" *Social Service Review* (1982) 56:527–528.
19. Karl Popper, *The Open Society and its Enemies* (5th ed.; London: Routledge and Kegan Paul, 1966).
20. J. J. C. Smart and Bernard Williams, *Utilitarianism: For and Against* (Cambridge: Cambridge University Press, 1973), pp. 28–30.
21. Smart and Williams, pp. 29–30.
22. John Rawls, *A Theory of Justice* (Cambridge: Harvard University Press, 1971), p. 114.
23. Rawls, p. 117.
24. See chapter 2.
25. Charles Fried, *Right and Wrong* (Cambridge: Harvard University Press, 1978), p. 130.
26. James Rachels, "Can Ethics Provide Answers?" *Hastings Center Report* (1980), 10:38–39.
27. Karl Raymond Popper, *Of Clouds and Clocks: An Approach to the Problem of Rationality and the Freedom of Man,* annual Holly Compton Memorial Lecture (St. Louis: Washington University, 1965), p. 2.
28. Richard Rose, "Disciplined Research and Undisciplined Problems," in Carol H. Weiss, ed., *Using Social Research in Public Policy Making* (Lexington, Mass.: Lexington Books, 1977), p. 23.

Index

Absolutism, versus relativism, 55-57
Actual duty, versus prima facie duty, 31-33
Act utilitarianism, 192; *see also* Utilitarianism
Additive goods, versus basic, nonsubtractive goods, 59-60
Allen, Francis, 127
Altruism, 27, 239-41
Annas, George, 234-35
Aretaic judgments, versus deontic judgments, 29
Aristotle, 29, 56, 80, 224, 242
Augustine, Saint, 210
Authoritative question of ethics, 23-27; *see also* Distributive question of ethics; Substantive question of ethics

Baby Doe, case of, 230, 261*n*7
Basic goods, versus additive, nonsubtractive goods, 59-60
Beneficence, principle of (Donagan), 163
Bentham, Jeremy, 15, 18, 19, 29, 211, 244; *see also* Utilitarianism
Berlin, Sir Isaiah, 39-40
Beveridge, Sir William, 47
Beveridge Report, 47
Biestek, Felix, 80
Bismarck, Otto von, 42, 46
Bok, Sissela, 216
Branch, Taylor, 223
Buchanan, Allen, 82

Califano, Joseph, Jr., 144
Carter, Rosemary, 82
Charity Organization Society, 143, 225
Chrysler Corporation, 43-45, 47
Cicero, Marcus Tullius, 33
Civil disobedience, justification of, 191
Cleisthenes, 45
Coates, Robert B., 130
Code of Ethics, NASW, 10-13, 31-32, 195, 200, 218
Cognitivist theories of ethics, versus noncognitivist theories of ethics, 14
Compensation, principle of, 52-53

Confidentiality, right to, 62, 100-10, 195-207
Consent, voluntary, 63; *see also* Informed consent
Contribution, principle of, 53-55
Corn Laws, 45
Crandall, Rick, 213

Deception, use of, 202, 216; *see also* Truth-telling; Whistle-blowing
Deontic judgments, versus aretaic judgments, 29
Deontological theory, 15-16; and obligation to obey laws, regulations, and rules, 192; and truth-telling, 210-11
Depression of 1870s, 46; of 1930s, 43, 47
Descriptive statements, relationship to evaluative statements, *see* 'Is-ought' problem
Dewey, John, 14
Diener, Edward, 213
Difference principle (Rawls), 51
Distribution of limited resources, 48-55, 84-94, 134-40
Distributive question of ethics, 27-29; *see also* Authoritative question of ethics; Substantive question of ethics
Donagan, Alan, 32, 33, 51, 163
Dostoevsky, Fyodor, 20
Duty to aid, 36-37
Duty to protect, 106-10
Dworkin, Gerald, 81

Egoism, 27
Elizabeth I, 143
Elizabethan Poor Law (1601), 8, 142, 225
Emancipated minor, concept of, 114
Eminent domain, 149-58
Emmet, Dorothy, 21-22, 57
Empedocles, 242
Empey, LaMar T., 130
English Poor Law Reform Bill (1834), 8, 143
Equality, principle of, 49-50
Equal opportunity, 49-50
Erickson, Maynard L., 130
Ethical analysis, goals of, 22, 226-29
Ethics committees, 229-36
Evaluative statements, relationship to descriptive statements, *see* 'Is-ought' problem
Evil, principle of least, 33

Figlio, Robert M., 130
Fleishman, Joel L., 221, 223
Foster, John, 131
Frankel, Charles, 36
Frankfather, Dwight, 172
Freedman, Benjamin, 232, 234
Fried, Charles, 185, 186-87, 240-41

Germany, development of welfare state in, 46
Gewirth, Alan, 58, 59-61, 84, 147, 155, 186, 193
Good, definitions of, 19, 30-31
Good-aggregative utilitarianism, 15; *see also* Locus-aggregative utilitarianism; Utilitarianism
Grossman, Maurice, 205-6
Grotius, Hugo, 152

Hamilton, Gordon, 201-2
Hedonistic utilitarians, 19; *see also* Ideal utilitarians; Utilitarianism
Hobbes, Thomas, 191
Hollis, Florence, 12
Hume, David, 26, 29, 56, 131

Ideal observer, 59; *see also* Moral point of view
Ideal utilitarians, 19; *see also* Hedonistic utilitarians; Utilitarianism
Independent variable, problem of (Gewirth), 58
Informed choice, condition of, 63; *see also* Self-destructive behavior; Paternalism
Informed consent, 111-21
Institutional ethics committees, 230
Institutional review boards, 230
Intuition, use of in ethical decisions, 14-15
'Is-ought' problem, 26, 58, 131, 226, 227

Jonsen, Albert, 236

Kant, Immanuel, 56, 70-71, 210, 213
Keynes, John Maynard, 46-47

Landrecht, 41-42
Laws, obligation to obey, 31, 63-65, 87-88, 94-100, 191-93
Laws of nature (Hobbes), 191
Levy, Charles S., 87
Lexical ordering, 238
Liability, professional, 112
Liberty: negative, 40, 78-79; positive, 40, 78-79, 139
Locus-aggregative utilitarianism, 15; *see also* Good-aggregative utilitarianism; Utilitarianism
Lying, *see* Deception, use of; Truth-telling

Marx, Karl, 28, 56
Mature minor, concept of, 114
Mencken, H. L., xvi
Metaethics, 14-15, 33, 35, 229; *see also* Normative ethics
Milgram, Stanley, 212-13
Mill, John Stuart, 15, 19, 40, 56, 81, 244
Miller, Alden D., 130
Minimization of suffering (Popper), 237
Mondeville, Henri de, 113
Moore, G. E., 19, 58
Moral point of view, 58-59, 226
Morgan, James N., 145

Natural duties, versus supererogatory actions, 239-40
Naturalistic fallacy (Moore), 26, 58
Navigation Acts, 45
Need, principle of, 51-52
Negative liberty, 40, 78-79; *see also* Positive liberty
Negative obligation, versus positive obligation, 38-40
Negative responsibility, versus positive responsibility, 182-84, 188
Negative utilitarianism, versus positive utilitarianism, 237, 239
Nietzsche, Friedrich Wilhelm, 56
Noncognitivist theories of ethics, versus cognitivist theories of ethics, 14
Nonsubtractive goods, versus additive, basic goods, 59-60
Normative ethics, 33, 35, 229; *see also* Metaethics
Nozick, Robert, 37

Obligation, negative and positive, 38-40
Ohlin, Lloyd E., 130

Palmer, Ted, 130
Passenger Acts, 45
Paternalism, 76-84; *see aso* Self-determination
Paul, Saint, 183
Payne, Bruce L., 221, 223
Peters, Charles, 223
Pinker, Robert, 47
Plato, 31, 45, 56, 113
Poor Law of 1601, *see* Elizabethan Poor Law (1601)
Poor Law Reform Bill of 1834, 8, 143
Popper, Sir Karl Raymond, 237, 243, 244-45
Positive liberty, 40, 78, 139
Positive obligation, versus negative obligation, 38-40
Positive responsibility, versus negative responsibility, 188
Positive utilitarianism, versus negative utilitarianism, 237
Poverty, extent of, 144-45
Prima facie duty, versus actual duty, 31-33
Principle of beneficence (Donagan), 163
Principle of veracity (Bok), 216
Privileged communication, 197-207; *see also* Confidentiality
Problem of authority (Frankel), 36
Property, right to retain, 65, 149-58
Prussia, development of welfare state in, 41
Pseudopaternalism, 83
Puffendorf, Samuel, 152

Rachels, James, 242
Rawls, John, 51, 191, 239-40
Regulations, obligation to obey, 63-65, 84-94, 188-97; *see also* Laws; Rules
Reif v. Weinberger, 116
Rein, Martin, 131
Relativism, versus absolutism, 55-57
Responsibility: negative, 182-84, 188; positive, 188
Ricardo, David, 8
Robison, James O., 130
Ross, W. D., 31, 32, 37
Royal Poor Law Commission, 8-9
Rozovsky, Fay, 117
Rules, obligation to obey, 63-65, 84-94, 188-97; *see also* Laws; Regulations
Rule-worship (Smart), 71, 184, 192

***S**algo v. Leland Stanford Jr. University Board of Trustees,* 113
Schloendorff v. Society of New York Hospital, 113
Self-destructive behavior, interference with, 63, 76-84
Self-determination, 63, 76-84
Sellin, Thorsten, 130
Settlement Acts, 45
Settlement House movement, 9, 143
Siporin, Max, 228
Situational ethics, 241
Smart, J. J. C., 71, 184, 237, 239
Smith, Adam, 8, 45, 58-59
Smith, Gerald W., 130
Socrates, 19, 31
Soyer, David, 80
Subpoena, obligation to obey, 205-7; *see also* Confidentality; Privileged communication
Substantive question of ethics, 29-34; *see also* Authoritative question of ethics; Distributive question of ethics
Suffering, minimization of (Popper), 237
Supererogatory actions, 239-40; *see also* Natural duties
Superintendent of Belchertown v. Saikewicz, 115

***T**arasoff v. Board of Regents of the University of California,* 106-10
Taxation, 65; *see also* Property, right to retain
Teleological theory, 15-20, 71, 192-93; *see also* Utilitarianism
Therapeutic privilege, 120
Triage, principle of, 51; *see also* Need, principle of
Truth-telling, 67-76; *see also* Deception, use of; Paternalism
Tukey, John, 244

Unworthy poor, versus worthy, 9
Utilitarianism, 15-20, 192-93, 237, 239

Veil of ignorance (Rawls), 51
Veracity, principle of (Bok), 216
Vigilante, Joseph, 14
Voluntary associations, 60, 64-65

Wasserstrom, Richard A., 191
Welfare state, growth of, 40-48
Wenk, Ernest A., 130
Whistle blowing, 216-23
Wigmore, John Henry, 201-2, 206
Wilder, Thornton, 224
Williams, Bernard, 182-3
Wilson, Suanna J., 207
Wittgenstein, Ludwig, 59
Wolfgang, Marvin E., 130
Worthy poor, versus unworthy, 9